# Solar Projects

## For Under $500

# Solar Projects

## For Under $500

Mary Twitchell

**A Garden Way Publishing Book**

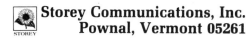

**Storey Communications, Inc.**
**Pownal, Vermont 05261**

*Design by Ann Aspell*
*Illustrations by Bob Vogel and David Sylvester*
*Cover photo by Didier Delmas.*

Copyright © 1985 by Mary Twitchell.

For additional information send all inquiries to
Storey Communications, Inc., Schoolhouse Road, Pownal, Vermont 05261.

*Printed in the United States by Alpine Press.*
*First printing, March 1985*

**Library of Congress Cataloging in Publication Data**
Twitchell, Mary.
    Solar projects for under $500.

    Includes index.
    1. Solar energy—Passive systems—Amateurs' manuals.
2. Building—Amateurs' manuals. I. Title. II. Title:
Solar projects for under five hundred dollars.
TH7413.T88 1984      697'.78      83-48971
ISBN 0-88266-363-1 (pbk.)

# Contents

## Foreword

**The Future of Solar.** The United States, with 6 percent of the world's population, consumes 35 to 40 percent of the world's mineral and energy resources. This disproportionate rate of consumption has resulted in our high standard of living and high-tech society, but these natural resources are now beginning to dwindle. As they do, we will be increasingly, perhaps devastatingly, affected.

We first began to examine seriously the negative impact of fossil fuels on our society in 1973 when our supply was threatened by the Arab oil embargo. In the intervening years we have had to confront the fact that many of our fuel reserves are situated in a very volatile part of the world; at any time their availability can be interrupted or terminated. And as both population and energy demand increase, so too will fuel prices. We have discovered that our dependence on fossil fuels pervades every aspect of our natural and economic environment; without fuel, there can be no production or distribution of goods. We also have discovered that burning fossil fuels is increasingly hazardous to our health and our environment. And the situation is not likely to improve.

For these reasons, a transition to renewable energy sources (wood and other biomass, solar, wind, and water) is essential. Of these, solar is the most promising; it is free, safe, clean, abundant, and available to all—rich and poor, city and country, apartment dweller and homeowner.

Some people are heeding the warning; energy-efficient homes are springing up. But because 60 percent of the housing for the year 2000 AD is already built, we must find ways to make our present structures more efficient.

**Solar is simple.** Solar devices are the simplest method of providing heat for the home, the garden, or the domestic hot water supply. All that is needed are a few tools and materials, and an unshaded, south-facing wall or roof or parcel of land.

**Solar saves.** Solar collecting systems will save you money. One-fourth of U.S. energy consumption is for home heating/cooling and domestic hot water; by installing a few inexpensive solar retrofits, plus insulation, weatherization, and conservation, you can decrease utility bills by at least 50 percent. A batch heater will cut water heating costs by 25 percent; thermal shutters and solar window collectors will substantially reduce bills for space heating; solar ovens and concentrating cookers provide three-course meals—free.

**Solar works in the garden, too.** American food production consumes 16 percent of the national energy pie, but this is wastefully high. Generally more energy (planting, cultivating, fertilizing, harvesting, canning, and trucking) goes into producing foodstuffs than the foodstuffs contain. Most of this expense can be reclaimed if food is produced locally for local consumption. This is possible with backyard cold frames and hotbeds which extend the growing season, and with solar pit greenhouses which offer year-round food production in almost all parts of the country.

Because the government is showing little interest in alternative technologies, the solution, or at least part of the solution, to the "energy crisis" lies in our effort—yours and mine—to participate in a technology better adapted to human need and human health—the solar technology.

**Organization of book.** This book is divided into three sections: solar for plants, solar for heating, and solar for the homestead. Within these groupings, we have arranged the building projects by skill; they progress from easy to more difficult, but none requires skills beyond those of a carpenter's apprentice.

We have included all the necessary information, from buying the materials to installing the final unit, in order to encourage readers to explore the possibilities of solar. The step-by-step directions are easy to follow and have been fully illustrated so that supplementary carpentry manuals aren't necessary. None of the projects costs more than $500, and even the most complicated can be built by two people in two weekends.

The essential tools will be found in any well-equipped workshop; many of the supplies you may already have on hand, or they can be purchased at your local hardware store or lumberyard.

We know that once you've completed your first solar project (be it a grow tunnel for vegetables, a reflective shutter, or a solar oven), you will want to build more. Before going on to a more complicated project, read through the variations at the end of each section; we hope these will spark your imagination and lead you to create some of your own solar designs.

# Solar for Plants

# Plastic Grow Tunnel

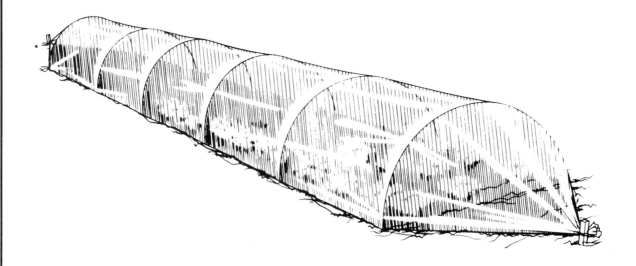

**Skills required:** Slight.

**Cost:** $0.15 per square foot of garden space covered.

**Amount of heat gain:** Soil temperature will be 5 to 10 degrees warmer than outside.

**What it does:** A grow tunnel will extend your gardening season by as much as two to four weeks. You'll be able to plant earlier, harvest later, and harvest more. Heat-loving plants such as tomatoes, peppers, and eggplants will get off to a stronger start. By planting cabbages, lettuce, or other greens early, you can harvest them much earlier. Grow tunnels also protect plants from garden pests and the wind.

The tunnel works best when it covers a bed no wider than four feet; for starting plants or growing lettuce, plastic six feet wide will give ample headroom. Rolls come 6, 10, and 20 feet wide, and 25, 50, and 100 feet long, and in other dimensions. The wider rolls are easily cut to give the required width.

The tunnel is made of a single layer of plastic stretched along the supporting rods. The plastic is pulled to one side during the day, then drawn over the bed at night or when there is a chance of frost.

Working with the directions that follow, you can design your own tunnel, from a small one to cover a crop of early lettuce to a lengthy one with headroom enough for a long row of pepper plants.

**How it works:** The grow tunnel works like a greenhouse. During the day, sunlight passes through the plastic and the heat is trapped inside, with much of it absorbed by the soil. At night, some of the heat flows back through the plastic, but the flow is slow enough to keep the temperature inside 5 to 10 degrees F. higher than the soil outside.

**Tips:** Remember to open the tunnel on hot, sunny days. Gather the plastic and carefully roll it to one side; otherwise the heat will cook the plants. (On clear days, inside temperatures may exceed outside temperatures by 40 to 50 degrees F.) Pull the plastic back over the supporting rods late in the afternoon. If it will be a cold night, cover the tunnel with tarps or old blankets to help retain the collected heat.

If winds are a problem, hoe soil up along the edges, to anchor the plastic.

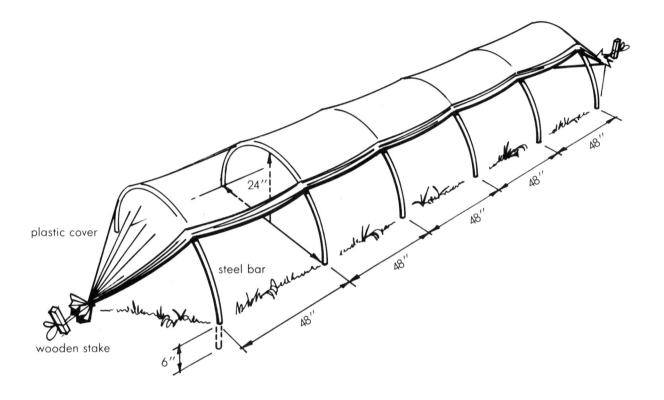

plastic cover

24"

steel bar

wooden stake

6"

48"

48"

48"

48"

48"

**Materials for one 4' x 20' bed:**

| Amount | Size | Item |
|---|---|---|
| 2 | ¼" x 20' | Hot rolled steel bars |
| 1 roll | 6' x 25' | 6 mil polyethylene plastic |
| 2 | 1" x 2" x 16" | Wooden stakes |
| 1 | 4' | Twine or wire |
| 1 | pint | Rustproofing paint |

**Tools:**
Tape measure
Scissors or utility knife
Paint brush or rag
Hacksaw
Hatchet

**Advantages:**
1. Practical for commercial as well as backyard gardens.
2. The simplest and cheapest of the cold frames.
3. Extends the growing season by two to four weeks.
4. Protects plants from cold, winds, insects, rabbits, and birds.
5. Hastens plant growth and increases yields.
6. Can be built to fit any size or shape of garden.

**Disadvantages:**
1. Limited seasonal use.
2. Plastic must be replaced after one or two seasons.
3. Demands attention. Must be opened on sunny day. Plants must be watered.

## How to build:

*These are directions for a tunnel covering a garden bed 4 feet wide and 20 feet long.*

## A. Building the Tunnel

**1.** Cut each of the two bars into three equal pieces, each 6'8" in length. Mark with a pencil. Lock the bar in a vise or place it on a low surface where you can hold the bar securely with one foot. Cut with a hacksaw.

**2.** Apply two coats of rustproofing paint to the bars with a rag or brush. Let dry.

**3.** Take the plastic and the six bars to the garden. Outline the bed with pegs and string. With a stick, mark "X's" along both sides at 4' intervals.

**4.** Begin at one end of the tunnel. Force one end of a bar 6" into the soil at the corner of the bed. Holding the top of the bar, bend it slowly, and insert it into the ground at the opposite corner of the bed. Press the end 6" into the ground. The bar should form a half-circle.

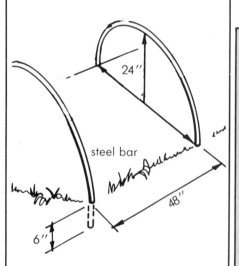

**5.** Insert bars at the five remaining locations marked along the bed. The bars should remain upright; if necessary, push them a little farther into the ground to ensure that they are firmly in place.

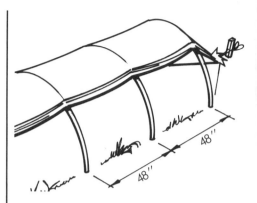

**6.** Drape the plastic cover loosely over the bars, centered so there is 2½' extra at each end. Gather the edge of the plastic at one end and tie it together with twine or wire. Point the ends of the two stakes.

**7.** With a hammer or hatchet, drive one stake in the ground beyond the tunnel and midway between the ends of the half-circle. Tie the knotted plastic to it.

**8.** Repeat Step 7 at the other end of the tunnel, pulling the plastic taut.

Water the plants if the tunnel remains closed for several days. When it's no longer needed, remove the tunnel. If you use it in the fall, dismantle it before winter, when the protected plants finally die.

Do not leave the plastic up during the summer. It will quickly disintegrate.

If you're careful, you should get two seasons of use out of 6 mil plastic. Four mil is cheaper, but much flimsier.

If possible, orient the tunnel east and west, to maximize the amount of south-facing plastic.

Prepare the beds as you always do, turning the soil and adding any needed fertilizer before erecting the tunnel.

## Other design possibilities

For taller or wider tunnels, increase or decrease the arch of the steel bars. If you are growing tomatoes, for example, decrease the width of the tunnel (or increase the length of the support bars) to give added headroom. Lettuce, radishes, spinach, or cabbage, on the other hand, need little headroom.

The supporting members can be as simple as slender saplings, mill edgings, or ½" plywood strips, all of them smoothed to avoid tearing the plastic. Leftover fencing can be arched to support the plastic, with the bottom edges of the plastic held by furring strips. Or dig a trench around the perimeter of the tunnel, then cover the edges of the plastic with earth.

For a sturdier structure, have a metal shop bend ⅝" electric conduit into a half-circle shape. These can be inserted directly into the ground, or they can be fastened with U-bolts to stakes driven into the ground at 6' intervals. Plastic conduit also can be used. For rigidity with larger structures, you may need a ridge of ⅛" cable stretched across the top of the conduit.

The arch is most commonly used because it is easiest to bend materials into that shape. However, an A- or inverted U-frame is possible, as long as there are no rough edges to tear the plastic.

To increase the heat-absorbing quality of the tunnel, place black plastic over the ground, and plant seeds or small plants through holes in it.

# Permanent Cold Frame With Three Possible Glazings:

- Using a Recycled Window

- Homemade Window Using Polyethylene Plastic Film

- Homemade Window Using Corrugated Fiberglass Glazing

- Hotbed Variation

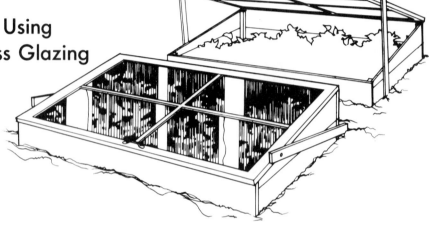

**Skills required:** Slight.

**Cost:** $30 to $35.

**Amount of heat gain:** This cold frame can extend the growing season by as much as three months.

**What it does:** Cold frames are an inexpensive form of solar greenhouse. On sunny days, they provide a warm environment for plants; on cloudy days, they moderate temperature swings and shelter the plants from chilling winds and nighttime frosts.

They are ideal for starting seedlings in the spring. These can be either hardy crops to be harvested directly from the cold frame, or crops that later will be transplanted in the garden—such crops as cabbage, lettuce, broccoli, and cauliflower.

The cold frame can be used to shelter flats which have been started elsewhere. It's a good place, for example, to harden off tomatoes before they are transplanted.

In northern climates, cold frames provide an ideal summer environment for melons, cukes, and other crops that thrive in the heat.

In late summer, plant the cold frame with hardy greens to harvest in October or November (or well after the first frost).

**How it works:** The heat of the sun is trapped beneath the glazing which causes internal temperatures in the cold frame to rise much more quickly than outdoor ambient temperatures. Once the window lid is shut, the insulation and thermal shutters decrease heat loss; adding thermal storage increases the accumulation and retention of heat for slow dissipation overnight to young plants.

**Tips:** The directions call for #2 pine; you may prefer to substitute cedar, cypress, or redwood which are more rot- and insect-resistant. If you use pine, it should be treated with Cuprinol (not penta or creosote; these wood preservatives are toxic to plants). When working with Cuprinol, wear gloves, and avoid breathing the vapor. Do not apply the preservative near planting beds.

**Advantages:**
1. Can increase the types of produce you grow.
2. Allows for a jump on the season—up to six weeks for vegetables and flowers.
3. Plants are hardier and stouter

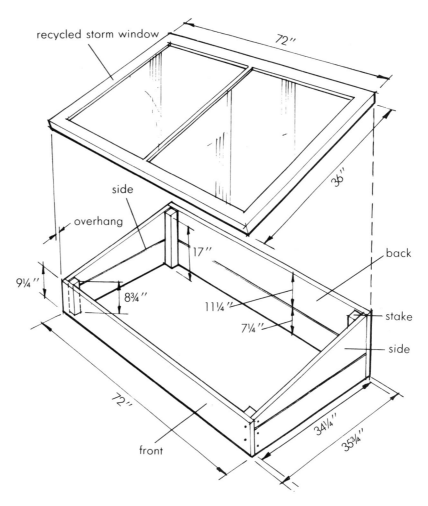

recycled storm window

72"

36"

side

overhang

17"

9¼"

8¾"

11¼"

back

7¼"

stake

side

72"

front

34¼"

35¾"

than those grown in greenhouses because of exposure to
hot and cold temperatures.
4. Can be used to harden off
plants before transplanting.
5. Good place to propagate and
multiply houseplants or to
start perennials for fall planting.
6. Can grow fall salad crop.
7. Use for wintering over semi-
hardy plants.
8. Use for winter storage.
9. Can convert cold frame to use
as hotbed (see instructions pp.
15-17).

### Disadvantages:

1. Although cold frame will extend the growing season, it
does not provide year-round
growing conditions in most
parts of the country.

### Materials for frame:

| Amount | Size | Item |
|---|---|---|
| 1 | 1″ x 10″ x 6′ | #2 pine |
| 1 | 1″ x 8″ x 12′ | #2 pine |
| 1 | 1″ x 12″ x 12′ | #2 pine |
| 1 | 2″ x 2″ x 5′ | #2 pine |
| 26 | #8 x 1¾″ | Wood screws |
| 1 | quart | Cuprinol |
| 2 | 2½″ | Loose pin hinges with screws |
| 1 | ¾″ x 12′ | Self-sticking foam weatherstripping |
| | | Door pull or screw-type knob |
| | | Scrap lumber (l x or 2 x) |
| | | Resorcinol or waterproof glue |

### Tools:

Fine-toothed handsaw or circular
  saw
Hammer
Screwdriver
Rafter square or try square
Combination square

Electric drill with #8 Screwmate
Straightedge
Tape measure
Paint brush
Utility knife

## How to build:

*These directions are for an 18½" (height) x 35¾" (width) x 72" (length) cold frame to be used with a 3' x 6' recycled storm window. If you want to use recycled windows of other dimensions, adjust the width and length measurements of the frame accordingly.*

*Directions are also given for making your own window with plastic film or corrugated fiberglass glazing. Good quality fiberglass will last 15 to 30 years; the polyethylene plastic will have to be replaced after two seasons, but is much cheaper.*

## A. The Frame

**1.** From the 1" x 8" x 12' board, cut three pieces; one piece should measure 72" and two pieces should measure 34¼". From the 1" x 12" x 12' board, cut one piece to 72".

To angle the sides of the cold frame for the window, lay the remaining piece of 1 x 12 flat on a work surface. Measure 34¼" in from one end of the board and mark (Point A). At Point A, draw a perpendicular line 2" long with the square (Line AB). With the straight-edge, draw a line from Point B to the further corner on the end of the board from which you measured.

Cut out the truncated triangle with a handsaw.

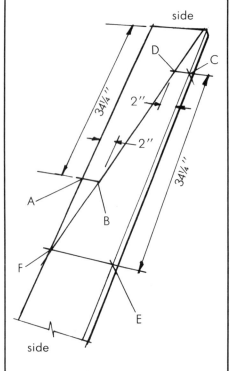

**2.** For the second side, measure down along the edge from the triangular point remaining on the 1 x 12 until there is a width of 2". Draw a square line (Line CD). At Point C measure along the edge of the board 34¼" to Point E. At Point E draw a perpendicular line the width of the board (Line EF). Connect Points D and F. Cut out the second side (piece CDFE).

**3.** From the 2 x 2 stock, cut two stakes to 17" and two to 8¾".

Coat all lumber with Cuprinol, a wood preservative.

**4.** Align the end of one of the longer stakes with the edge of your work surface. On top, place one of the rectangular sides (1" x 8" x 34¼"), and one of the angled sides with its actual 11¼" width over the stake. Adjust so that both side pieces are edge to edge lengthwise, with the 1 x 8 (actually 7¼") flush with the bottom of the stake. The side boards should also be flush with the edge of the stake. (A temporary second stake can be slipped under the side boards to keep them level while they are being assembled.)

With an electric drill and a #8 Screwmate, drill holes, two per board, which are ¾" in from the outside edge. Remove boards and apply a thin layer of glue to adjoining surfaces. Then screw through the sides into stake using #8 x 1¾" wood screws.

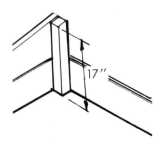

**5.** The other end of the side will be screwed into a shorter stake. Position stake so that it aligns with the sawn ends of the side boards, and is flush with the bottom edge of the 1 x 8. Drill holes ¾" in from the sawn ends. There should be one hole into the tapered end of the 1 x 12 and two into the rectangular 1 x 8. Glue and screw together.

Repeat this assembly for the second side, remembering that the stakes must be on the opposite side of the boards, so that all four stakes will be on the inside of the frame when it is assembled.

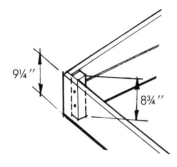

**6.** Rest one of the sides on the 1 x 8 edge and perpendicular to a surface against which you can push when screwing front and back pieces into stakes. The shorter stake will face you.

Position front 1 x 10 board with its sawn end flush with the side. The outside edge of front piece should be in line with the angle of the side. Adjust front if necessary. Drill two holes 7″ apart and 1½″ in from edge. Remove. Apply glue to adjoining surfaces. Check for square and screw together with 1¾″ screws. Screw front to other side in the same manner. Check corners for square.

**7.** Rotate frame so that the front is flush with a surface against which you can push. Position the 1″ x 8″ x 72″ back piece flush with outside edges of the 1 x 8 sides. Drill two holes 1½″ in from edge and 5″ apart. Glue and screw together with 1¾″ screws, checking for square. Drill, glue, and screw other end of 1″ x 8″ x 72″ board into stake. Check for square.

Rest 1″ x 12″ x 72″ board edge to edge lengthwise on top of 1 x 8 board. On each side, drill two holes 1½″ in from the edge of the board and 6″ apart. Glue and screw into stakes.

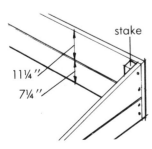

## B. The Glazing

### I. Using a Recycled Window

<table>
<tr><td colspan="3">Materials:</td></tr>
<tr><td>Amount</td><td>Size</td><td>Item</td></tr>
<tr><td>1</td><td>3′ x 6′</td><td>Recycled storm window</td></tr>
<tr><td colspan="3">If the window is in poor repair, you will need:</td></tr>
<tr><td colspan="3">Materials:</td></tr>
<tr><td>Amount</td><td>Size</td><td>Item</td></tr>
<tr><td>1</td><td>pint</td><td>Exterior enamel trim paint<br>Glazing compound<br>Glazier's points</td></tr>
</table>

**Tools:**

Paint scraper        Hammer
Putty knife          Paint brush
Chisel

### How to repair:

**8.** The 3′ x 6′ storm window should be carefully inspected before it is mounted on the cold frame. Scrape down to remove peeling paint and loose glazing compound. If the glazing compound is missing or easily removed, the window will have to be reputtied.

Check that along the edges of each pane where the glazing compound has been removed there are two glazier's points. Replace if necessary. Glazier's points are available from any glass retailer and are pressed into the wood with a putty knife. Some points come with a special "pusher" which is aligned with the triangular point, then tapped into place with a small hammer.

Cracked panes should be replaced or air will leak through the cracks. Chisel out the bits of glass and old putty. Have a new pane cut ⅛″ smaller than the length and width of the opening so that the glass will fit easily.

To secure the glass, knead the glazing compound until it is soft and pliable. Then roll it between your hands to form a long, ⅛″ thick rope-like bead. Lay the bead around the frame to fill the groove in which the glass will rest. This cushions the glass and corrects irregularities in the frame.

**9.** Set the pane in place and tap in the glazier's points, using two per side for small panes or one point every 6″ for larger ones. Run a bead of compound to fill the crack between the face of the frame and the glass. The caulking should hide the points. Bevel the edges with a putty knife to form a triangle that is flush with the top surface of the wood and extends about ¼″ out onto the glass.

Collect the excess compound in your hand; it can be reused.

Paint the frame and caulking with an exterior enamel trim.

## II. Homemade Window
## Using Polyethylene Plastic Film

**Materials:**

| Amount | Size | Item |
|---|---|---|
| 1 | 2″ x 2″ x 10′ | #2 pine |
| 1 | 2″ x 2″ x 12′ | #2 pine |
| 1 | 56′ | 22 gauge wire |
| 1 | 78″ x 78″ | Polyethylene plastic of 4 or 6 mil |
| 1 | ¼″ x ¾″ x 20′ | Screen molding |
| 6 | #8 x 1¼″ | Wood screws |
| 1 | box | ¾″ brads |
| 1 | quart | Cuprinol |
| | | Resorcinol or waterproof glue |

**Tools:**

| | |
|---|---|
| Backsaw | Utility knife |
| Chisel | Electric drill with ⅛″ bit and #8 |
| Hammer | Screwmate |
| Staple gun and staples | Wire cutters |
| Handsaw | Scissors |
| Combination square | Paint brush |
| Tape measure | Screwdriver |

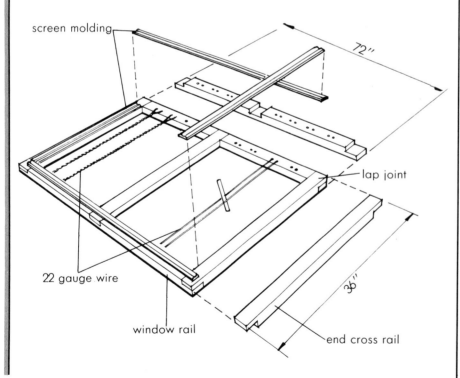

*screen molding*

*22 gauge wire*

*window rail*

*end cross rail*

*lap joint*

*72″*

*36″*

## How to build:

**1.** Cut the 2″ x 2″ x 10′ board to get three 36″ pieces; cut the 2″ x 2″ x 12′ board in half, each piece 72″.

On the three pieces 36″ in length, mark and square off a line 1½″ in from each end. Lay one of the pieces flat with the squared line facing up. On the two edges draw lines with the combination square from the 1½″ mark down 3/4″. Continue this line to the end of the board. Draw similar lines at the other end of the board.

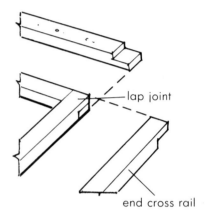

*lap joint*

*end cross rail*

**2.** With the backsaw, make several cross cuts from the squared line to the end of the board, sawing down only to the ¾″ mark. Remove the sawn section from the end to the square mark with a hammer and wood chisel. Or the lap joints can be made by making two cuts with the backsaw, one cut across the grain and one with the grain.

Repeat this procedure at both ends of the other 36″ pieces.

**3.** Mark, saw, and chisel the ends of the 2″ x 2″ x 72″ pieces in the same manner.

On one of these long window rails, measure in from one end and make square lines at 35¼″ and at 36¾″. Mark the edges to a ¾″ depth as was done to the other end joints; saw halfway through the stick, and chisel out the joints as before. Do the same to the second long rail.

**4.** Lay the two 72″ rails parallel and 33″ apart. Set the three 36″ pieces in place across them. The joints should be flush and square. Check the fit. Chisel out any high spots to level the joint faces.

Coat these pieces with Cuprinol wood preservative.

**5.** Once the window rails are dry, assembly can begin. The window frame will be held together with #8 x 1¼″ wood screws, one per joint. Drill holes to prevent the wood from splitting. Remove, apply glue, and screw together.

**6.** Wire supports between the longer rails are necessary to prevent water from puddling on a sagging lid. There should be four equally spaced wire supports for each half of the window.

For each wire support, drill two holes about ½″ apart in each of the two long rails. The holes should be opposite each other. Cut eight pieces of 22 gauge wire, each approximately 7′ long. On one rail thread a wire from the top down through one hole and back up through the adjacent hole. Then stretch the longer end of the wire to the opposite long rail. Feed it down one hole and back up through the adjacent hole. Bring the two wire ends towards the middle of the frame and twist them together. With the two wires lying side by side, in-

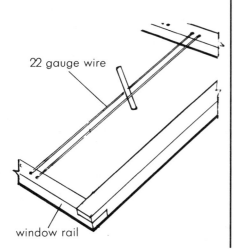

22 gauge wire

window rail

sert a nail or stick in between, and twist the wires together until they are taut. Do not overtighten. Release nail. Although wires may untwist a little, they will still remain taut.

Repeat this process until all eight support wires are in place.

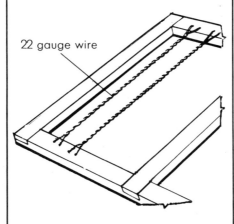

22 gauge wire

**7.** It is necessary to wrap the entire lid in plastic film to protect it from weather, and to prevent the plastic from being torn away by the wind. The process will go much faster if you have a helper.

To double glaze the window frame, you will need a 78″ x 78″ piece of plastic; 20′ of ¼″ x ¾″ screen molding; and a box of ¾″ brads.

From the screen molding, cut two lengths to 70½″ and three lengths to 33″. Position the window with one of the longer rails parallel to the edge of your work surface. Center the sheet of plastic side-to-side on top of the window frame. There will be a 3″ overhang on each side. One edge of the plastic should be flush with the outside edge of the longer rail away from you. Drape the plastic over the frame and let it fall down between yourself and the work surface.

Along the longer rail closer to you, staple the plastic to the window frame. Then center a 70½″ strip of screen molding on top of the plastic ¾″ in from the outside edges

of the window. Tack in place with brads every 6″.

**8.** Wrap the plastic around underneath the window and up to overlap the initial plastic edge along the longer rail. Staple the two thicknesses of plastic to the window frame. They should overlap. Allow some slack because the plastic will shrink in cold weather. Center the second long wooden strip ¾″ in from the edges of the window frame, and drive in brads. The wooden strip should cover both layers of plastic.

**9.** Along one end cross rail, staple plastic to frame. Fold the 3″ overhang around window edge and staple edge of plastic to frame. Then nail one of the 33″ strips of wood to end cross rail. It should butt against the two longer strips and be ¾″ in from edge of frame.

Draw plastic before stapling along other end cross rail. Fold overhang over edge of window and staple. Nail down wooden strip between two longer strips and ¾″ in from edge of window. Middle wood strip is nailed over middle cross rail to secure the plastic. Trim off any excess plastic with scissors.

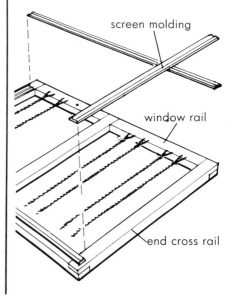

screen molding

window rail

end cross rail

## III. Homemade Window
## Using Corrugated Fiberglass Glazing

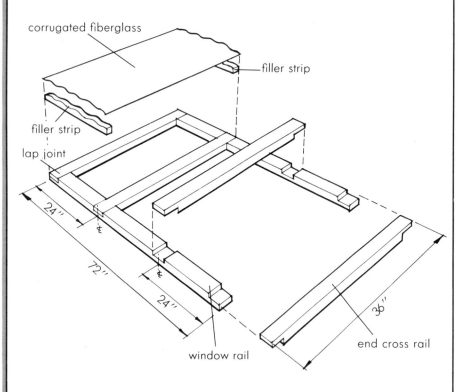

corrugated fiberglass

filler strip

filler strip

lap joint

24"

72"

24"

window rail

end cross rail

36"

### Materials:

| Amount | Size | Item |
|---|---|---|
| 2 | 1" x 3" x 72" | #2 pine |
| 4 | 1" x 3" x 36" | #2 pine |
| 8 | #8 x ⅝" | Wood screws |
| 1 | 26" x 9' | Corrugated fiberglass |
| 1 | 12' | Foam plastic corrugation filler strip |
| 5 doz. | 1¾" | Aluminum screw shank (or ring shank) nails with neoprene or fiberglass washers |
| 1 | tube | Fiberglass sealant |
| | | Resorcinol sealant |

### Tools:

| | |
|---|---|
| Backsaw | Tape measure |
| Chisel | Caulking gun |
| Hammer | Screwdriver |
| Handsaw | Crayon |
| Jigsaw (optional) | Electric drill and #8 Screwmate |
| Combination square | |

### How to build:

**1.** Cut 2½" laps ⅜" deep in both ends of the two long (72") and four short (36") pieces. Cut on the flat side. Cut two 2½" wide notches, ⅜" deep in the flat side of each long piece; each of these notches should be centered 24" from either end. (See p. 10 for directions on sawing these notches.) The short cross members will support the overlap joints of the fiberglass panels. Drill holes with #8 Screwmate and assemble frame, using glue and one ⅝" wood screw at each joint.

**2.** Saw fiberglass into three pieces, each 36" long. Use a fine-toothed handsaw or jigsaw.

Lay 6' of filler strip along the back and front edges of the frame. On top of the filler strips, lay the fiberglass, with the center panel last. The panels will overlap the inside cross rails one corrugation.

Along the back and front edges of the fiberglass strips, mark for nail holes in every third corrugation. Use a crayon. Marks should be made on the ridges (not valleys).

Also mark at 5" intervals along the top of the ridges nearest the side edges and along the overlapped ridges.

Lift off panels, leaving filler strips in position. Drill all nail holes in the fiberglass panels, except those in joint overlaps. Lay the panels down on the frame with the center one on top. Check the positioning. Then remove the center panel and nail down the outer panels along the outside edges. Use 1¾" aluminum ring shank nails with neoprene washers.

Apply fiberglass sealant to inside ridges. Lay center panel on top. Drill marked holes and nail down overlaps.

If you want a double layer of glazing, staple a layer of polyethylene plastic to the undersurface of the frame.

## C. Completing the Cold Frame

**10.** Now that you have completed one of the three types of windows, apply the ¾" self-sticking weather-stripping along the outside perimeter of the window's undersurface. Do not apply along what will be the hinged edge because it will act as a shim and prevent proper closure of window.

**11.** Take frame and window to where you intend to locate cold frame. Align so that the front faces solar south.

Position window on top of the frame walls so that it is centered. The north edge of window should be flush with outside edge of north wall of cold frame; there will be a ¼" overlap on the south to shed water.

Measure in 8" from each end along the north edge of window, and mark. Position a hinge to the inside of one of these marks, and so that the pin can be removed. With a pencil, mark the screw holes. Position second hinge similarly and mark the screw holes.

Remove window. Using a nail as a center punch, make shallow pilot holes in the centers of the pencil marks along the edge of the window. Attach the hinge leaf to the window using the screws provided.

Replace sash on top of cold frame walls. Line up other leaf over the pencil marks. Make pilot holes and set the remaining screws.

**12.** Attach door pull or screw type knob to top of south window rail.

**13.** From a scrap of lumber, cut two sticks 3" long. These can be used to prop up the window frame in warm weather.

**14.** To check that the weatherstripping will do its job, put a piece of paper on top of the weatherstripping. With the window

The soil should be reasonably level, well drained, free of large stones, and enriched with lots of organic matter. You also may want to add as much as one-fourth sand; sand retains heat and will keep the soil porous.

Soil in the cold frame is generally much drier than in an open garden. Give the cold frame thorough waterings in spring and summer. In fall, the growth of plants decreases. It may stop in winter. Plants will need only minimal watering during these seasons.

Plan the location of the cold frame carefully. Ideally, it should be easily accessible and close to the kitchen and/or garden.

Other considerations include exposure. A cold frame should have full sun between 9 a.m. and 3 p.m. If it can't face directly south, face it in a southeasterly direction to get the early morning sun.

Cold frames located against the south side of a house have the added advantage of the building as a windbreak. Or, built into or against a north slope, they will benefit from the wind protection and the added insulation of the earth.

Remember to prop up the window on sunny days even if outdoor temperatures are cool. Wait ten minutes before checking the temperature inside. Then adjust window if necessary.

When outdoor temperatures soar, plants in the cold frame can be shaded with cheesecloth stretched between the frame walls with the window open. This will greatly reduce the sunlight but still allow good ventilation.

closed, you should be able to pull out the paper with some effort. If the paper slips out easily, look for cracks between the window and frame. Add weatherstripping until the seal is tight.

**15.** You may wish to protect the glazing when the cold frame is not in use. (Extreme heat will cause polyethylene plastic to disintegrate; snow loads may weaken or tear it.) Remove the two hinge pins and lift off the window for storage.

### Other design possibilities

**Thermal Storage.** Whenever the entire area of the cold frame isn't being used, heat storage materials can be added. By absorbing heat during the day and releasing it at night, they usually increase cold frame temperatures by 5 to 10 degrees F.

Along the north wall, place as many one-gallon water jugs or bricks as you have room for. Paint

their surfaces flat black so they will absorb more heat.

**Insulation.** Cold frames lose their heat very quickly. To retain more of this heat, fill grain or plastic bags with straw, leaves, or any other coarse material. Place the bags around the walls, and even over the window if you don't mind moving eight bags or more every day. Hay bales around the frame and a blanket over the window may be even easier.

Although many frames are bermed with earth for conserving heat, the soil tends to bend, warp, and rot the wood more quickly.

Rigid insulation (polystyrene or urethane foam) is very effective. Cut 1" to 2" insulation boards to fit around the outside of the north, east, and west walls; the pieces should be wide enough to extend below the frost line.

**Shutters.** Plants in the cold frame can be further protected by adding a thermal shutter beneath the window lid. Cut a piece of 1″ Thermax, a rigid insulation, to the inner dimensions of the cold frame. Then cut it in half. With the two pieces lying flat on top of each other, tape along one of the longer edges with aluminum duct tape.

Measure 1¼″ up from the bottom of the cold frame on all sides. Butt 2 x 2 wooden strips against the line and nail into frame with 7d finish nails along all four walls.

At night unfold the shutter and rest it on the support rails; during the day fold it in half and store against the back wall, or remove. If there are several cold, cloudy days in succession, leave the shutter closed; the plants will survive unharmed.

**Lid Opener.** Greenhouse suppliers now carry thermostatically controlled lid openers. These adjust the window opening to permit sufficient ventilation in the cold frame. The device is powered solely by the heat build-up in the cold frame; it will open the lid when the inside temperature exceeds 68 degrees F. and will close the cover when outdoor temperatures fall below 65 degrees F.

**Solar Pod.** Solar Pod kits and complete assembly instructions are available from Solar Survival, Harrisville, NH 03450. They are expensive but the pieces have been precut and are easy to assemble.

The curved roof of the pod allows for increased sunlight; the double glazing and 2″ insulation make the cold frame even more effective at retaining above freezing temperatures.

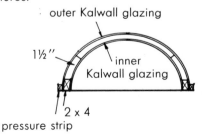

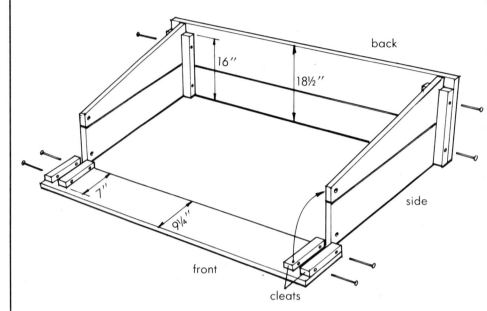

*Knock Down Cold Frame*

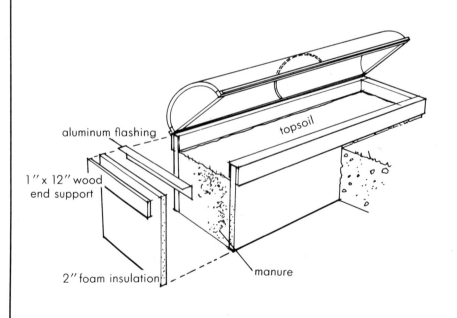

*Solar Pod*

**Knock-Down Cold Frame.** If they aren't used all summer, cold frames may take up valuable space; if so, build a knock-down cold frame that can be dismantled in minutes.

Instead of using stakes for the corner supports, cut four strips of 1 x 1 stock to 16" and four strips to 7".

Lay the 1 x 10 front board flat on your work surface. Align one of the 7" pieces flush with the end and bottom edge of the 1 x 10. Drill, glue, and screw into front piece with 1¼" screws.

After the first cleat is in place, measure toward the center of the board ¾". Draw a parallel line. Place the second cleat flush with this pencilled line, leaving a ¾" gap between cleats. Drill, glue, and screw into front.

Do the same at the other end of front board with one cleat flush with the edge and a ¾" gap between it and the second cleat.

Lay the 1 x 8 and 1 x 12 back boards edge to edge lengthwise on your work surface. Align the 16" cleats flush with ends of the boards and the bottom edge of the 1 x 8. Leave ¾" space and position the two remaining cleats. Drill, glue, and screw into back boards with 1¼" screws.

Assemble cold frame on flat surface. Space the front parallel to and 34¼" away from the back. Slip 1 x 8 side pieces down between back and front cleats. Slide the angled 1 x 12 in on top of each side.

You will need helpers to push back and front together so that the boards are tight. Drill two holes in each of the back corners with a ⅜" bit. Drill through outside cleat, 1 x 8 side, then the inner cleat. The second hole should pass through the cleats and 1 x 12 side. Do the same at front corners.

Slip 8d nails into these holes to hold the cold frame together.

Build the window lid in the same manner as described on page 9.

# Hotbed

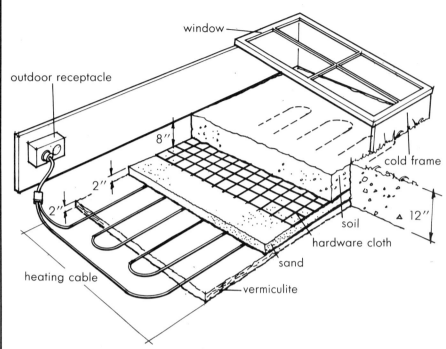

*Hotbed with Soil Heating Cable*

**Skills required:** Slight, and, depending on the method you use, some knowledge of wiring.

**Cost:** The cost of building a Permanent Cold Frame ($30 to $35), plus the cost of a heat source. There are three possible heat sources: manure, light bulbs, or heating cables. Manure should be free; if it must be trucked, that may be a small additional expense. Light as the heat source includes the expense of light bulbs, bulb receptacles, and the extension cord. Heating cables cost $30 to $50.

**Amount of heat gain:** Manure will raise soil temperatures in the frame 10 degrees F. above outside soil temperatures; light bulbs will prevent the soil from freezing; and, with heating cables, temperatures will remain between 72 and 74 degrees F., or at whatever reading the thermostat is set for.

**What it does:** Hotbeds are built like cold frames; they differ only in that they use means of heating other than the sun.

At night and on cloudy days hotbeds are warmer than cold frames, and they may also be more expensive and elaborate.

**How it works:** Like the cold frames, the glazing of the hotbed traps the sun's energy during the day. This causes temperatures within the box to rise more quickly than those outside. At night, temperatures in a cold frame fall steadily, but not as quickly as those outside. The addition of heat storage materials and insulation can further slow, but not stop, this process. Consequently, in the worst of winter, cold frames will freeze.

Hotbeds prevent this by having their own source of heat. In northern climates electric heating cables are more reliable than manure or electric lights for insuring the plants' safety.

Most seeds do not need light to germinate; but many need 70 to 75 degree F. temperatures. Light bulbs heat the air and therefore are not as effective as either the manure or the heating cables which provide bottom heat. This heat, given off to the soil at the seeds' depth, promotes germination and fosters strong root systems in the seedlings. With bottom heat protecting the roots, many seedlings can take near-freezing air temperatures.

**Advantages:**
1. Can double as a regular starter bed or added growing space.
2. Promotes faster germination of seeds.
3. Bottom heat (as with manure and heating cables) encourages quick germination and seedlings with strong root systems. If their roots are heated, many seedlings can withstand near-freezing temperatures.
4. Heating cables are a safe, clean, and convenient way to establish a hotbed; electric lights provide even, reliable heat; manure is free.

**Disadvantages:**
1. Must watch hotbed carefully so that it is never too hot or too cold. If temperatures get above 75 to 80 degrees F. while the plants are small and there is no ventilation, the plants will die.
2. Electrically heated hotbeds are much more expensive than manure; initially, manure smells; and light bulbs will break if you are careless.

**Tips:** Hotbeds are best for peppers, tomatoes, eggplants, and other heat-loving plants.

Choose a site with well-drained soil and preferably on ground that slopes away from the bed. Without adequate drainage, water may collect in the pit. This will slow plant growth and delay manure fermentation.

## How to build:

*Follow the directions on pp. 6-15 for building a Permanent Cold Frame.*

## A. Manure: Heat from Decomposition

1. Take the cold frame to where you intend to locate it, but do not set it in place.

In the soil, mark off the approximate location of the frame, being sure the window will tilt toward the south.

Dig down 30" under the area where the frame will be erected. The hole should be 6" wider and longer than the outside dimensions of the frame. In the bottom add 4" of fresh manure with as much as one-third hay or straw bedding. Pack down and dampen if manure is dry. Add a second 4" layer and tamp down. Wet again if necessary. Continue to fill the hole in the same way to within 6" of ground level. Then finish off with rich soil.

2. Position the cold frame over the soil to which you have just added the manure.

Remove the hinge pins and lid. Lid should be left off cold frame for the first week to let fumes of the manure escape when it heats up. After one week, test soil temperatures with a thermometer. Wait until temperatures have cooled to 90 de-

Orient the hotbed so that it is fully exposed to the sun and in the warmest spot possible—a southeastern exposure is best. Good windbreak protection on the north is also desirable.

The greatest danger with hotbeds is overheating and rapid drying of the soil; be sure to water the bed each morning with a fine spray. However, do not overwater. Soil should be kept just moist enough to prevent plants from wilting.

If water will be a problem, lay lengths of 4" drainage tiles around the perimeter, and slope them away from the bed.

grees F. Then plant seeds and replace lid.

While the manure is rotting, the bed will maintain its heat (usually for six to eight weeks); when the bed begins to cool, it will have to be rebuilt with fresh manure. Manure hotbeds are best operated twice annually, once in the early spring and once in the late fall. (In the winter it is very difficult to work manure into frozen soil.)

The success of this method varies with the diet of the animal from which the manure comes, the type of animal, and the amount of bedding in the manure (the less bedding, the hotter the pile).

## B. Soil Heating Cables

1. Take the cold frame to where you intend to locate it, but don't set it in place.

2. There are two kinds of heating cables: plastic- and lead-covered; both give satisfactory results. A standard 60' cable will heat a 6' x 6' or 6' x 8' bed, and is available from a garden or greenhouse supplier.

To install the cable, excavate to 12" below the soil level of the cold frame site. In the bottom lay 2" of vermiculite. This will insulate the frame from cold air entering below; it will also allow water to drain away from the cable.

On the inside of the frame, install an outdoor receptacle. The wiring should conform to the National Electrical Code; if you aren't familiar with wiring procedures, hire a qualified electrician.

Put the frame in place and carefully lay the cable. The spacing of loops (usually about 8" apart) depends on cable wattage and the size of the growing bed. Read cable instructions carefully. Avoid kinks which may break or damage the cable. Do not let one cable cross over another, and do not shorten the cable, which may cause it to overheat and burn out.

Plug in the cable. Then cover cable with a 2" layer of sand. On top of the sand, lay a sheet of ½" mesh hardware cloth or chicken wire. This will prevent the cable from being damaged inadvertently by gardening tools.

On top of the hardware cloth, add an 8" layer of rich soil. Bury the remote bulb of the thermostat in the soil layer; it should not come in contact with the cable.

3. Lay the window over the cold frame and mount hinges and weatherstripping following instructions on p. 13.

## C. Electric Lights

1. Take cold frame to where you want to locate it and set in place. Do not hinge window.

Fasten 25-watt frosted light bulbs to strips of lumber mounted along the inside perimeter of the frame. Or suspend the lights from non-electric wire to hang bulbs 10" to 12" above the soil. Use one 25-watt bulb for every 2 square feet of garden space. Run an extension cord from the frame to an outdoor electric receptacle. Put window in place.

When there is a prolonged cold snap or frost prediction, plug in the light bulbs. They will provide enough heat to keep hotbed temperatures above freezing.

### Other design possibilities

**Basement Window Cold Frame.** You can build a three-sided cold frame and butt it against a cellar window. When freezing weather threatens, partially open the window; the cellar heat should be enough to protect the plants.

# A-frame: Portable Cold Frame

**Skills required:** Slight.

**Cost:** $20, using two recycled windows that measure 44¼″ x 40¾″.

**Amount of heat gain:** The A-frame cold frame can extend the growing season by as much as three months.

**What it does:** This cold frame can be used in the same way as the previous one (see "What it does" p. 6). It is, however, even cheaper to build and has the added convenience of being portable.

Before the ground thaws, set out your A-frame. Leave the windows closed. After a few warm days, the soil in the cold frame will thaw and you can begin planting hardy crops. As the weather warms, move the frame, and this time plant less hardy crops in it. When these can survive outdoor, nighttime temperatures, move the frame again and plant heat-loving vegetables. At the end of the season, use the A-frame to give protection where it is most needed.

Using this method, you will greatly extend your growing season.

Because the A-frame is so portable, you can start more crops in it than in the Permanent Cold Frame.

**How it works:** The sun's rays penetrate the glazing which traps the heat within the A-frame. As a result, inside temperatures rise more quickly than outdoor temperatures. When outdoor temperatures cool, so too do those in the cold frame, but more slowly. Usually this is sufficient extra heat to prevent the plants from freezing. If more protection is needed, cover the frame with bags of leaves, hay bales, or a blanket.

**Tips:** Ventilating the cold frame is a "must" on sunny days even when it is cold outside; however, on cloudy or cold, windy days, leave it closed.

If you don't believe temperatures will get inordinately hot, leave a thermometer in the cold frame to monitor temperature swings.

**Advantages:**
1. Gives plants an early start and increases the types you can produce.
2. Inexpensive.
3. Portable.
4. Easily disassembled for storage.
5. May add manure to soil bed and use as hotbed.
6. Good for starting herbs and for fall salad crop.

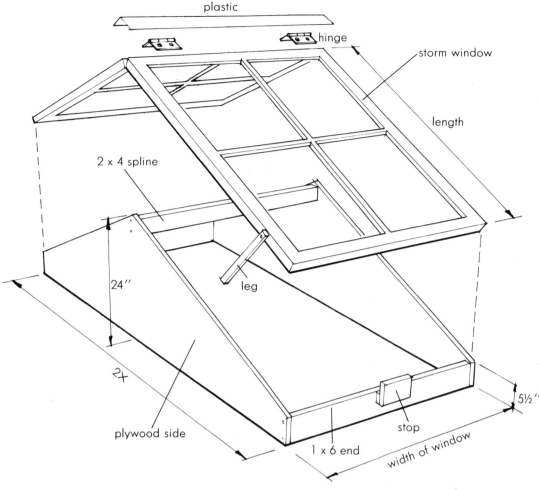

plastic

hinge

storm window

length

2 x 4 spline

24″

leg

2X

plywood side

1 x 6 end

stop

width of window

5½″

7. Possible to use for winter storage of vegetables.

8. For a minimal amount of care, the cold frame lengthens your growing season considerably. It is usually needed only for the one or two "killer" frosts which come in the month before the last frost and the month after the first frost.

**Disadvantages:**

1. Doesn't withstand cold temperatures as well as Permanent Cold Frame with shutters and insulation. And an A-frame is hard to insulate if you want it to be portable.

2. Must prop open during peak heat periods of day and close whenever frost or severe cold snap threatens.

3. Demands constant care and watering.

**Materials:**

| Amount | Size | Item |
|---|---|---|
| 1 | ½″ x 4′ x 8′ | CDX plywood |
| 2 | 44¼″ x 40¾″ | Storm windows |
| 1 | 1″ x 6″ x 8′ | #2 pine |
| 25 | 1½″ | Drywall or wood screws |
| 1 | pint | Resorcinol or waterproof glue |
| 2 | 4″ | Simple butt hinges |
| 1 | 2″ x 4″ x 4′ | Fir, spruce, or pine |
| 1 | 5″ x 44¼″ | Clear polyethylene plastic |
| 1 | quart | White exterior oil-based paint |
| 1 | quart | #10 Cuprinol wood preservative |

**Tools:**

| | |
|---|---|
| Fine-tooth saw or circular saw | 2 C-clamps |
| Hammer | Electric drill |
| Tape measure | Phillips driver for electric drill |
| Straightedge | #8 Screwmate |
| Protractor | Staple gun and staples |
| Rafter square | Slotted head screwdriver |
| Try square | Paint brush |

## How to build:

The overall dimensions of the cold frame are 44¼″ (width) x 72⅝″ (length). Your dimensions will differ if you are using different-sized windows.

*Recycled storm windows of any size can be used as long as you have two of the same dimensions. To make it easier for the reader to adapt the directions for windows of other sizes, parentheses follow all dimensions which will have to be adjusted.*

*Fill in these blanks by first determining the width and height of your windows. (You will want the frame width to be the longer dimension because this means the sides of the cold frame will be smaller and therefore cast less of a shadow on the growing bed.) If your windows each measure 5′ x 2′, for example, the longer dimension (5′) should be substituted in the parentheses wherever there is a "W," and the shorter dimension (2′) wherever there is an "H." Then do the arithmetic processes indicated, and put your own answers in the blanks provided.*

## A. Laying Out the Plywood

**1.** Lay the sheet of plywood flat on a work surface. Along the 4′ dimension, measure up 5½″ (Line AB). Along the 8′ dimension, measure 72⅝″ from the corner, and mark. From this mark, draw a perpendicular 5½″ long (Line DE), using a rafter or combination square.

Mark the center between these two lines (36⁵⁄₁₆″ from either line). At the center, mark a perpendicular line with the rafter square 24″ long (Line CF). Then draw the angled lines between Points C and B; C and E. These lines should each be 40¾″ long.

**2.** Cut out plywood side with a circular saw or handsaw.

**3.** Mark out a second piece of the same shape on the remaining plywood, and cut out.

## B. End Pieces

**4.** Cut the 1 x 6 into two pieces, each of which measures 43¼″ in length (W − 1″ = _____).

**5.** Also cut the 2 x 4 to 43¼″ (W − 1″ = _____).

## C. Assembly

**6.** From a bottom corner edge of one plywood side, measure up ¾″ and mark first screw hole; do likewise at 2″ intervals, for the remaining two screw holes. Holes should be ⅜″ in from the plywood edge. Drill holes with a #8 Screwmate.

Clamp a stop to your work surface. Lay one of the 1 x 6s on edge with one end against the stop. Apply glue to adjoining surfaces. Place plywood against end of 1 x 6. Align edges carefully; with the try square, check that the corner makes a perfect right angle. Then screw together with 1½″ drywall or wood screws.

**7.** In the same manner, screw opposite edge of plywood into the end of the second 1 x 6. Check frequently that unit is square.

**8.** With both ends of the cold frame facing you, lift the second side piece of plywood into place. Drill, glue, and screw together through the plywood into the 1 x 6s.

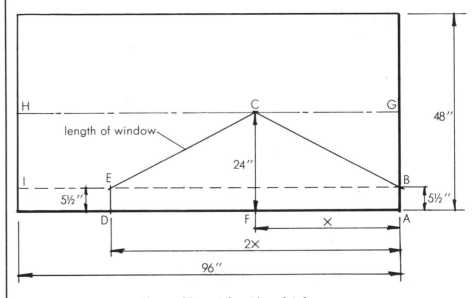

***Plywood layout for sides of A-frame***

# Different Windows

1. Measurements in the directions will vary for windows of other dimensions. To adjust the measurements, lay a sheet of plywood flat on a work surface. Along both 4' dimensions, measure up 5½". Connect these points, BI, using a long straightedge. Your line will run parallel to the factory edge along the 8' dimension.

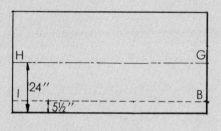

2. Again measure along both 4' dimensions 2' from the factory edge; parallel to the first, draw a second line with a long straightedge running the length of the plywood (Line GH).

3. Measure the shorter dimension of your window. Hold one end of the tape measure at Point B. Swing the tape in an arc until the height dimension on the tape intersects with Line GH. Mark this point (Point C) on Line GH.

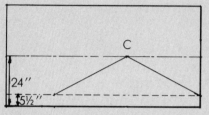

4. These directions for laying out the sides are for maximum use of the 4' x 8' sheet of plywood, but before continuing, you should check that the tilt of the cold frame windows will provide a satisfactory solar angle for early spring and late fall growing.

To determine this angle, position a protractor using Line BI with B as the perpendicular and Line BI as the horizontal. The angle should be between 25 to 40 degrees for optimum use of the cold frame in all but the coldest winter months; this translates into a window height of 27" to 51".

If your window is less than 27", decrease the distance between Points B and G until the angle between Lines BI and BC is 40 to 45 degrees at most. If your window is more than 51", increase the distance between Points B and G until the angle between Lines BI and BC is at least 25 degrees. In such a case, two sheets of plywood will be needed, one for each side.

(Cold frames can be made with the glazing tilted towards the sun at less than a 25 degree angle, but they are less efficient. Angles greater than 45 degrees are best if you live in a climate where you can use the A-frame during the worst of winter, December through March. The cold frame in these directions has not been designed for optimum efficiency during those months.)

5. Once you have established Point C, draw a line (Line CF) parallel to Line AG.

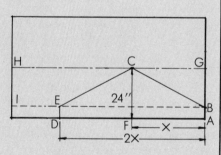

6. From Point A, measure the distance to Point F. Measure this same distance from Point F along the factory edge to Point D. Mark and draw a perpendicular 5½" long (Line DE).

7. Connect Points E and C; Line BC should equal CE. If they don't, remeasure.

**9.** A top support is needed. Align the 2 x 4 spline so that it is flush with but does not protrude above the sides of the apex.

Drill, glue, and screw together with 1½" drywall or wood screws, screwing through the plywood into the ends of the 2 x 4.

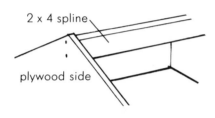

2 x 4 spline

plywood side

## D. Glazing

**10.** Lay the storm windows in place so that their edges meet tightly at the apex of the plywood. You may need to brace them in place.

On the outside of the top rails of the windows, and 4" in from either side, mount the two hinges so that the windows will be able to fold back on themselves. The hinges will span the triangular space between the windows, so be sure the hinges are wide enough.

To prevent water and cold drafts from passing into the cold frame through this triangular gap, staple a piece of 5" plastic over the opening.

**11.** You will need stops where the windows meet the 1 x 6s. Gather some small scraps of lumber or plywood, and screw or nail them to the center of both 1 x 6s. They will prevent the bottom of one window from slipping off the 1 x 6 when the other window is opened.

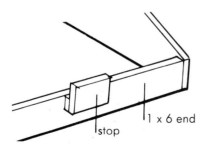

1 x 6 end

stop

**12.** You may also want to attach knobs or rope handles to the bottom rail of the storms to make them easier to open.

**13.** Give the frame two coats of Cuprinol to protect the wood. Let dry.

Check the windows carefully; they may need to be painted and/or the panes reputtied.

Paint the inside of the cold frame with two coats of the white paint. This will help reflect light into the frame. Paint the outside surfaces whatever color you like. Be sure to use an oil-based paint; Cuprinol is hard to cover with a latex paint.

**14.** From either scrap lumber or the remaining plywood, cut four strips 3" wide and 7" to 9" long. Screw these legs into the bottom of the windows along the sash stile on either side. Use only one screw. These legs may be used to prop the windows open during warm weather.

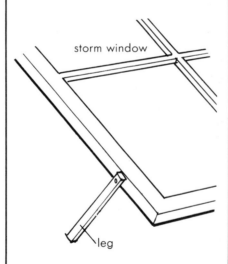

storm window

leg

## E. Setting the Cold Frame in Place

**15.** Before setting up the cold frame, prepare the soil for an area

of approximately 4' x 7' (which will vary according to the overall width and length dimensions of your cold frame). The 4' dimension will run east/west.

Work the soil until it is loose and friable, adding compost, lime, or other fertilizer, if you intend to enrich the soil. Mark rows and plant seeds. Water, if necessary.

**16.** Over this area, place the cold frame. Be sure that chilling breezes won't get in under the sides or ends of the frame; bank soil around the box from the outside. With a tape measure, check the inside diagonals of the box. If they aren't equal adjust the frame until it is square; the earth will keep it in position so the windows will sit properly.

**17.** With the windows doubled back on each other, lift them over the cold frame and position the lower one against one of the stops. When the bottom rail is in place, rest the windows against the plywood sides. Carefully unfold the top window up over the spline. It will rest on the plywood sides with its bottom rail against the second stop.

**18.** To hold the windows open, swing both legs so that their ends rest on the ground. It is also possible to swing the south-facing window up over the 2 x 4 spline and let it rest on top of the north-facing window. This position is good on windy days.

**19.** Once there is no danger of frost, remove the windows by doubling them over one another. Then lift off. You may need two people, one at either end, to lift off the box because the soil may have compacted around the frame.

In the fall when there again is

danger of frost, place the cold frame box over the plants that need protection, and install windows.

When the cold frame is no longer needed, store it where it will be protected from unnecessary weathering.

## Other design possibilities

Other easily portable cold frames include:
  bottomless one-gallon milk jugs
  hay bales
  recycled windows

If you can't find old storm windows for the Portable A-frame, make your own using the directions on pp. 10–12. If you have only one window, the north wall can be built of plywood and shuttered to permit ventilation in the cold frame.

# Window Greenhouse

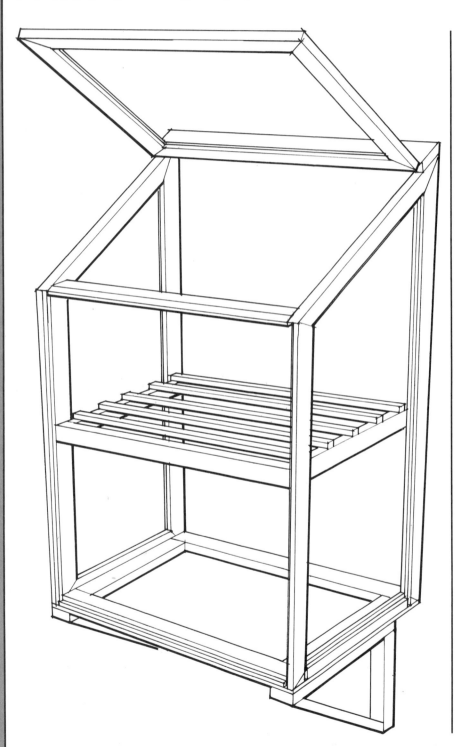

**Skills required:** Moderate.

**Cost:** $50 to $80.

**Amount of heat gain:** Usually heat loss exceeds heat gain.

**What it does:** The window greenhouse is placed over any south-facing window to provide space for seedlings and houseplants. Because of its bay window design, the window greenhouse receives more sunlight than a south-facing window. During the day, sunlight entering the greenhouse is converted into heat; any excess can be vented into the house.

Window greenhouses are ideal for those who don't have the time or land for a full-sized greenhouse, particularly for those living in apartments. They are best suited for plants that don't take up much room such as herbs and cherry tomato plants, and for seedlings started in late winter to plant in early spring. Window greenhouses also can be used for houseplants or for holding tender outdoor plants over from one season to the next.

If the greenhouse is added to a window without an existing storm window, it will act as a second layer of glazing and reduce heat loss from the inner window. In northern climates, however, extremely cold temperatures may necessitate leaving the inner window open to heat the greenhouse with furnace-heated house air. This practice keeps the plants alive; it also increases heat loss through the greenhouse glazing, making the annual heat gain of the greenhouse negligible, if any at all. During cold winter nights, it is preferable to bring the plants into the house so that the inner window can be shut, but this is often inconvenient.

**How it works:** The increased glazing of a window greenhouse allows more sunlight (heat) to reach the plants than a vertical window would.

**Tips:** The window greenhouse should be installed on a south-facing window that is exposed to full sun from 9 a.m. to 3 p.m. Check carefully for buildings, trees, etc., that might block the light.

Before building the window greenhouse, check local regulations; some communities have city ordinances prohibiting protruding structures. Also check your insurance policy to be sure it has no relevant restrictions.

**Advantages:**
1. Attractive and convenient.
2. Acts as a storm window.
3. Ideal for city apartments.

**Disadvantages:**
1. Fairly expensive for limited growing space; would be better to invest in storm windows or movable insulation for south-facing windows.
2. Difficult to maintain ideal greenhouse conditions; can become very hot in summer, very cold in winter. In fact, greenhouse may be unusable in summer because of overheating.
3. Caulking and weatherstripping are important for control of unwanted ventilation; they will need to be checked frequently and replaced when necessary.
4. Plants on upper multiple shelves will filter out sun and limit ventilation to plants below.

**Materials:**

| Amount | Size | Item |
|---|---|---|
| 4 | 1″ x 2″ x 12′ | #2 pine or redwood |
| 1 | 2″ x 4″ x 10′ | Pine, fir or spruce |
| 1 | ¼″ x 1¼″ x 15′ | Furring strip |
| 1 | ⅜″ x 3′ x 3′ | CDX exterior plywood |
| 1 | ¾″ x 15″ x 22½″ | Thermax insulation |
| 4 pcs. | ⅛″ | Double-strength glass (cut to fit) |
| 2 | 2½″ | Fixed butt hinges |
| 4 | 2½″ | Lag bolts and washers |
| 4 oz. can | | Wood putty |
| 9 | 16d | Common nails |
| 2 oz. | 10d | Finishing nails |
| ⅜ lb. | 6d | Finishing nails |
| 1 oz. | 4d | Finishing nails |
| 3 oz. jar | ¾″ | Brads |
| 20 | 2″ | Wood screws |
| 40 | 1″ | Wood screws |
| 1 tube | | Latex caulking |
| | | Glazier's points |
| | | Glazing compound |
| | | Resorcinol or waterproof glue |
| | | Sandpaper |
| | | Wood preservative or enamel paint |

**Tools:**

Router with ³⁄₁₆″ diameter pilot, rabbeting bit and arbor OR circular saw with edge guide
Try square
T-bevel gauge (optional)
Handsaw or adjustable miter box and backsaw
Protractor or protractor-type cut-off guide
2 C-clamps
Hammer
Vise
Nail set
Plane
Awl
Screwdriver
Tape measure
Combination square
Marking gauge
Carpenter's level
Electric drill with #6 and #8 Screwmates, ¼″ bit
Sawhorses (optional)
Ratchet handle and socket wrenches
Putty knife
Caulking gun

5. The smaller the greenhouse, the greater the temperature fluctuations and the more difficult it will be to control the environment.
6. Like bay windows, too much surface area in which to lose heat; to achieve any heat gain may have to close off greenhouse at night, but this leaves the plants out in the cold. In addition it is impossible to insulate greenhouse sufficiently at night to keep plants warm.

# How to build:

These directions are for a 54¼" (H) x 27" (W) x 18" (D) window greenhouse which is designed to be screwed into the side and top blind stops of a double-hung window. The greenhouse fits in the same spot of the frame as the storm window; if your window has a storm, it will have to be removed before the greenhouse is installed. Don't remove the sashes, however, unless you have a casement window.

To determine the width of your greenhouse, measure on the outside from blind stop to blind stop. Then measure the height from the blind stop along the top to a point directly below it on the window sill. If you wish to decrease the greenhouse depth to 12" or 16", adjust the side dimensions given in these directions [i.e., SHELF SIDE (A), BOTTOM SPACER (C), LID SIDE (H), SIDE BOTTOM (J), and SIDE TOP (I).]

Directions are given for only one shelf. With the shelves spaced 11" apart, this greenhouse can easily handle two additional shelves (more if you wish).

All the shelves are made in the same way. For slatted shelves, allow 5' of 1" x 2" stock and approximately 15' of ¼" x 1¼" strips for each shelf.

Glass shelves also can be used, and are preferable because they allow more sunlight to reach plants on the lower shelves. Have the glass cut to the dimensions of the shelf frame minus ⅛" for tolerance. For each shelf frame you will need two SHELF SIDEs (A) and one SHELF FRONT (B).

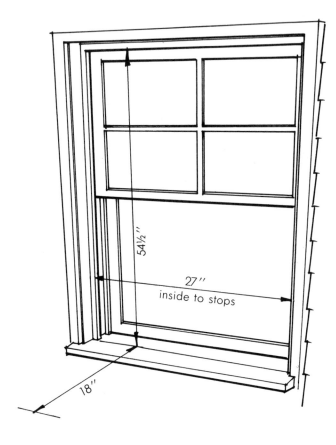

## A. Cutting the Pieces

**1.** Cut the first 12' strip into the following lengths and label as indicated:

| Amount | Length | Label |
|---|---|---|
| 2 | 17" | SHELF SIDE (A) |
| 2 | 25½" | SHELF FRONT/ BOTTOM BACK (B) |
| 2 | 15" | BOTTOM SPACER (C) |
| 1 | 27" | TOP CROSS-PIECE (D) |

The remainder is scrap.

**2.** Lay flat on its broad side and clamp the second 1" x 2" x 12' strip to your work surface. Mark for a ¼" deep and ⅜" wide rabbet lengthwise of the board. Use marking gauge or combination square.

To cut the rabbet with the router, screw a rabbeting bit onto the arbor, then screw a ³⁄₁₆" diameter pilot to the bit. Insert in router and set router for ¼" depth. Cut rabbet.

If you will be making the rabbet cuts with a circular saw, adjust the depth of the blade to ¼". Set the edge guide for a cut ⅜" in from the edge of the board. Make the first cut lengthwise.

Turn the board on edge and clamp to two sawhorses for the second lengthwise cut. Set the depth of the saw blade to ⅜" and the edge guide for a cut ¼" in from the edge of the board.

**3.** Cut a similar rabbet lengthwise of the third 1" x 2" x 12' board and set it aside.

**4.** With the fourth 12' strip on edge, clamp it to your work surface or to two sawhorses. Along one edge remove a ¼" deep x ⅜" wide rabbet with either the router or circular saw.

From this rabbeted 12' strip, remove two lengths each 25½" long with a handsaw or circular saw. Label them BOTTOM FRONT(L) and TOP FRONT (L). Set aside.

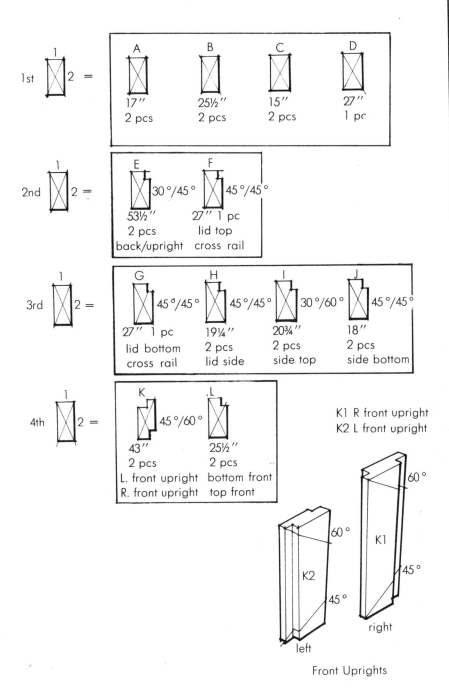

1st  1|2 =

| A | B | C | D |
|---|---|---|---|
| 17″ | 25½″ | 15″ | 27″ |
| 2 pcs | 2 pcs | 2 pcs | 1 pc |

2nd  1|2 =

| E | F |
|---|---|
| 30°/45° | 45°/45° |
| 53½″ | 27″ 1 pc |
| 2 pcs | lid top |
| back/upright | cross rail |

3rd  1|2 =

| G | H | I | J |
|---|---|---|---|
| 45°/45° | 45°/45° | 30°/60° | 45°/45° |
| 27″ 1 pc | 19¼″ | 20¾″ | 18″ |
| lid bottom | 2 pcs | 2 pcs | 2 pcs |
| cross rail | lid side | side top | side bottom |

4th  1|2 =

| K | L |
|---|---|
| 45°/60° | |
| 43″ | 25½″ |
| 2 pcs | 2 pcs |
| L. front upright | bottom front |
| R. front upright | top front |

K1 R front upright
K2 L front upright

Front Uprights

**5.** It will be necessary to make a second rabbet in the remaining length of 1″ x 2″. Lay the strip flat and clamp to your work surface. The existing rabbet should be facing down and be on the side closer to you. Along the top edge away from you, cut a second ¼″ deep x ⅜″ wide rabbet lengthwise. Leave this board on your work surface in order to make the angled end cuts.

## B. Cutting the Angles

**6.** At the end of the board, place the protractor and mark for a 60 degree left cut. Cut off triangle with circular saw or handsaw, or with miter box and backsaw. (If you are using a protractor-type cut-off guide, set it for a 30 degree left cut.)

Measure down along the front

edge of the board 43″ and mark. Set the protractor to 45 degrees right. Draw the angle to align with the mark. Cut with handsaw or backsaw and miter box. This should leave a board 43″ long with a 60 degree cut at one end and a 45 degree cut at the other. Label LEFT FRONT UPRIGHT (K) and set aside.

**7.** Mark the end of the remaining length with the protractor set at 45 degrees left and cut. From the apex, measure along the front edge 43″. Mark. Set the protractor to 60 degrees right (or to 30 degrees right if you are using a protractor-type cut-off guide). Draw angle and cut with saw. Label RIGHT FRONT UP-RIGHT (K). Set aside.

**8.** Place on your work surface one of the two 12′ strips which was rabbeted the entire length. Position it with the rabbet facing you and down towards the work surface. With the protractor set at 30 degrees right (or 60 degrees right if you are using a protractor-type cut-off guide), mark angle at end of 12′ strip. Cut with saw. From the apex, measure down along the back edge 53½″. Mark. Set protractor to 45 degrees left. Draw angle. Cut and label RIGHT BACK UP-RIGHT (E). Set aside.

**9.** Set protractor to 45 degrees right. Mark angle on end of remaining length and cut. Measure along the back edge 53½″ and mark. Set protractor to 30 degrees left. Draw angle and cut. Label LEFT BACK UPRIGHT (E). Set aside.

This should give you two pieces of the same length which if laid flat-surface to flat-surface will have rabbets along both outside edges and be cut to 30 degrees at one end and to 45 degrees at the other.

**10.** On the remaining piece, set the protractor to 45 degrees right. Mark and cut angle. Measure along back edge 27″ and mark. Line up protractor with this mark for a 45 degree left cut. The cut will angle towards the first cut. Cut and label LID TOP CROSS RAIL (F). Set aside.

The remainder of this strip is scrap.

**11.** Place the third 12' strip (also with one lengthwise rabbet) on your work surface. The rabbet should be facing up and be on the side near you. At the end of the board, set the protractor to 45 degrees right. Cut. Then measure from the apex along back edge of board 27" and mark. Readjust the protractor so that it reads 45 degrees left. Align with mark and draw angle. It should angle toward the first cut. Cut.

Label LID BOTTOM CROSS RAIL (G) and set aside.

**12.** Adjust protractor to read 45 degrees right. Cut a 45 degree angle. From the apex measure 19¼". Set the protractor for 45 degrees left. Mark angle. Cut. Label LID SIDE (H) and set aside.

Cut a second identical 19¼" section with two 45 degree angled ends. Label LID SIDE (H) and set aside.

**13.** With the remainder of the board flat on your work surface and the rabbet facing up and facing you, set the protractor to 60 degrees right. Mark and cut angle. Measure along back edge 20¾". Mark. Set protractor to 30 degrees left and draw angle. Cut and label LEFT SIDE TOP (I). Set aside.

**14.** Set protractor to 30 degrees right. Mark angle on end of remaining section of 12' strip (rabbet should still face up and towards you). Cut. Measure 20¾" along back edge. Mark. Set protractor to 60 degrees left. Mark. Cut and label RIGHT SIDE TOP (I). Set aside.

**15.** Set protractor to 45 degrees right. Mark angle on end of remaining section of 12' strip. Cut.

Measure along back edge 18". Mark. Set protractor to 45 degrees left. Mark. Cut and label SIDE BOTTOM (J). Set aside.

Cut an identical 18" length with two 45 degree cuts, one on either end. Label SIDE BOTTOM (J). Set aside.

## C. Side Assembly

**16.** On a flat work surface lay RIGHT BACK UPRIGHT (E) with rabbet facing up and in towards center. Both ends will also angle toward the center. Eighteen inches to the left, place RIGHT FRONT UPRIGHT (K) with its ¼" deep x ⅜"-wide rabbet towards the center. At the bottom, position an 18" SIDE BOTTOM (J) with the rabbet up and facing the center. At the top place a 20¾" SIDE TOP (I). With its rabbeted edge up and facing the center, it will slip into the 30 degree cut of the BACK UPRIGHT (E) and the 60 degree cut of the FRONT UPRIGHT (K).

Apply glue to the mitered ends of BOTTOM and FRONT pieces. Place the two lengths in a vise and tighten to hold them firmly. Check for square. Readjust if necessary. Nail together with two 4d finishing nails near the end of each rail. Countersink nails with nail set. Double check corner for square.

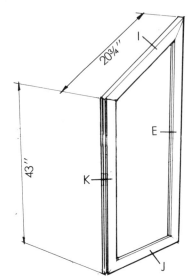

Follow the same procedure for gluing and nailing the other three corners. If side is assembled correctly, there will be a continuous rabbeted edge inside on all four sides.

Assemble the left side frame. Check the bottom angles for square, and set aside.

## D. Shelves

**17.** To construct the wooden slatted shelves, stand one of the 17" SHELF SIDES (A) on end or place it upright in a vise. Set a 25½" SHELF FRONT (B) perpendicular to the SHELF SIDE (A) with the edges flush. Remove and apply glue to adjoining surfaces. Replace and hold it square. Nail through SHELF FRONT (B) into SHELF SIDE (A) with two 6d finishing nails. Countersink heads.

Glue and nail other end of SHELF FRONT (B) into the second SHELF SIDE (A) in the same fashion.

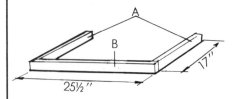

**18.** Lay the U-shaped frame on your work surface. Check for square. From the ¼" x 1¼" furring strips, cut seven lengths, each 25½" long. Lay the first strip along the edge of the SHELF FRONT (B) and nail into SHELF SIDES with two ¾" brads at either end. Space the remaining furring strips approximately 1½" apart and nail to frame, being sure that the frame remains square. (The wider the spacing between the slats the better, because more sunlight will reach the plants on the bottom shelf. Decide what size of pot you will be putting on these shelves, and if possible, increase the spacing of the slats.)

Make as many shelves as you will need, and set aside.

## E. Greenhouse Assembly

**19.** Position one of the sides on your work surface with the continuous routed edge up. Measure in from both edges along SIDE BOTTOM (J) 1½". Mark. Between these two marks, place the 15" BOTTOM SPACER (C) on edge and slip under the SIDE BOTTOM. Apply glue to adjoining surfaces. Reposition BOTTOM SPACER (C). Align bottom edges. Nail through SIDE BOTTOM (J) into SPACER (C) with three 6d finishing nails evenly spaced and ⅜" in from the outside edge. Countersink nail heads.

Glue and nail second BOTTOM SPACER (C) to other side frame in similar fashion.

**20.** Rest both sides on edge of FRONT UPRIGHTs (K) 25½" apart with the routed sides facing in. One side should be against a wall or a surface against which you can nail.

Lay BOTTOM BACK (B) on edge on top of the two BOTTOM SPACERs (C). Apply glue to all adjoining surfaces. Then nail BOTTOM BACK (B) into BOTTOM SPACER (C) with two 10d finishing nails; nail through BACK UPRIGHT (E) and SIDE BOTTOM (J) into BOTTOM BACK (B) with 6d finishing nails. Position nails so they don't hit one another within the joint. Countersink nails.

Rotate sides and nail BOTTOM BACK (B) into other side.

**21.** Turn unit over so that it rests on edge of BACK UPRIGHTs (E) and BOTTOM BACK (B). Place BOTTOM FRONT (L) on edge. It should align with side rabbets and edges of mitered corners. Apply glue and nail through BOTTOM FRONT (L) into BOTTOM SPACERs (C) with two 10d finishing nails. Then nail through sides into BOTTOM FRONT (L). Avoid nailing through rabbet. Check for square.

Nail other end of BOTTOM FRONT (L) in place. Countersink nails.

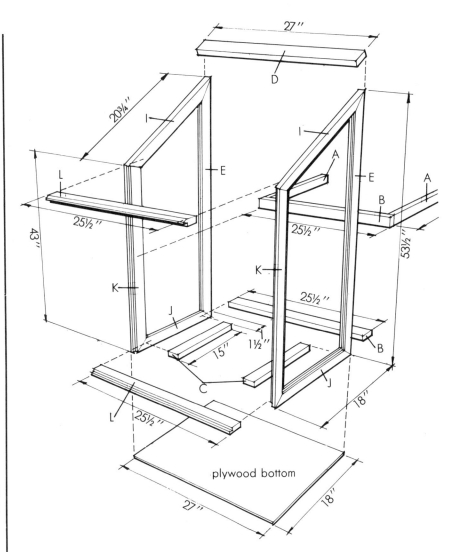

plywood bottom

**22.** Measure 22¾" from bottom of window greenhouse along outside edges of FRONT and BACK UPRIGHTs (K and E). Make squared marks with the combination square. Draw an "X" on the side of the line away from the end from which you measured.

Rest unit on one of its sides. Insert shelf so that the 17" SHELF SIDEs (A) cover the "X's" and are flush with the square lines you have just drawn. The SHELF FRONT (B) will run between the FRONT UPRIGHTs (K); the shelf slats will face the top of the unit; and the ends of the SHELF SIDEs (A) will be flush with the BACK UPRIGHTs (E). You may need a helper to steady the shelf while you nail it into place. Apply glue to adjoining surfaces. Realign edges. Nail through SHELF

SIDE (A) into BACK UPRIGHT (E) with two 6d finishing nails.

Rest unit on other side. Nail through FRONT UPRIGHT (K) into SHELF FRONT (B) and SHELF SIDE (A).

Follow same procedure to secure other side of shelf. Countersink nails.

**23.** Position greenhouse upright on the floor. Set the 27" TOP CROSS-PIECE (D) flat on top of the 20¾" SIDE TOPs and flush with the edges of the mitered corners. Apply glue to adjoining surfaces. Nail into SIDE TOPs (I) with two 6d finishing nails per side. Countersink nail heads.

**24.** Nail TOP FRONT (L) into place. It will complete the rabbeted edge along the front of the greenhouse.

Position TOP FRONT (L) perpendicular to front mitered corners. Mark the lengthwise edge of the TOP FRONT (L) for a 60 degree bevel to match the angle of the SIDE TOPs (I). Remove with a plane.

Apply glue to adjoining surfaces. Align rabbeted edges, being sure TOP FRONT (L) is level. Nail through SIDE TOPs (I) into TOP FRONT (L) with two 6d finishing nails. Countersink.

If you want to install other shelves, do so now. Follow instructions as in Step 22.

## F. The Lid

**25.** Assemble the pieces for the lid. There will be two 27″ LID CROSS RAILs (F and G) and two 19¼″ LID SIDEs (H). All four are cut with 45 degree end cuts and are rabbeted. Place on work surface with rabbets up and facing into the center of the lid.

Assemble in the same fashion as sides. Use vise to hold adjoining pieces; glue and nail together. Check for square.

**26.** Rest lid on top of angled sides and butting against TOP CROSS-PIECE (D). Clamp lid to sides temporarily with two C-clamps. Measure in from each end along TOP CROSSPIECE (D) 3″ and mark. Position one of the hinges so that its outside edge aligns with one of these marks. With a pencil, trace the circumference of each of the screw openings. Remove hinge. Center an awl in each of the circles and tap with a hammer. Reposition hinge over holes and fasten with screws provided with the hinges. Screw second hinge in place following the same steps.

## G. The Plywood

**27.** From the plywood, cut a piece 18″ x 27″ for the bottom of the greenhouse.

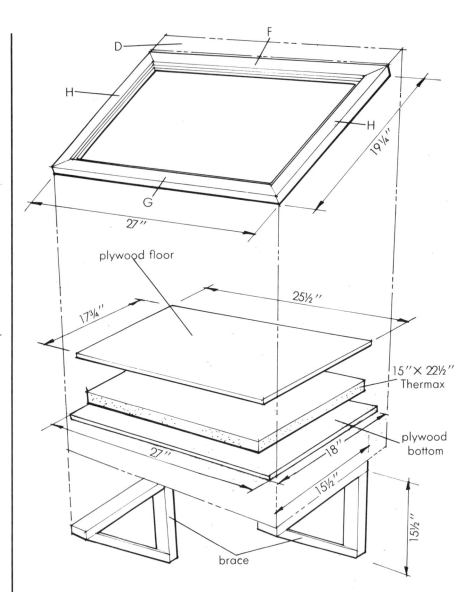

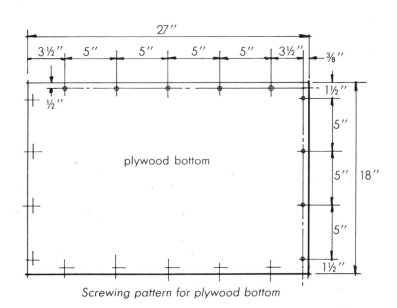

Screwing pattern for plywood bottom

Rest greenhouse on edge of BACK UPRIGHTs (E). Plywood bottom should align with outside edges of BOTTOM FRONT (L), SIDE (J), and BOTTOM BACK (B) pieces.

Drill holes with a #6 Screwmate. Follow diagram for positioning to prevent screws from later interfering with one another. Apply glue to adjoining surfaces and screw together with four 1" x #6 wood screws along both sides and five along both ends.

**28.** Apply wood putty to all nail and screw holes, and to either side of the BOTTOM FRONT (L) in both mitered corners. Check all joints and fill as needed. Let dry, then sand down wood filler.

## H. The Braces

**29.** From the 2" x 4", cut four lengths of 15½". Set aside. Lay the remainder of board flat. Loosen the wing nut on the circular saw and set saw for a 45 degree bevel cut. Tighten nut and cut bevel across one end. Then measure along top edge 20⅞". Make a square mark. From the other side of the 2" x 4", cut another 45 degree bevel along the squared line. The beveled cuts should angle towards each other.

Cut an identical 20⅞" length with both ends angled to 45 degrees.

**30.** Stand one of the 15½" lengths on end. Perpendicular to it, place a second 15½" length. Align all edges and nail together with three 16d nails.

Rest the "L" shape flat on one leg. The 20⅞" length should fit between the two legs. Nail together with three 16d nails on each end.

**31.** On the outside of the window where the greenhouse will be installed, extend the line of the blind stops along the sill by positioning the rule-blade of the combination square flush against the stop. Continue line from the sill to exterior

house wall. Using a level, draw a line 17" long down the house wall. Be sure it is plumb.

Draw a line from the opposite blind stop down the exterior house wall in the same way. The lines should be 27" apart.

Position one of the braces to the center of one of these lines. The upright member of the brace should be flat against the exterior house wall, flush against the sill, and flush with the line. Mark where the bottom of the sill meets the brace. Do the same on the second brace. Measure this distance; filler strips will be cut to this length.

**32.** To determine the thickness of the filler strips, align one end of a level with the inside edge of one of the blind stops. Then hold the combination square against the sill and read the distance from the bottom of the sill to the bottom of the level. This equals the amount the brace will have to be built up in order to hold the greenhouse level.

Cut the filler pieces from 2" x 4" and plywood scraps. Nail them to the horizontal member of the brace, flush with the sill line.

## I. Pre-Installation

**33.** Prime and paint all wood to match house or trim. Use exterior trim or shutter enamel paint, or a clear or pigmented exterior wood preservative stain. Let dry.

**34.** Reposition braces below sill and flush against lines on house wall. With the electric drill and bit, drill two holes 12" apart in each brace. Insert lag bolts and washers. With the ratchet, screw the braces to the house wall. Check that the braces are level with each other.

**35.** Set the greenhouse in place on top of the braces. The BACK UPRIGHTs (E) should rest against and be flush with the inner edge of the blind stops.

Drill screw holes with a #8 Screwmate through the BACK UPRIGHTs (E) into the blind stops every 6". Screw together with one screw on each side. Tighten them just enough to hold greenhouse in place while holes are drilled into the braces.

**36.** Measure 3" (or the distance from the inner edge of the blind stop to the outer edge of the sill). Mark this distance on the inside edge of the BOTTOM SPACER (C). From there measure in towards the center ½" for the placement of the first screw. Drill holes every 4" to 5" with a #6 Screwmate.

Drill holes on both sides through the plywood and into the braces.

Remove temporary screws in blind stops. Return to work area with window greenhouse.

## J. Installation of the Glass

**37.** Measure for the glass. There will be four pieces of double-strength glass. To calculate the dimensions, measure the width and length from the edge of the rabbets of each frame (two sides, front, and lid). From these measurements, subtract ⅛" for tolerance.

**38.** Set greenhouse on its bottom. Work the glazing compound so that it is pliable. Then roll it between your hands to form a long rope-like bead. Lay the ⅛" bead around one of the side frames to cushion the groove in which the pane will rest.

Lift pane into place. Have a helper hold the glass while you tap in the glazier's points, using one point every 6". Fill the cracks between the frame and the glass with a second bead of compound. The caulking should hide the points. Bevel the edges with a putty knife. Collect the excess compound and reuse.

Install the front and other side glass panel in the same way.

Set the glass into the lid. Tap in the points and caulk with glazing compound.

## K. Installation

**39.** It will take two people to move the greenhouse to the house window where it will be located. Lift greenhouse into place on top of braces. Be sure BACK UPRIGHTs (E) align with blind stops.

From the inside of the house, screw through BACK UPRIGHTs (E) into the window blind stops using the drilled holes and 2" screws.

Also use the drilled holes to screw bottom piece of plywood into the 2" x 4" braces. Use the 1" screws.

**40.** Cut a piece of ¾" Thermax to 15" x 22½". Drop in between the BOTTOM SPACERs (C) and BOTTOM FRONT (L) and BACK (B) pieces.

**41.** Cut a 17¾" x 25½" piece of plywood and set it on top. It should fit between the SIDE BOTTOM (J) pieces and align with the outside edge of the BOTTOM BACK (B). Plywood should rest flush with front rabbeted edge.

Drill holes with the #6 Screwmate according to the following pattern.

Apply glue to adjoining surfaces and screw together with three 1" screws along the back and front, and four 1" screws along both sides.

Caulk all seams between greenhouse and house window frame.

If glass shelves are to be used, carefully insert them so that they rest on the SHELF SIDEs (A).

### Other design possibilities

**Location.** South-facing windows are optimum. However, if you have only east or west windows, you should close in the north wall and lid with plywood and insulation.

**Size.** Window greenhouses can be attached with "L" brackets to the window trim.

**Glazing.** A second layer of glazing can be installed by stapling plastic to the wooden frame. The plastic should be on the inside.

Greenhouses also can be glazed with ¼" clear acrylic plastic. This decreases the danger of window breakage, appreciably lightens the weight of the unit, and simplifies construction. See "Window Collector" for glazing installation details (p. 84).

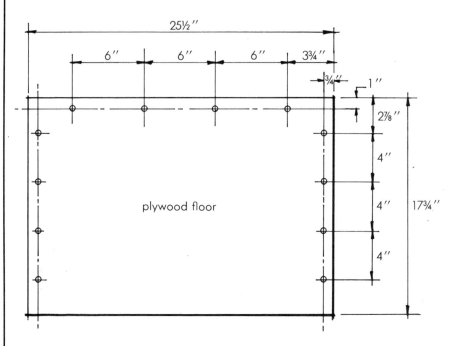

*Screwing pattern for plywood floor*

It is essential that the window greenhouse be vented frequently. Not only will opening the top lid let excess hot air escape, but it will set up air currents that in turn will reduce the chance of fungus infections.

Be sure that all lumber is straight and free of knots. Redwood is preferable; it isn't affected by rot and usually blends well with most architecture.

Pay attention when nailing the pieces together. Be sure the nails are staggered so that when two pieces are joined, the nails won't strike one another.

It is also important that the greenhouse be built square or the glass won't fit. Check the angles frequently with the try square.

There are a number of angles that must be cut. For marking these you can use an ordinary protractor or a protractor-type cut-off guide. Or the angles can be taken off either protractor and set on a T-bevel gauge, and the bevel gauge used to draw all similar angles.

**Heat Sink.** If your window greenhouse produces excess heat during the day, you may wish to store this heat in the greenhouse for nighttime use. Dark colored bricks or bottles filled with sand or filled with water to which a dark food coloring has been added can be used. These materials will act as a heat sink, causing the greenhouse to warm up and cool off more slowly.

**Opener.** Attach two 6" scrap pieces of plywood or 1" x 2" stock to the SIDE TOPs approximately 1" from the back of the TOP FRONT. Use only one screw or carriage bolt and washer for each prop stick. The sticks will swivel to hold the lid in the desired position.

**Weatherstripping.** If the lid doesn't fit tightly, weatherstrip around the edges of the LID SIDEs and BOT-TOM with $\frac{3}{16}$" x $\frac{1}{4}$" pressure-sensitive foam weatherstripping. Also add a hook and eye so that the lid will fasten tightly to the TOP FRONT.

**Screen.** You may want to staple insect screening to the SIDE TOP, TOP FRONT, and TOP CROSS-PIECE to keep birds and insects out when the lid is open. Gaps will have to be left for the lid prop sticks.

# Solar Pit Greenhouse

**Skills required:** Moderate to extensive.

**Cost:** Approximately $500 for an 8′ x 12′ pit greenhouse on a pier foundation.

**Amount of heat gain:** Temperatures in the greenhouse will stay above freezing all year except during winter cold snaps in northern climates.

**What it does:** Solar pit greenhouses are partially sunk below grade to take advantage of the moderating temperatures of the earth. They are built with a pitched, glazed, south roof for heat collection, and an insulated north roof for greater heat retention.

These structures combine all the advantages of a ground-level greenhouse, while being extremely energy-efficient. For cool-weather plants, it is possible to rely solely

on solar radiation for year-round growing conditions, and warm-weather crops can be grown successfully with only a small amount of supplemental heat. Sometimes a few light bulbs or a small electric heater is enough to raise temperatures the needed 10 to 15 extra degrees F.

The greenhouse is invaluable as a growing season extender. Plants can be brought in from the garden in the fall to keep well past early winter, or in early spring plants can be started in the greenhouse and later transplanted into the garden.

**How it works:** This greenhouse has been designed to capture and hold as much of the sun's energy as possible. In most climates, solar radiation should be sufficient to heat the greenhouse year-round.

The south-facing roof is set at a 45 degree angle for the full benefit of the winter sun; the 60 degree slope of the north roof bounces additional light (heat) to the plants below, and is responsible for a 20 percent increase in plant yields. Reflected light is also gained by painting all interior surfaces white and will add 5 to 10 percent to greenhouse productivity. In northern climates, some reflected light enters the greenhouse from snow allowed to collect along the knee wall.

In addition to direct solar radiation, the greenhouse is warmed by the earth below. The gravel of the walkway and the earth of the benches also function as thermal storage materials. They absorb daytime heat and release it gradually at night.

The insulation around the perim-

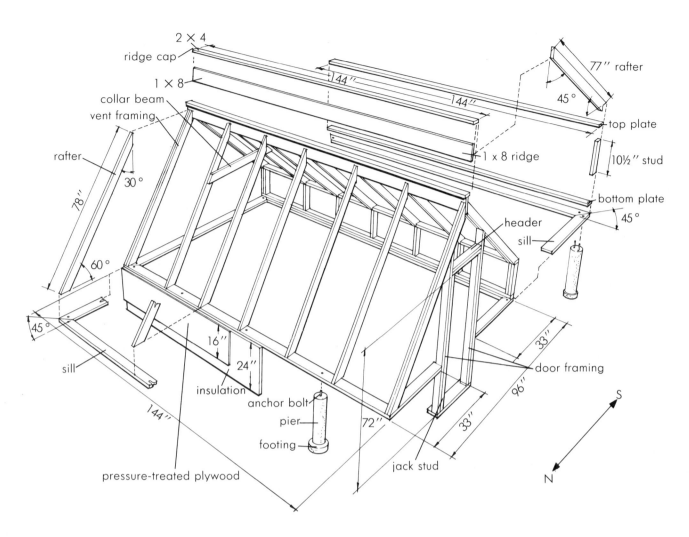

2 × 4
ridge cap
1 × 8
collar beam
vent framing
rafter
78″
30°
60°
45°
sill
144″
insulation
16″
24″
anchor bolt
pier
footing
pressure-treated plywood
144″
144″
77″ rafter
45°
top plate
10½″ stud
1 × 8 ridge
bottom plate
45°
header
sill
door framing
33″
96″
72″
33″
jack stud
S
N

eter and in the north roof will lock in the heat; even if outdoor temperatures go below freezing, the greenhouse should never go below 40 degrees F.

**Tips:** The greenhouse should receive the full winter sun with a minimum of three hours of sunlight a day. A hill, tree, building, or earth berm on the north side for a windbreak will protect the greenhouse from cold north winds and cut down on the need for expensive heating. Evergreens to the south, however, may cast shadows. Deciduous trees, because they lose their leaves, are usually no problem in winter; in summer, they may block the sun which will moderate greenhouse temperatures.

The greenhouse door should not face the prevailing winds. In the

following directions, the door is located on the west wall. Adjust the instructions if the prevailing winds on your site are from the west.

Directions call for a 45 degree slant on the south roof. It is an easy pitch to construct. In northern climates, it is the best angle for greenhouses which will be used primarily in spring and fall. The ideal angle for winter growing conditions, however, is equal to your latitude plus 10 to 15 degrees. At this angle, the greenhouse makes the best use of the weak, low-angled sunlight.

If you wish to adjust the roof angle, you will also have to adjust the height of the knee wall.

Although this greenhouse has a 60 degree pitch on the north roof and a 45 degree pitch on the south roof, there are other options. In-

stead of pitching both sides, the north wall can be vertical, with a 45 degree south-facing roof. Such a design allows more head room, more vertical growing area, and heat storage along the north wall.

An 8′ x 12′ pit greenhouse is minimal. If it is built any smaller, temperatures will rise and fall very rapidly, making an energy-inefficient greenhouse. Larger greenhouses are possible but as the size increases, so too does the expense.

Use pressure-treated lumber for all members. Avoid oil-borne preservatives such as creosote, which is toxic to plants. Water-borne preservatives are recommended.

Choose the 2 x 6s for the sill carefully; the sill is the important connection between the piers and the roof framing. The boards should be straight and free of cracks.

## Materials:

| Amount | Size | Item |
|---|---|---|
| 4 | 1″ x 4″ x 10′ | Common pine |
| 1 | 1″ x 6″ x 12′ | Common pine |
| 1 | 1″ x 8″ x 12′ | Common pine |
| 1 | 2″ x 3″ x 8′ | Pressure-treated fir, pine or spruce |
| 1 | 2″ x 3″ x 10′ | " |
| 3 | 2″ x 4″ x 12′ | " |
| 34 | 2″ x 4″ x 8′ | " |
| 1 | 2″ x 6″ x 6′ | " |
| 10 | 2″ x 6″ x 8′ | |
| 2 | 2″ x 6″ x 12′ | " |
| 1 | 2″ x 12″ x 10′ | " |
| 2 | 2″ x 12″ x 8′ | " |
| — | 6″ diameter and long enough to extend below frost line for 13 holes | Sonotubes |
| 17 | ½″ x 8″ | Anchor bolts |
| 5 sheets | 2″ x 2′ x 8′ | Tongue-and-groove blue rigid styrofoam insulation |
| 3 | 10′ | Drip edge |
| 1 roll | 8″ x 50′ | Flashing |
| 1 roll | | 15 lb. roofing paper |
| — | 4′ x 46′ | Flat fiberglass glazing (Kalwall Sunlite .040) |
| 4 sheets | ½″ x 4′ x 8′ | Pressure-treated plywood |
| 4 sheets | ½″ x 4′ x 8′ | CDX exterior plywood |
| 2 | 3″ | Butt hinges |
| — | 6″ x 24″ x 40′ | Foil-faced fiberglass insulation batts |
| — | — | Concrete |
| 3 bundles | | Asphalt shingles |
| 2 oz. | 4d | Galvanized common nails |
| ⅓ lb. | 6d | " |
| 2¼ lbs. | 8d | " |
| 1 lb. | 10d | " |
| 2 lbs. | 16d | " |
| 1 lb. | 2d | Galvanized roofing nails |
| 160 | 1″ | Aluminum nails with neoprene washers |
| 1 roll | 2″ | Duct tape |
| 2 tubes | — | Silicone caulking |
| 1 | | Hook and eye |
| — | 9 cu. ft. | Pea gravel |
| 1 | ½″ x 26′ | Rebar |
| 1 | 12″ x 12″ | Screened and louvered aluminum vent |
| | | Roofing cement |
| | | Staples |

## Tools:

Tape measure
Wire-cutting shears
Caulking gun
Mason's cord
Hammer
Handsaw
Circular saw with plywood blade
4′ carpenter's level
Line level
Plumb bob
Chalkline
Hoe
Vise
Combination square
Hatchet
Shovel
Electric drill and bits
Protractor or protractor-type, cut-off guide
Vise grips
Hacksaw
Marking gauge
T-bevel
Staple gun
Rafter square
Utility knife
Chisel
Post hole digger (optional)
Mattock (optional)
Jigsaw (optional)

**Advantages:**

1. Low profile blends in with almost any environment.
2. Requires little or no heat from a source other than the sun.
3. Efficient design because the walls are beneath the ground. Temperatures below the frost line are about 50 degrees F. year-round, which is significantly warmer than the outside air in winter.
4. Good wind protection.
5. If movable insulation is used, heat loss is cut in half.
6. If pit isn't used for growing plants in winter, it can be used for storage of root crops.
7. Labor-saving method of construction because there is no need to build benches or a floor, and the walls have been greatly simplified.
8. Easier to build and more economical and efficient to operate than a regular greenhouse.
9. Because there is no artificial heating, pests are generally kept to a minimum.
10. Watering can be done quickly.
11. Plants grow in almost perfectly-simulated natural conditions.

**Disadvantages:**

1. Performs better than an above-ground solar greenhouse only in extremely cold weather.
2. Well-drained site must be chosen to avoid collection of water in trench.
3. If attached to house, you may have to dig several feet below house foundation and this procedure may cause problems.
4. Cannot grow towering plants because of limited space.

## How to build:

*Directions are given for an 8' x 12' pit greenhouse with a 60 degree north-facing roof pitch, and a 45 degree roof and knee wall to the south.*

## A. The Foundation Lines

**1.** Decide the general location of the greenhouse. Then establish the building corners using a measuring tape and four 2" x 4" x 2' wooden stakes.

Locate one corner of the building and drive in a stake. With the tape, measure and mark the other three corners, marking each with a stake. (The 8' dimension will run north/south, the 12' dimension will run east/west.) Drive a nail into the top of each stake. Run mason's cord between the stakes; tie off at each nail.

**2.** To ensure that the perimeter lines are square, measure the diagonals which should be equal. Or measure 3' from one corner stake along the string, and mark. From the same corner, measure along the other string 4' and mark. The distance between these two points should be 5' if you have a perfect right angle. You may have to adjust the corner stakes several times before you find the exact locations.

**3. Batter Boards.** Batter boards are erected beyond the corners to hold the building lines which mark the outside edges of the building. You will need twelve 2" x 4" stakes 4' in length. Pointing the ends with a hatchet will make the stakes easier to drive into the ground. You will also need eight 1" x 4" ledger boards, each approximately 5' long.

Use a hammer or axe head to drive in the stakes 4' beyond each greenhouse corner and parallel with the sides of the building. The middle stake should form a right-angle triangle with the other two stakes. Level the tops of the stakes with a carpenter's level placed on top of a straightedge. Fasten the ledger boards to the stakes with 6d nails, and with a carpenter's level check that the top edges are horizontal.

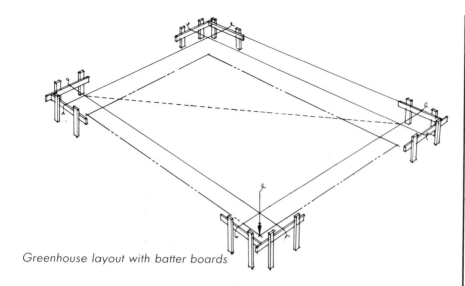

*Greenhouse layout with batter boards*

**4.** To check that the sets of batter boards are in the same horizontal plane, use a straightedge and a 4' carpenter's level, or pull a cord taut between opposite ledgers. Attach a line level to the middle of the cord; a set of batter boards may have to be tapped in farther before they are level with each other.

**5.** At one corner adjust the lines to the batter boards so that the point where the cords intersect is directly over the nail of the corner stake. This is done by dropping a plumb bob from the intersection and adjusting the cords until the plumb bob lines up with the nail.

**6.** Mark with a pencil where the cords hit the ledgers. Fasten the cord to nails driven into the back of the ledgers. Or with a handsaw, cut saw kerfs ¼" deep where the lines touch the batter boards. This allows the strings to be easily removed while you are digging and to be replaced whenever you need to know the exact building perimeter.
Repeat the process at the other corners. Be sure the lines are pulled taut.

**7.** Check again for squareness by measuring from one intersection of two strings diagonally to the other intersection. Then measure the other diagonal. If the two measurements are the same, the corners are at right angles. If you have to move the strings to get a right angle, remember you will have to adjust two strings.

## B. Excavation

**8.** Remove the corner stakes and cord; leave the batter boards and building lines in place. Determine which wall will have the door. Locate and mark the center of the west wall (or whichever wall will have the door). Measure 15" to each side and mark. From these two points, lay out the center aisle of the greenhouse which will be 30" wide x 9' long. The aisle should extend to within 3' of the outside of the west wall.
Dig out this area to a depth of 3'. (To make excavation easier, temporarily remove the west wall building line.)

**9.** From a depth of 32", extend the excavation another 50" westward beyond the pit door to provide a gradual rise of almost 5' to ground level. This provides space for a stairway of five treads. (The extent of the stairway excavation can be decreased if you prefer using a ladder or a set of steps with more vertical rise.) Add and level 4" of pea gravel in the center aisle walkway.

## C. Marking for the Post Holes

**10.** Replace the west wall building line. To mark for the post holes, begin in the southwest corner. Measure 2¾" from the corner along the south building line. At right angles from this point and towards the north building line, measure 2¾".

*Excavation for the aisle and stairway*

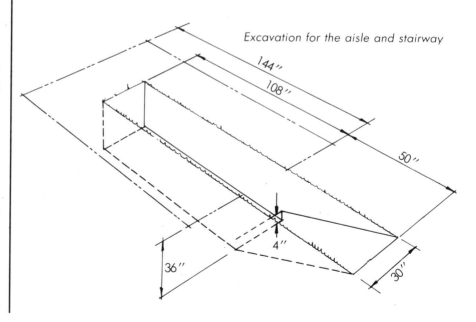

Mark this point with a stake. It represents the center of one of the corner foundation piers.

The center of all foundation piers will be 2¾" inside the building lines.

Holes for the 6" piers along the north and south walls (or five piers per side) should be dug as shown on the illustration. Along the wall without the door (the east wall), center one middle post. Along the opposite wall (the wall with the door), there will be two holes spaced 39" from the outside edge of the corner pier to the inside edge of the door pier (or 33" o.c.). Drop a plumb bob to locate the position of these two piers, and mark with stakes. The top of the two support piers for the door will be 1½" below the level of the gravel to allow room for the door sill (2 x 6) which will be added later.

Remove the building lines.

## D. The Footings

**11.** The footings, a concrete mass necessary to support each pier, should be twice the diameter of the pier and 6" to 8" thick. Footings must extend below the frost line. Check your local building codes for average annual frost penetration in your area. In northern sections of the country it is often 4' or more.

To determine the depth of the excavation, measure to the frost line from the highest corner of the building; the lower piers later will be backfilled and graded to create an even soil depth around the perimeter.

**12.** Dig the holes approximately 12" in diameter and to a depth below the frost line. The two holes at the entrance should be 18" below the level of the pit. Use the perimeter of the holes as the forms for the footings. Before you pour the concrete, make sure the holes are exactly where they should be. With the building strings attached, and using a plumb bob, also check

### Estimating Concrete Needs

To estimate the amount of concrete necessary to fill one Sonotube, use the following formula:

pi x radius$^2$ (of Sonotube in feet) x depth (in feet) divided by 27 equals cubic yards.

Multiply this by the number of piers.

To estimate for the footings with the dimensions given in feet, multiply: width x length x thickness divided by 27 to determine the number of cubic yards of concrete you will need for one footing. Multiply this by the number of footings.

that you can get the 6" piers plumb and centered on the footings in the hole and still be aligned with the outside edge of the building.

Clean out the bottom of the holes. The footings should be poured on undisturbed dirt, otherwise the greenhouse may settle slightly.

**13. Concrete.** Because of the small amount needed, it's easier to buy bags of ready-mix concrete. But if you wish to mix it yourself, use these proportions:

1 part cement
2 parts sand
3 parts gravel or stone.

The sand and gravel must be clean and free of debris.

Concrete can be mixed by hand on a flat, clean surface or in a metal wheelbarrow. Wear rubber gloves and boots to protect yourself from the caustic action of the cement.

Mound the dry materials and make a depression in the middle. Add water gradually to the depression as the dry ingredients are turned in toward the middle with a hoe or shovel. Add water until the mixture is liquid enough to flow easily when shoveled and the aggregate is completely coated with paste.

The amount of water determines the strength of the concrete. Too much will make the concrete weak and flakey; too little will cause the

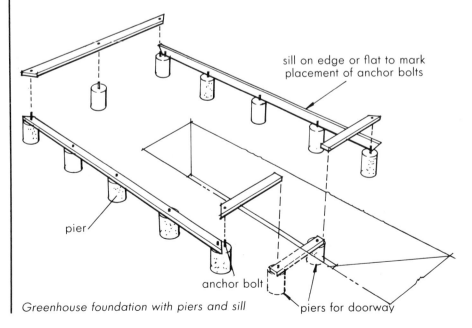

*Greenhouse foundation with piers and sill*

sill on edge or flat to mark
placement of anchor bolts

pier

anchor bolt

piers for doorway

mixture to set up too quickly. Add the water a little at a time, mix thoroughly, then add more as needed. The mixture should be plastic, not runny, and there should be no dry clumps.

To test, draw the hoe through the concrete in a series of jabbing motions. Little ridges will stay raised when the mix is correct. If the mixture is too wet, the concrete will fall back quickly, in which case, add more gravel and cement. If the mixture is too dry, the ridges won't be smooth and even.

Pour 6" to 8" of concrete into each of the holes. Before it hardens, insert a length of rebar in the center of the footing.

**14. Rebar.** In order to tie the footings and concrete piers together and to strengthen both, use the ½" metal reinforcing bars (often called rebar).

Cut the bar into eleven 2' lengths and two 1' lengths. The latter two are for the entrance pier footings. In the vise bend one end of each to form a "J" hook. Check the position for each reinforcing bar with the layout lines, then place one bar, J-hook down in each pier footing. Check the position of each bar; the concrete, as it gradually hardens, will hold the bars in position. Let concrete cure for at least two days—six is better. Keep it moist during this time.

## E. Piers: Sonotubes

**15.** To position the Sonotubes, use the layout lines as a guide. Place the cardboard tubes on top of the footings with the bars sticking up into the tubes. Backfill with earth around the bottom of the tubes. Use 2 x 4 bracing around the tops.

**16.** On each tube mark the height of the concrete to be poured. To do this, use a string and line level. Begin in the corner where the

ground is highest, and on the tube mark 4" above the ground. This line represents the top of the foundation and the bottom of the sill. Stretch the string with the line level attached from corner to corner, marking on the foundation tubes where the level string-line crosses. The level can be checked with a water hose and bulb attachment. It's important to get these level, since the level of the building itself depends on it.

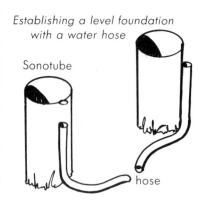

*Establishing a level foundation with a water hose*

**17.** Once the level line has been established, drive a nail through each tube at the correct height, then cut off the tubes a few inches above the nails. With the string stretched and leveled along the west wall, measure down 37½" to establish the top of the concrete piers for the door supports. Mark location. Remove excess tubing a few inches above the nails. Sonotubes can now be filled with concrete.

## F. Anchor Bolts

**18.** After the concrete has been poured, an anchor bolt must be set in the center of each pier including the two door piers, and held in place until the concrete hardens. These bolts are used to attach the sill to the foundation. The threaded top is attached to the sill with a washer and nut; the L-shaped hook

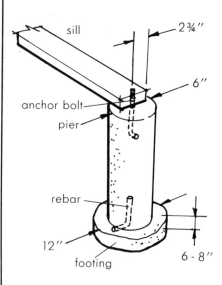

at the bottom is set in the concrete pier.

Place the anchor bolt with the screw threads exposed just enough so that it will extend through the sill (1½") and a nut and washer can be placed on it. No concrete should harden on the exposed threads. Check periodically with a square to make sure the bolts remain perpendicular and in line.

**19.** At the corner piers, two sill plates will come together to form a mitered corner. Here there should be two anchor bolts embedded in the concrete to secure each of the 2 x 6s. Set these bolts off-center, close to, but not on, the building corner.

The bolts should not interfere with the rafters or studs. If they do, notches can be cut later in the framing members to make them fit around the bolts.

Let the foundation piers harden, usually for a day or two. Even after two days, the concrete will still be soft (although hard enough to frame on), so be careful that you don't chip or crack it with a hammer.

The cardboard of the Sonotubes can be left to rot below the surface of the ground; above ground it can be cut off with a utility knife.

## G. Foundation Insulation

**20.** Replace the building lines. Mark with stakes for a trench beginning ¼" outside the building lines. (The trench will be flush with the outside edge of the foundation piers.) The narrow trench should be approximately 20" deep and go around the perimeter of the greenhouse (with the exception of the door opening). Use a shovel or mattock to remove the soil.

**21.** Into the trench, place the rigid insulation so that it extends to the top of the piers. The tongue-and-groove sheets are easily cut with a knife, and lock together for a tight fit. Tape adjoining sheets with duct tape.

Cut one sheet of the pressure-treated plywood into three 16" x 8' strips. Cut a second piece of the plywood into 16" strips as needed. Partially backfill against the insulation, then lay these strips lengthwise in the trench against the foam insulation. They should extend to the top of the piers.

The plywood will provide a structural cover for the foam to keep the pressure of the earth (especially during freezing) from breaking the insulation.

Remove any temporary bracing for the piers, and backfill around the piers and plywood. Tamp down the earth, being careful not to damage the insulation.

## H. Sill Construction

**22.** For the sill, which connects the concrete piers with the greenhouse walls and roof, measure the two 2" x 6" x 12' boards to be sure each is exactly 12' in length. Cut to length if necessary. Center one 2" x 6" x 12' sill along the north wall next to the anchor bolts. With a combination square, draw the exact thickness of the bolts on the sill. Using a tape measure, mark the distance to the center of each bolt from the outside edge of the sill. (The bolts will be centered on the 2 x 6.) Drill holes the same size or slightly larger than the anchor bolts. Use a drill and ½" or ⅝" bit. Then cut both ends of the sill to a 45 degree angle, with the cuts angled toward each other.

**23.** Cut 6" squares of asphalt shingle and place on top of the concrete piers. They will stop moisture from the ground that is absorbed by the concrete from reaching the sills and rotting them.

**24.** Slip the sill over the bolts; add washers and tighten the nuts. If the bolts should extend above the nuts, they can be cut off with a hacksaw.

**25.** For the east wall sill, butt a 2" x 6" x 8' length against the outside corner of the north sill. Check for square. Mark and drill holes for the anchor bolts. Cut both ends to a 45 degree angle. Slip the sill over the bolts, add washers, and tighten the nuts.

Follow the same procedure for securing the 2" x 6" x 12' south wall sill to the anchor bolts.

**26.** For the west wall (or the wall with the doorway), cut two pieces, each 33", from a 2" x 6" x 8' length. Mark for the anchor bolts. Cut the end of the sill that will fit against the north wall sill to a 45 degree angle. Leave the square cut on the other end. Then secure to pier. The unsecured end will later be nailed to the door framing.

Follow the same procedure for the second 33" length which will run from the southwest corner of the greenhouse, and later be nailed into the door framing.

**27.** Cut a length of 2" x 6" to 30" for the door sill. Before drilling for the anchor bolts, be sure the outside of the sill lines up with the west wall building line. Then secure to piers.

## I. Framing

**28. The South Wall: The Knee Wall.** You will need nine 2" x 4" pieces, each 10½" long, and two 2" x 4" x 12' plates. The wall will be built on a flat surface and later lifted into place.

Lay the plates edge to edge for marking the placement of the studs. From one end measure in 1½" and draw a square line with an "X" to the side closer to the end from which you measured. Measure in another 1½" and do the same. The rest of the plate will be marked out

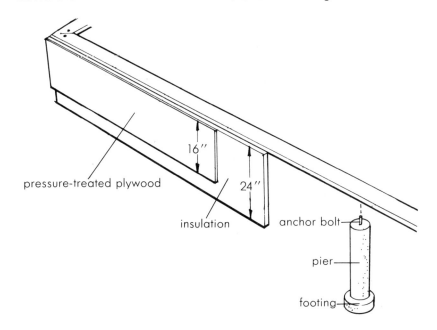

pressure-treated plywood

insulation

16"

24"

anchor bolt

pier

footing

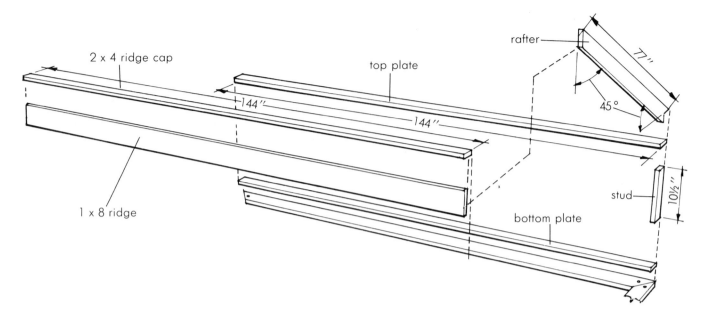

2 x 4 ridge cap

top plate

rafter

7"

45°

144"

144"

1 x 8 ridge

stud

10½"

bottom plate

for the studs every 24″ o.c., with a double stud at the opposite end. Copy the stud placement lines on the second plate.

**29.** Lay one plate and a 10½″ length on edge. One end of the stud should rest against a nailing surface, the other should be lined up as precisely as possible with the square mark on the plate. Endnail through plate into the stud with two 16d nails.

Continue until all studs have been nailed to the plate. Rotate the partially finished wall 180 degrees so that the plate now rests against the nailing surface. Align the second plate and endnail through it into each of the studs. Be sure they align with the "X's."

**30.** Set the wall on the sill, line up the outside edge of the bottom plate with the outside of the sill. Be sure the wall is plumb. Then secure it to the sill with two 10d nails driven through the plate every 2′.

**31.** Mark both the sill on the north wall and the top plate on the south for the placement of rafters. Use the same 24″ o.c. spacing, and mark "X's" wherever a rafter will be nailed. Again, there will be double rafters at both ends.

Mark out the same rafter spacing on both sides of the 1″ x 8″ x 12′ board that will be used for the ridge.

**32. Ridge Cap.** Lay on edge the 1″ x 8″ x 12′ ridge which has just been marked for the rafter spacing. Center a 2″ x 4″ x 12′ board on top to form a "T" and nail together with 10d nails spaced every 24″. Set aside.

**33. The Rafters.** For the north roof, cut one 2 x 6 to 6′6″ with a 30 degree angle, called a plumb cut, on one end, and a 60 degree cut on the other. The cuts should angle toward one another.

**34.** For the south roof, cut one 2 x 4 to 6′5″. Both ends will be cut to 45 degree angles. The 45 degree cut at the top of the rafter, called the plumb cut, allows the rafter to rest tightly against the ridge. The 45 degree cut at the bottom of the rafter will be a combination of seat and plumb cuts, called a bird's mouth. This cut allows the rafter to fit around the top plate for a stronger joint.

**35.** Test these pattern rafters by fitting them into place at their bases. Then join them at the top against a

short piece of 1-by stock, representing the ridge. If the fit is satisfactory, cut eight more of each rafter.

**36.** Once all the rafters have been cut, build four sets of double rafters. Select four straight south rafters and four straight north ones. Lay them in groups of two on top of each other (i.e., two groups of two north rafters, two groups of two south rafters). Nail together with 10d nails, staggered at 16″ intervals. These will support the roof at the east and west ends of the building.

**37.** Lay scrap boards or 2-by stock between the bench areas to span the 30″ center aisle. These will give you something to stand on while nailing the rafters into the ridge.

**38.** With the ridge cap on the ground, set the marking gauge to 6¼″ and draw a line parallel to the edge of the 1 x 8 ridge board on both sides. The mark will be 1″ below the 2 x 4 ridge cap.

On the ground attach a double set of north rafters to the ridge. Align them with the "X's" on the end of the ridge board. Be sure the 30 degree plumb cut is at the ridge and that the top of the cut is flush with the 6¼" line that you have just drawn. The bottom of the rafters will extend below the ridge board. End-nail together with 10d nails. With the plumb cut at the ridge, toenail a double set of south-facing rafters into the opposite side of the ridge with 8d nails.

**39.** One foot from the other end of the ridge, nail a scrap 2" x 4" board to hold the ridge up temporarily. With helpers, lift the ridge into place. Once the ridge plus rafters are in place, adjust the span until the north-facing rafter ends are flush with the outside edge of the sill, and the bird's mouths of the south-facing rafters are firmly seated on the top plate.

Have a helper raise (or lower) the 2 x 4 support until the ridge is level. Then toenail the rafters into place on the sill (for the north roof) and the top plate (for the south roof), using two 8d nails per connection. Along the north sill you may have to notch or drill out the rafter ends to accept the nuts of the anchor bolts.

With the ridge still level, attach the double set of rafters at the other end of the ridge in the same manner. Be sure the rafters do not go above the 6¼" mark; this gap to the ridge is for the roofing materials. The ridge is now self-supporting and the support pole can be removed.

Fill in the intermediate rafters, a pair at a time.

Rafters 24" o.c. is a modular spacing that allows you to use 4' x 8' sheets of plywood. Be careful in the rafter layout; you want to ensure that later when the roof is added, the edges of the plywood will land exactly on the rafters for a good nailing surface. If you are sloppy, the plywood will run off the rafters and create time-consuming problems.

**40. Collar Beams.** Cut three lengths of 1" x 6" to 42". They will tie the second, fourth, and sixth pairs of north and south rafters together. Raise the first collar beam to a comfortable height and into place along the second set of rafters. Level, and mark the tops which will have to be trimmed to match the roof angles. Remove this triangle at both ends, and use the board as a pattern for the other two collar beams. Again lift into place, level, and nail both ends into a pair of rafters with 8d nails.

To maximize the use of space, you can hang plants from these members; therefore be sure you place the collar beams high enough so you won't hit your head.

## J. Framing for the Door (West Wall)

**41.** The first step in framing the door is to cut two 2 x 4s, one for the north side of the door, the other for the south side. Each will start flush with each end of the door sill, run flush against the outside edge of the 2 x 6 sill, then be cut at the proper angle at the top so that it can be nailed to the double rafter.

**42.** Put a 2 x 4 in position on the north side of the entrance on top of, and at the end of, the door sill. Position it against the sill, then check it with a level; it should be plumb. Mark on it the contact line, then cut. Repeat for the framing on the south side of the door, cutting that angle at 45 degrees. Nail both into place, using 8d nails to toenail into the door sill, then position the outer edge of each 2 x 4 flush with the outer edge of the rafter, and nail with 8d nails.

**43.** This procedure results in two parallel 2 x 4s spaced 27 inches apart.

**44. Jack Studs.** Cut two 2 x 4s to 72". They will rest flat against the vertical studs you've just nailed into position. Toenail them into the door sill with 8d nails and facenail them into the vertical studs with 10d nails staggered every 16".

Cut two 2 x 4s to 27". Nail together with 10d nails. This is the header which will go over the top of the rough opening for the door.

Rest the header on top of the 72" jack studs. Nail through the longer vertical uprights into the header with 16d nails. This completes the door framing.

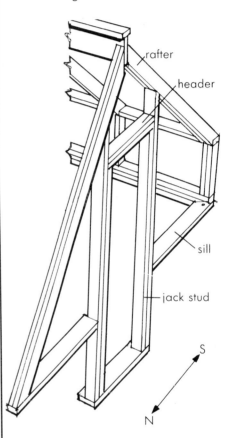

## K. Gable Studs

**45.** Gable studs are necessary on the east wall to support the roof. They too must be carefully measured and nailed because it is easy to get a crown in the rafter.

**46.** Measure in from the northeast corner of the greenhouse along the sill. At the 36" mark, draw a squared line with an "X" on the side closer to the corner from which you measured.

Hold two 2 x 4s against the squared line so that they cover the "X." With the studs vertical, mark the angle at which they meet the north-facing rafters. Cut this angle on both 2 x 4s. Nail together so they form one double stud, and nail them into position on the sill and the sloping rafters above.

**47.** Measure from the southeast corner along the sill. At the 36" mark, draw a squared line with an "X" on the side closer to the corner from which you measured. Repeat instructions in paragraph above.

## L. The Vent

**48.** Cut a 2 x 4 into a 24" length and a 12" length. Also cut a 2 x 4 to 18" in length, mark a 45 degree bevel on one end, and cut.

Rest the 24" length flat on a surface and from one end measure in 12". Mark a square line with an "X" on the opposite side of the line from the end from which you measured.

Rest the 18" length flat on a surface with the shortened side up. Measure in from the square cut end 12". Make a square line with an "X" on the side of the line opposite the end from which you measured.

**49.** Butt one end of the 12" length on edge and against a sturdy surface. Perpendicular to it, rest the 24" length on edge so that the 12" length covers the "X." Nail together with two 16d nails. Rotate so that the 24" length is against the nailing surface. Place the 18" piece on edge and perpendicular so that the 12" board covers the "X" and is flush with the square line. Nail together with two 16d nails.

This is the framing for the vent. To nail, lift vent frame into place so that the 18" length fits between the gable studs and the rafters. Have a helper hold the framing while you toenail the bottom crosspiece into the studs. Check for level and then nail the top crosspiece into the double studs on the south side and into the north double rafter.

## M. Flashing

**50.** Cut strips of flashing: two to 12' and one to 8' and two to 3'. Bend them to fit over the insulation and plywood covering along the greenhouse perimeter. Nail into sill with roofing nails spaced every 12". Tamp down earth and slope it slightly so that water will drain away from the foundation.

## N. The North Roof

**51.** The north roof will be sheathed in CDX plywood. Start roofing at the bottom and at one corner. Run a full ½" x 4' x 8' sheet horizontally across the rafters for greater strength. The plywood should be flush with the bottom of the rafters and the end walls of the building, and should overlap only one-half of the fourth rafter. Tack the top corners in place. Snap chalklines to indicate positions of the rafters and nail sheet into place with 8d galvanized nails spaced 12" apart along the rafters.

**52.** Measure the width from the piece of plywood decking which is in place to the roof ridge. It should be approximately 30". From a second sheet of plywood, cut an 8' strip to fit. Align this sheet with the first and with it flush against the roof ridge. Mark for rafter placement, and nail into place.

**53.** Cut a third sheet to butt against the first two sheets and run vertically down the roof. Nail in place.

## O. Drip Edge

**54.** Along the bottom and sides of the plywood decking, nail the 6" drip edge in place. Begin with the bottom plywood edge and work up along the gable ends.

Drip edge can be cut with tin snips or a hacksaw. Whenever two

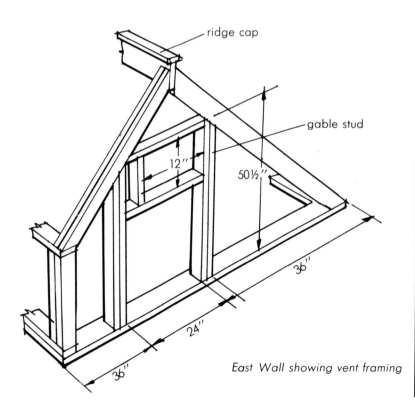

East Wall showing vent framing

ridge cap

gable stud

12"

50½"

36"

24"

36"

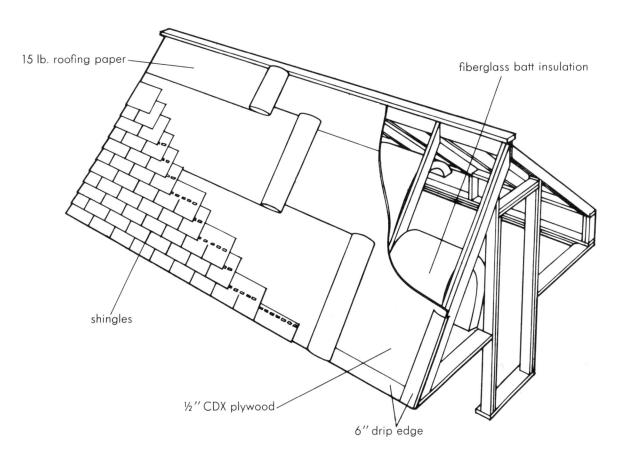

15 lb. roofing paper

fiberglass batt insulation

shingles

½″ CDX plywood

6″ drip edge

strips meet, overlap them by 3″ to 4″. Use 1″ galvanized roofing nails, spaced every 12″, and drive them in as far as possible from the outer metal edge.

## P. Felt Paper

**55.** Unroll the felt paper and cut a 12′ length. Align this with the sides and bottom edge of the plywood. Staple to plywood. Cut a second piece to 12′. Let it overlap the first by 4″ and staple it to the decking. Continue stapling felt paper until the north roof is completed to the ridge.

## Q. Shingles

**56.** To shingle the north wall, you will need: a straightedge (a rafter square is good); a utility knife for cutting the shingles; and a chalkline for marking the shingle courses.

For the starter course, cut the shingles lengthwise just above the tar tabs. Invert the shingles so that the tabs face toward the ridge and the tar tabs face up. Place this row so it overhangs the metal drip edge by 1/2″. Nail into place along the lower edge with 1¼″ galvanized roofing nails. Be sure the nails pass through the plywood, not just the drip edge.

**57.** Lay the next course on top of the starter course, with the mineral surface up and the tabs facing toward the sill. Begin even with the drip edge. Nail in place with four nails placed above the tab slots.

**58.** Measure up 5″ on both ends of the first course and snap a chalkline. This marks the lower edge of the second course of shingles. For the first shingle in this row, center one of the tab cutout slots between two of the slots in the first row. Mark the excess that overhangs the drip edge. Turn the shingle over, and using the rafter square for a

straightedge, cut the shingle. Reposition so that the edge of the shingle aligns with the chalkline and nail in place. Continue across the row using full shingles. The last shingle will have to be cut to fit. Continue up the roof, being sure the slots in one row are centered between the slots in the next.

**59.** At the ridge, the last row of shingles will have to be cut lengthwise to fit. Cover the nail heads with blind roofing cement. When you are finished, no nail heads should show.

## R. Roof Insulation

**60.** Insulate the north wall from the inside of the greenhouse. Use foil-backed fiberglass batts. Cut to length and staple the batts through the tabs into the sides of the rafters. The foil-side should face the inside of the greenhouse.

## S. Building the Door

**61.** Cut two 2 x 3s to 68¾"; two more to 23¾" and one to 20¾". Endnail the top and bottom rails to the sides with two 16d nails. Center the middle rail between the side rails and endnail in place.

**62.** Cut two pieces of ½" exterior plywood to the outer dimensions of the frame (71¾" x 23¾"). Lay the frame on a flat surface with one sheet of plywood on top. Be sure the plywood aligns with the corners. Then nail into the 2 x 3 frame with 4d nails spaced every 6" and ¾" in from the plywood edge. Be sure to nail plywood to the middle cross-rail.

Turn the door over so that it rests on the plywood. Stuff foam, batts, or loose insulation in the recesses. Foam is recommended because of its high insulative value. Then nail second piece of plywood on top of the frame.

## T. The Benches

**63.** Cut eight 2" x 4" x 4' lengths. Point the ends with a hatchet. Drive them in one foot deep at 4' intervals along the edge of the trench, with two posts opposite the doorway. Between the posts and earthen walls, lift in sheets of pressure-treated plywood to shore up all three walls.

Turn over the soil in the bench area and enrich it with compost and manure.

## U. Blocking for the South Roof

**64.** Cut four lengths of 2 x 4 to 20-¼" and eight to 22½". These will be used as blocking between the south-facing rafters to support the roofing.

Measure along the outside edge of the rafters from the plate toward the ridge 29". Draw square lines along the sides of the rafters, with "X's" to the ridge side of the lines. Align one 20¼" length with the square marks in the first rafter bay. Toenail the blocking into the end rafter with two 8d nails, then end-nail through the second rafter into the blocking with 16d nails. Repeat the process until there is a line of blocking across the south roof.

**65.** The second row of blocking will go between the rafters at the ridge. Nail into place in the same way.

## V. Glazing the East and West Walls

**66. West Wall.** Begin at the north-west corner. Cut a triangular piece of fiberglass that will cover the sill and the rafter above, as well as the door framing. After double-checking the measurements, lay them out on the fiberglass. Use a felt-tipped pen or razor knife. Cut the glazing with sharp wire-cutting shears or a fine-toothed saw. Then apply an even bead of silicone to the wood framing members to be covered.

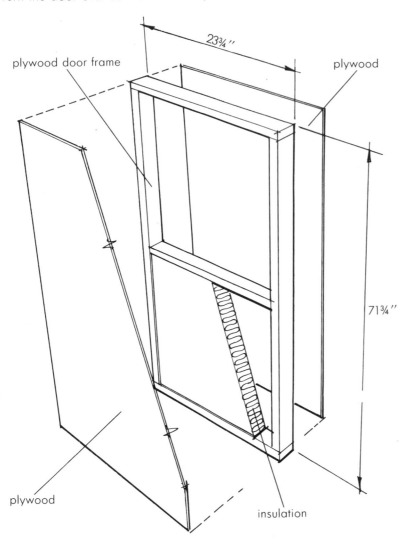

plywood door frame

plywood

23¾"

plywood

71¾"

insulation

**67.** You will need helpers to hold the edges of the fiberglass while it is being aligned. Nail the top edge to the end rafter in the center. Use a gasketed nail but do not drive it home. Recheck that the sides and bottom fit properly. Nail one outside edge, but drive the nails in only halfway. Pull slightly on the remaining edges—bottom and side. Temporarily center a nail on these two edges. Then nail down the glazing, beginning from the center of the rafter and sill and working to the edges. Place nails ¾" in from edge of fiberglass.

Pull diagonally on the four corners of the sheet to avoid leaving any bulges. Space the rubber-gasketed nails approximately 8" apart and angle them out to put tension on the sheet. Do not nail fiberglass from the header up along the door framing to the rafters until later.

**68.** Cut the second west wall sheet to reach from the knee wall and sill to the rafter above. Again, glazing should cover door framing (to the southwest). Lay bead of adhesive over the wooden members which will be covered by the glazing. Install the triangular second panel in the same way; do not tack down above the door framing.

**69.** Cut a piece of fiberglass material to cover the area above the door. It should be wider than the opening so that it will overlap the first two panels by 3" on each side. Apply a bead of silicone on top of the existing fiberglass. Set the newly cut panel on top and nail through both layers of glazing with the rubber-gasketed nails. Be sure you nail through the glazing into the door framing.

**70. East Wall.** For the east wall (or the wall with the vent), check your dimensions before cutting the fiberglass. Cut and install the first triangular panel which will run from the northeast corner to the first gable stud. Use the same proce-

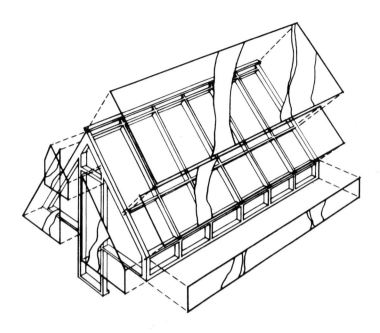

dure as outlined above. Do not nail into the gable studs.

Cut a second triangular panel to size for the southeast corner. Apply caulking and nail in place.

Cut a third piece to fit between the two gable studs. Apply a bead of caulking over the first two sheets; position the third and nail along the bottom and side. Do not nail along the lower stud of the vent bracing.

Cut a piece to fit around the vent, and secure.

Fit the 12" x 12" vent into the opening and nail into framing.

## W. Glazing the South Knee Wall and Roof

**71.** Cut a 4' x 12'4" piece of fiberglass and a second that is 2'9" wide and 12'4" long. Set aside.

**72. The Knee Wall.** Cut the remaining piece (1'3" x 12'4") to 12' long. Apply caulking, center panel, and nail into studs, sill, and top plate with rubber-gasketed nails.

**73. South-facing Roof.** Apply caulking to framing members and lift 2'9" x 12'4" panel into place so that it is centered with a 2" overhang over the top plate. Nail into

place; do not nail down the top corners or along the top edge.

Apply caulking to framing members and to top edge of first fiberglass panel. Lift the 4' section into place along the ridge. Center the panel and nail into rafters and blocking. Along the bottom edge there will be a 2" overlap; be sure to nail through the two sheets into the blocking.

## X. Hanging the Door

**74.** Mount the two 3" hinges on the side rail of the door. Place hinges 8" from top and bottom, and place them so that the door will swing inward. On the door, outline the leaf of the hinges. With a hammer and chisel, remove wood in the cutout to the depth of the hinge. Then screw hinges to door.

Lift door into place, the hinges should be on the north side. To center the door, rest the bottom on a match book or sliver of wood so that clearance is equal top and bottom. Outline the leaf of the hinges on the 2 x 4 jamb. Remove door. With a hammer and chisel, remove wood in the cutout to the depth of the hinge. Replace door. Predrill and screw to frame.

Open and close the door to be sure it swings freely.

Mount a hook on the door and an eye on the jamb for securing the door shut.

## Y. The Stairway

**75.** Dig four holes 6″ in diameter and 3′ deep at the top and bottom of the stairway slope.

To make the stringers, cut two pieces of 2 x 12 to 59″ long. Trim the ends to fit the slope of the entrance ramp. For the treads, nail 9″ pieces (five/side) of 2 x 4 to form braces on both stringers. The braces should be nailed 7″ apart from the top of one brace to the top of the next.

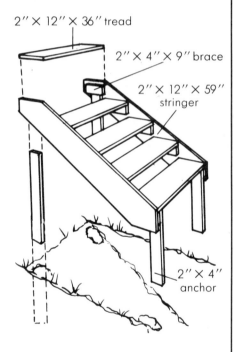

2″ × 12″ × 36″ tread

2″ × 4″ × 9″ brace

2″ × 12″ × 59″ stringer

2″ × 4″ anchor

**76.** Make five 36″ treads from 2 x 12s, and nail them in place on the top edge of the braces.

Set the stairway in place on the slope. Nail lengths of 2 x 4s to the inside of the stringers; they will extend into the holes you've dug. Place a few rocks in the bottom of each hole. Then fill with wet concrete to hold the stairway in place.

Provision should be made in advance if you want electricity and water in the greenhouse. Water pipes will have to be laid below the frost line to prevent freezing in winter; you may even want to install a small sink. Electric outlets are handy for lighting, for use of a ventilating fan, and for heating in an emergency.

The directions given here are for a detached greenhouse. Attached greenhouses, however, are easier and cheaper to build. Because they are attached to a building, one less wall is necessary. In addition, the north wall is protected by the adjoining building which may even provide additional heat to the greenhouse. Electrical and plumbing service lines between the buildings also can be easily hooked up. However, a trench 3′ deep must be dug for the pit. When this is dug along or even below a house foundation wall, problems may develop. There may also be difficulty (or excessive expense involved) in cutting an entrance into the basement. Check with a contractor before you attempt an attached pit greenhouse.

Detached greenhouses are ideal when your house lacks good southern exposure, and can be located close to the vegetable garden or tool shed for greater convenience. They provide a spacious environment for the plants and for the gardener; with the 60-degree pitch and shiny surface of the north wall, additional light bounces from the north wall to the plants below.

Locate the pit greenhouse where it is easily accessible and on high ground; avoid siting it at the bottom of a hill where frost pockets are likely to occur. A greenhouse built on a knoll or hillside may avoid the need for stairs into the pit. High ground also reduces drainage difficulties. If water (either run-off water or a high water table) is likely to be a problem, add tiles along the footings, sloped away from the foundation. Cover these with building paper and backfill with 6″ to 8″ of coarse gravel. If the pit is very muddy, add 12″ of small stones in the bottom of the excavation. Then cover with crushed stone or pea gravel.

### Other design possibilities

**Foundation.** In sandy soils, you may have to construct a full concrete block foundation; however, this will substantially add to the expense. Wooden posts which have been treated can also be used instead of the concrete piers.

**Glazing and Insulation.** Glazing on the east and west walls contributes a considerable amount of light, especially in the spring and fall. In cold northern climates, however, the heat loss at night may be so great that these walls should be insulated and sheathed with a second layer of fiberglass or polyethylene film added to the knee wall.

The south-facing roof provides substantial heat and light during the day but is also responsible for much of the heat loss. Internal or external shutters or curtains to be drawn at night will keep more heat in the greenhouse. Rigid shutters with an insulation core can be made and clipped into place.

Commercial or homemade flexible curtains are another option. They are made with multiple layers of plastic film and insulation sandwiched between fabric. Usually they are installed to run in tracks to either side of the glazing. Less expensive and more efficient is a thermal blanket to be drawn across the greenhouse one to two feet above the plants. This blanket holds the heat away from the glazing and from the roof peak.

**The North Wall.** To increase the intensity of reflected light from the north wall, staple heavy duty aluminum sheets to the rafters. Also paint all interior surfaces white to reflect more light to the plants.

The north wall can be finished off with a vapor barrier (in which case, use kraft-backed fiberglass batts) and plywood or masonite. It then should be painted with a glossy white enamel.

Outside the greenhouse, you may want to add burlap bags filled with leaves or straw around the north wall to provide increased wind protection.

**Ventilation.** It is important that there is moving air in the greenhouse to prevent disease, and in the summer to exhaust excess heat. By leaving the door ajar, a cross draft will be established with the vent on the east wall. If this isn't sufficient, install a fan above the door.

# Solar for Heating

# Exterior Reflective Shutter

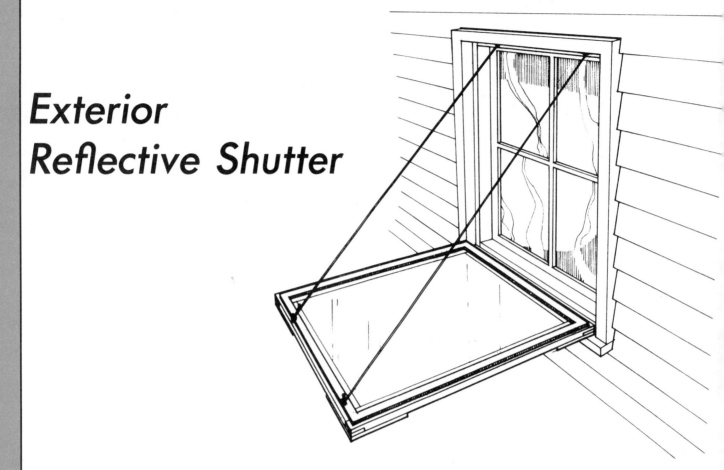

**Skills required:** Slight.

**Cost:** $1.00 per square foot.

**Amount of heat gain:** 3/4 gal. oil/ft.$^2$/heating season.

**What it does:** Exterior reflective shutters can be constructed to cover any glazed area, but they only make sense on south-facing glass where the reflective value of the shutter can be utilized to increase the solar radiation through the glazing.

**How it works:** With the shutter tilted to the right angle during the day, rays of sunlight that would not pass through the glazing now hit the reflective foil. Since they bounce off at the same angle as they hit, they are reflected in through the window; this increases the heat gain.

At night with the shutter closed, heat is trapped inside the house, and because of the thermal resistance of the insulation, conductive heat losses through the glass are greatly reduced. These shutters will cut heat loss through single pane windows by eight and through double-glazed windows by four.

**Advantages:**
1. Cheap.
2. Simple.
3. Rugged.
4. Easy to construct.
5. Lightweight.
6. No moisture condensation as with interior thermal shades, curtains, and shutters.
7. Does not take up valuable interior house space.
8. Instant heat as soon as sunlight hits the reflector.
9. Heat gain even during overcast weather.
10. Marked decrease in heat loss through glazing.
11. Adaptable to any window size including the large glass expanse of greenhouses.

**Disadvantages:**
1. Sun must be out for peak performance.
2. Questionable aesthetically.
3. Prevents heat gain from reflection off snow.
4. Have to contend with rain, ice, wind, snow, which may interfere with operation of shutter. May have to remove snow.
5. If it is a first-floor shutter, ground below may be obstructed. Also may interfere with outdoor pedestrian traffic.
6. Must adjust twice a day.
7. To operate, must either go outdoors or put up with small heat loss from the through-the-wall holes.
8. Design must be strong enough to withstand the elements.
9. May want to remove for summer.

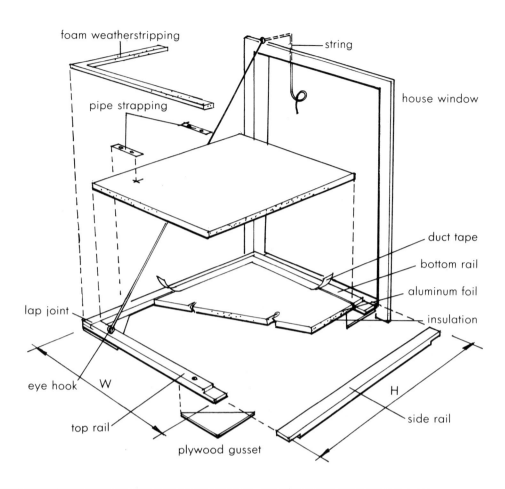

foam weatherstripping

pipe strapping

string

house window

duct tape

bottom rail

aluminum foil

insulation

lap joint

eye hook

W

top rail

plywood gusset

H

side rail

| Materials: | | | Tools: |
|---|---|---|---|
| | | | Staple gun |
| Amount | Size | Item | Hammer |
| | | | Handsaw |
| — | 1″ x 2″ | #2 pine | Screwdriver |
| 1 set | 1″ | Utility hinges of galvanized steel | Backsaw |
| ¼ lb. | ⅝″ | Wood or drywall screws | Marking gauge or combination |
| — | 1″ x 4′ x 8′ | Foil-faced polyisocyanurate foam board | square |
| 1′ | | Pipe strapping | Utility knife |
| 1 pint | | Cuprinol-20 wood preservative | Straightedge |
| 1 roll | 2″ | Aluminum foil tape | #8 Screwmate |
| 1 | | Tie-down (available at marine supply stores) | ¼″ drill and bit |
| | | Adhesive-backed foam sealing strips, felt weather- | Try square |
| | | stripping, or plastic weatherstripping | Clamps |
| | | Scrap plywood | |
| | | Resorcinol or waterproof glue | |
| | | Heavy string | |
| | | Staples | |

Depending on your installation, you also may need:

| 2 | | Pulleys |
|---|---|---|
| 4 | | Eyehooks |
| 4 | | Teenut fasteners |
| 1 | ¾″ | Dowel, cut to window width |
| 1 | 4d | Nail |

# How to build:

*Overall dimensions will depend on your specific window opening.*

It is important that the shutter fit tightly between the exterior side jambs or against the window casing. Choose 1 x 2s that are straight with small or no knots. Sometimes knots can be avoided if measurements are carefully worked out so that the knot is left as scrap.

Instead of pine, fir, or spruce, you may wish to use moisture- and warp-resistant woods such as redwood or cedar.

To determine the amount of lumber you will need, decide whether the shutter will sit between the side jambs (possible if you don't have aluminum combination storms) or against the exterior window casing. If the shutter will fit between the side jambs, add height to width of window opening, and multiply by two. For shutters that will close against the casing, add the height plus width of the window opening plus 6″; then multiply by two.

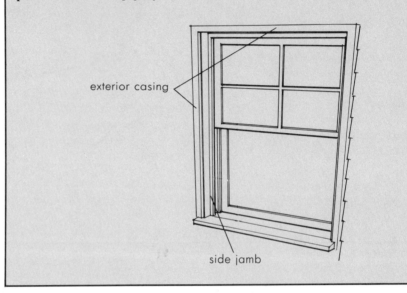

exterior casing

side jamb

## A. The Frame

**1.** Cut the 1″ x 2″ side pieces to the height of the window opening if the shutter will fit between the side jambs. If the shutter will fit against the casing, add 3″ to the height of the window opening. Cut the top and bottom pieces to the width of the window (plus 3″ if the shutter will fit against the exterior casing).

**2.** At the ends of each piece and always on the same side, cut two lap joints; this will give a flush fit when the rails are mated. Across the face of the side rails measure in from the end of each piece 1½″ (the width of the lumber) and mark. Set a marking gauge (or combination square) to ⅜″ and mark this distance from the end of the rail to the width of the cut.

**3.** With a backsaw, saw down the center of the side rail with the saw kerf to the waste side. Make a second cut on the face side just inside the marking line.

Do the same for both cross rails (top and bottom rails).

**4.** Assemble the frame. Apply resorcinol or waterproof glue to facing surfaces of the joints, clamp to work surface, and check with a try square that the joint is square. Drill two holes per joint with a #8 Screwmate. Screw together with ⅝″ screws.

Assemble the rest of the frame, being sure that all four corners are square.

**5.** To add rigidity, cut four equilateral triangles with a hypotenuse of 5" or more. Use scrap plywood for these gussets. Align these, one at each corner of the frame. Drill holes, then screw into frame, being sure that for each gusset there are at least two screws going into each of the adjoining legs of the frame.

**6.** Treat the frame with two coats of Cuprinol or paint to match the color of your house trim.

## B. Insulating the Shutter

**7.** Put the frame on a work surface with the gusset-side down. Measure the inner width and length, and cut the 1", foil-faced polyisocyanurate foam to fit inside frame. Use a utility knife and a sturdy straightedge to make the cuts.

**8.** Slip the insulation into the frame against the gussets.

**9.** Place aluminum foil tape around the edges on both sides between the wood rails and the insulation to seal the frame against moisture. The tape also should be used wherever the foam isn't protected by the aluminum foil cover because the foam is ultra-violet degradable in direct sunlight.

**10.** To further secure the insulation, cut 3" lengths of pipe strapping. Screw these into the wooden frame at 2' intervals on the side without the gussets. Allow them to project 2¼" onto the insulation. These will prevent the insulation from slipping out of the frame.

**11.** If the shutter will fit against the exterior casing, run adhesive-backed foam sealing strips or plastic weatherstripping along the edge of the frame. When the shutter is closed, the foam will press against the exterior casing of the window.

If the shutter will close between the side jambs, staple felt weatherstripping to the exterior edges of the shutter.

## C. Mounting Shutter on Window

**12.** Hold the shutter in place against the window to determine where the hinges will go. The shutter will hinge on top of, or against, the sill, depending on your window, and swing down from the top. Mount the hinges on the shutter.

Decide whether you want to operate the shutter from inside or outside the house.

**Opened from Inside.** For shutters that will be operated from inside the house, mount two eyehooks along the inside edge of the top rail 4" in from either edge. Be sure

the hooks won't interfere with closing the shutter tightly.

Run one end of the string through the eyehook and knot it. Measure off at least three times the length of the shutter and cut the string. Cut a second piece of string to the same length and tie to the other eyehook.

**13.** Hinge the shutter to the sill and, with the shutter closed against the window, estimate where the holes will be for the cord to enter the house. Drill holes through window sash and carefully hammer the teenut fasteners into the holes from the inside and the outside. These will prevent the movement of the cord from enlarging the holes. Thread the cord through the holes.

**14.** Inside the house, staple the ends of the two strings to a ¾" dowel, cut to the width of the window—a scrap of 1 x 2 will do also.

Cut a piece of pipe strapping 3" long. Bend it in a half-circle around the dowel, leaving a 1" lip. Drive a 4d nail into the center of the dowel. Mount the curved piece of pipe hanger wherever convenient (on the sill, apron, or baseboard). It should line up with the dowel nail.

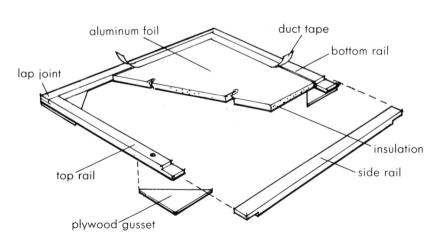

aluminum foil — duct tape — bottom rail — lap joint — top rail — plywood gusset — insulation — side rail

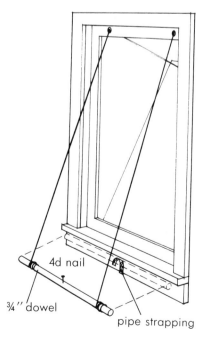

¾" dowel — 4d nail — pipe strapping

At night with the shutter resting against the window, slip the nail head through one of the holes in the pipe hanger. During the day, let out enough string so that the shutter is angled for sun reflection into the house, and hold this position by again threading the nail through the pipe hanger.

**Opened from Outside.** You may prefer opening and closing the shutter from outdoors; it does prevent air leakage through the holes in the top rail of the window sash.

You will need a tie-down to which you will fasten the cord that controls the position of the shutter. Mount this at a convenient height to one side of the shutter, and on the house siding. You can fabricate a tie-down with coat hanger wire and a pair of pliers, then screw it to the house siding.

**15.** Screw in two eyehooks on the top of the top rail of the shutter. Position them 4" from either end of the shutter. Align these with two pulleys mounted on the house siding just above the shutter. Cut a piece of strong cord about six times the length of the shutter, tie one end firmly to the eyehook further from the tie-down. Run the cord through the pulley above that eye-

hook, then across and through the other pulley, loop it to the tie-down, then back through the second pulley and to the eyehook directly beneath it.

**16.** By releasing or pulling the doubled cord, the shutter can be adjusted to any angle; it can also be left flush against the siding during the summer. You may prefer to remove the shutter entirely for summer.

## Other design possibilities

**Dimensions.** If the shutter won't interfere with sunlight reaching the windows below, it can be built to as much as twice the height of the window to further increase heat collection. Shutters also can be built with a greater thickness of insulation.

**Operation.** Tight-fitting shutters may be difficult to open. Additional weight on the top of the shutter (a piece of metal, hardwood, etc.), or an exterior pull cord will alleviate this problem.

Instead of maintaining the shutter tilt with cords, it may be easier to let it rest on a pole, concrete blocks, etc., but these methods depend on how large the shutter and,

when opened, how close to the ground it is.

Shutters also can be closed by hand, and held in place with butterfly latches or by a hook latched at the top.

Shutters for large windows may need extra support to prevent warping. Instead of the gussets, back the frame with ¼" exterior plywood, or canvas, or ⅛" tempered masonite to minimize the extra weight.

The optimum tilt of the shutter in winter is 5 degrees below the horizontal; however, this angle should be adjusted throughout the year. The tilt will be greatest in December when the sun is lowest in the sky. Never leave the shutter perpendicular to the window. Rain and snow will collect and may damage the shutter.

**Seal.** It may be difficult to get a tight seal between the shutter and the window. In older houses, foundations may have shifted and windows gone out of square, or there may be an uneven accumulation of paint, or your shutter frame may not be exactly square. If weatherstripping doesn't solve the problem, add 1½" x ¼" battens around the exterior of the frame for shutters that fit between the window jambs. The battens should form a tight seal against the window casing.

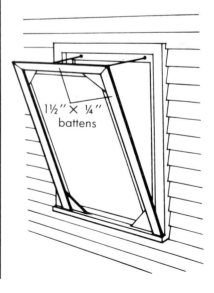
1½" X ¼" battens

---

Before constructing a reflective shutter for a south-facing window, check that the shutter won't be shaded and that nothing will interfere with its hinged action (i.e., shrubs, trees, eaves of adjoining roofs, etc.). Second-floor shutters are less prone to shading; however, they may block sunlight to the windows below.

There are many kinds of rigid insulation, but none has as high an insulating value as the polyisocyanurate foams (trade names: Thermax, R Max, High R, etc.). Many of the rigid insulations produce toxic gases when exposed to temperatures above 200 degrees F. For this reason, homeowners have been discouraged (or legally prevented) from using them for interior insulation. However, it can be argued that it is safe to apply the insulation to the exterior of the house, since by the time the fire reaches the exterior walls, smoke inhalation is a much greater danger than toxic fumes from any exterior shutter. In the section "Other design possibilities," shutter designs that do not use the foam are described.

**Materials.** Shutters can be made without any insulation. To the frame, screw a piece of ½" CDX plywood, and to the plywood, glue or tape a reflective surface such as Mylar, polished aluminum sheets (such as aluminum printing plates from an offset printer), aluminum foil, or merely aluminum or white paint. If aluminum plates are used, clean them with paint thinner to wash the aluminum clean of residual ink.

# Double-hung Windows

## And Other Prefabricated Units
- Bay Window
- Sliding Patio Doors
- Solar Glassed-in Porch

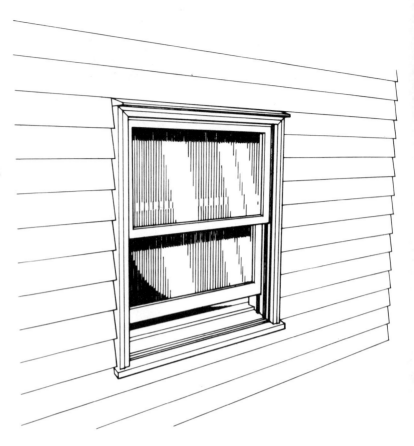

**Skills required:** Moderate. You should know something about house wall construction or have a carpentry manual handy.

**Cost:** Depends on window size and type.

**Amount of heat gain:** In the course of a year, north-facing windows will lose more heat than they gain; south-facing glass, however, will gain more heat than it loses.

Adding windows to the south wall of a house is an easy way to increase heat gain; to decrease heat loss when installing new glazing, observe the following:
- Measure accurately for a plumb and square fit of window in rough opening.
- Insulate around the rough opening (along side and head jambs, and beneath sill).
- Add a storm window or use thermopane glass which will cut heat loss in half.
- Weatherstrip all movable parts

from inside the house, and on the outside apply plenty of caulking between frame of new unit and house siding.
- Provide movable nighttime insulation (thermal shades, shutters, or curtains).

**What it does:** Windows can be added on any wall of the house; on the north, east, and west walls they provide natural light and ventilation; on the south wall they provide light, ventilation, as well as a net heat gain over the year.

**Tips:** You should know if the wall into which you will be putting the window is load-bearing. On houses with hip or flat roofs, all the walls carry some weight. Houses with gable roofs, however, have load- and non-load-bearing walls. The bearing walls on gabled houses run with the roof eaves. They are usually the longer house walls, and run perpendicular to the joists and rafters. Non-bearing walls, the

short walls, run parallel to the joists and rafters. You can determine which way the joists run by checking the direction of the ceiling members in the cellar; then go to the attic. The joists (which support the floor) and the rafters (which support the roof) should also be going in the same direction.

In non-bearing walls, the window opening can be as wide as you wish. For large windows to be added to bearing walls where two or more wall studs will have to be cut, you should first consult a contractor; temporary bracing and a well-designed header may be necessary. For installing the double-hung window in these directions, only one wall stud is cut. If the directions are followed, there will be no weakening of your house wall.

Most houses are of wooden stud construction even though they may be sheathed with shingles, aluminum siding, stucco, or brick. The directions given here are for buildings of stud construction.

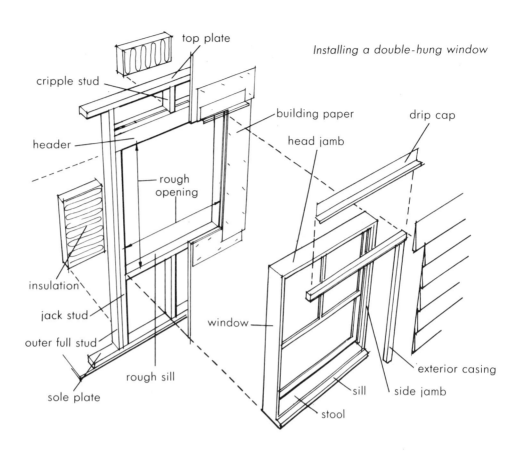

top plate

cripple stud

header

rough opening

insulation

jack stud

outer full stud

sole plate

rough sill

building paper

head jamb

drip cap

window

exterior casing

sill

side jamb

stool

**Materials for installing a double-hung window**
**With an interior wall of sheetrock:**

| Amount | Size | Item |
|---|---|---|
| 1 | | Double-hung window |
| 4 | 2″ x 4″ x 8′ | Pine, fir, or spruce |
| 1 | 2″ x 6″ x 8′ | Pine, fir, or spruce |
| 1 | 6″ x width of window | Aluminum flashing |
| 1 lb. | 16d | Common nails |
| ¼ lb. | 8d | Galvanized casing nails |
| ¼ lb. | 8d | Casing nails |
| ½ lb. | 8d | Common nails |
| ½ lb. | 10d | Common nails |
| | ½″ | Plywood scraps |
| | 1″ x 2″ | #2 pine scraps |
| | | Interior wall covering to match exist-ing covering |
| | | Shims |
| | | Sandpaper |
| | | Sheetrock nails |
| | | Joint compound |
| | | Perforated tape |
| | | Staples |
| | | Polyethylene plastic |
| | | Wood putty |
| | | Silicone caulking |

**Tools:**
Circular saw
Pry bar
Chalkline
Tape measure
Screwdriver
Hammer
Carpenter's level
Handsaw
Metal shears
Steel rule or straightedge
Utility knife
6″ putty knife
10″ putty knife
Countersink
Staple gun
Drill and bits
Caulking gun
Rafter square
Miter box (optional)

## How to build:

*Trace heating ducts, plumbing, and electrical lines to be sure they won't interfere. In some cases, you can determine their presence by inspecting the wall from the basement. Electrical lines can be easily moved; ducts and pipes are more difficult. If you are unsure about the location of your electrical lines, switch off the breaker for the area in which you will be working before cutting into the wall.*

*Windows come in two standard thicknesses: 4½" to match wallboard interiors, and 5⅝" to match plaster ones. Choose the correct thickness.*

## A. Preparing the Interior Wall

**1.** Purchase the new window. Included with the window unit will be instructions giving the dimensions for the rough opening in the house wall.

Mark the dimensions of the rough opening on the interior house wall. Locate the nearest studs beyond the sides of the opening.

Within this area, remove the baseboard and, if present, the base shoe and base cap at the floor. (The base shoe is a narrow strip fastened to the bottom of the baseboard; the base cap is fastened above it.) Also remove any ceiling molding.

To remove, insert a screwdriver between the molding and wall. Tap with a hammer. This should loosen the nails. Work along the molding until it can be pried from the wall. Be careful not to break or splinter the molding. It will be reused.

**2.** Along the center of the studs to either side of the window opening, snap vertical chalklines from floor to ceiling. With a utility knife, score the plaster or wallboard along the chalkline from floor to ceiling. Remove this section of wall covering with a pry bar. If there is lath to be removed, set the circular saw blade to a depth of ¾" (or whatever depth will cut through the lath but not into the stud), and cut along either side of the opening.

If the wall cavity is filled with insulation, remove it.

## B. Window Location

**3.** Usually the standard height from the window head to the finished floor is 6'8" so that the heights of windows and doors are the same. This distance can be transferred to the outside of the house by drilling pilot holes through the sheathing. If there are existing windows, place the new window at their height. Otherwise, choose a convenient working height for the window.

**4.** On the outside of the house, establish a level line for the top of the window. Measure the width of the window unit between the outer edges of the casing. Add ¼" for clearance. On the house wall, draw lines for the window width, using a level to be sure they are plumb.

**5.** To establish the length of the window, measure the window unit from the top of the casing to the bottom of the sill. Complete the window outline on the exterior wall and cut away siding (leaving the sheathing) with the circular saw set to the maximum depth of the siding.

## C. Sheathing

**6.** On the back side of the window unit, measure the width of the top and side casings. Subtract these measurements from the existing opening in the siding. Center the new measurement marks on the sheathing (which may be covered with building paper). Be sure lines are square and plumb. Then cut hole in the sheathing.

There should now be a lip of sheathing against which the window will rest, and an opening just large enough for the window jambs to slip through.

**7.** If there is a stud passing through the window opening, it will have to be cut. For a window opening of less than 2' in width cut into the first floor wall of a one-story house, this stud will have to be cut back 5½" above the rough opening. The 5½" distance allows space for a 2 x 6 header which will be added later (see page 61 for various header sizes).

A second cut through this stud will be necessary 1½" below the opening in the sheathing. This cut allows space for a 2 x 4 rough sill.

Work loose the section of 2 x 4 to be removed. Be careful not to damage the sheathing in the process.

## D. Framing the Rough Opening

**8.** Working inside, align the outer full studs 1½" out from the edge of the window opening in the sheathing. Toenail into top and sole plates with 16d nails.

**9.** Cut two jack studs to run from the top of the sole plate to the top edge of the window opening in the sheathing. Nail them into the outer full studs with 10d nails. The jack studs should stand against the sheathing, even with the bottom of the full stud and even with the sheathing opening.

**10.** The member used to span the top of the window opening is called a header. It is sized according to the weight above it and the distance it will span. See table below.

Cut two header boards to the horizontal distance between the outer studs. Because these boards will rest on edge and must be as thick as a stud is wide, you will need ½" plywood filler material.

Make a sandwich, with the plywood between, and nail together with 10d nails. Nail on both sides and stagger the nails every 10".

**11.** Set the header on top of the jack studs. Using two 16d nails on

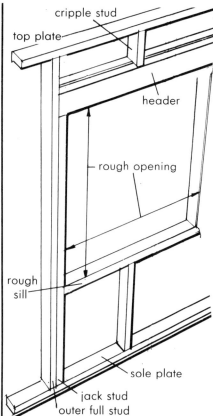

each side, nail through the full stud into the header.

**12.** Toenail the cripple stud (the stud length left above the window) into the header with 8d nails.

**13.** There will be a rough sill (2 x 4) set perpendicular to the jack studs, flush with and below the bottom of the window opening. Cut sill to length, and toenail into jack studs.

**14.** Check for level, then with 16d nails nail through the sill into the end of the cripple stud below the window.

## E. Drip Cap

**15.** Window openings exposed to rain need to be flashed. Sometimes the drip cap comes as part of the window unit. If you have to buy your own, you might want to purchase standard aluminum drip cap (which is pre-bent), or you can make your own. With metal cutting shears, cut a strip of 6" aluminum flashing, long enough to cover the exterior head casing. Lay the length of flashing on a 2 x 4 with a ½" lip projecting. Bend the lip 90 degrees. Turn the flashing over, extend it another 1½" (or the depth of the casing), and along the length of the flashing make a second 90 degree bend.

**16.** Above the window opening, slip the 4" flat section of flashing up between the sheathing and siding.

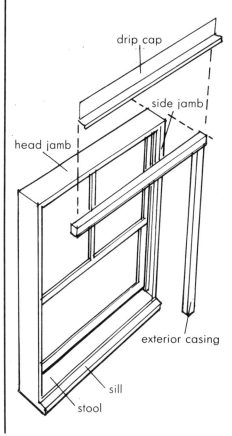

### Header Spans

| Load above Opening | Maximum Span in Feet | | | | |
|---|---|---|---|---|---|
| | 4 | 6 | 8 | 10 | 12 |
| Roof | 2 x 4 | 2 x 6 | 2 x 8 | 2 x 10 | 2 x 12 |
| One story | 2 x 6 | 2 x 6 | 2 x 10 | 2 x 10 | 2 x 10 |
| Two stories | 2 x 10 | 2 x 10 | 2 x 12 | — | — |

## F. Setting the Window

**17.** Place the window unit, exterior casing down, on a flat surface and check for square. If the unit isn't square, clamp one side to a work surface, and gently push against the jamb corners to square it. Tack a 1 x 2 diagonal brace between side and head jambs. Tack a second between side casing and sill. The braces shouldn't interfere with setting the window in place.

**18.** From outdoors, tip window unit into place, pushing it up under the flashing. The exterior casing should fit firmly against house sheathing.

**19.** If the jambs are less than the thickness of the walls, including the interior finish material you plan to use, add strips of wood to the jambs to bring them flush with the finished interior wall. Cut wood strips to the proper length; glue and nail them to the jambs with 4d finishing nails.

**20.** Center window between the jack studs. From outside, raise the window until the head jamb hits the header, then check with a level. Nail the lower of the two corners to the header with 8d galvanized casing nails. Lower the other corner until the unit is level, and nail that corner in place.

**21.** You will need a helper outside the house to hold the window securely against the sheathing. On the inside, again check for level and squareness to be sure nothing has moved. Insert shims between the finish sill and the rough sill. Drive 8d casing nails through the finish sill and shims into the rough sill below.

**22.** Plumb the window, front to back, and on each side insert at least two shims between the side jamb and the jack stud.

**23.** Fill the gaps between the jambs and the studs with plenty of fiberglass insulation.

Over the loose insulation around the window add a vapor barrier of plastic film. Staple the polyethylene between the studs and window jambs.

Insulate between the cripple studs, with the paper side of the fiberglass batts facing into the room. Use the tabs on either side to staple the insulation to the studs. Staple polyethylene over the insulation for a vapor barrier.

**24.** Fasten the exterior casing (top and sides) to the rough frame (jack studs and header) with 8d galvanized casing nails at 12" intervals. Countersink nails and fill holes with wood putty.

**25.** With silicone caulking, caulk between flashing and casing, casing and exterior siding.

## G. Interior Finish

**26.** To replace the wallboard below the window, measure the width between existing pieces of wallboard, and the height between the sole plate and the sill of the window. Mark dimensions on the face side of the wallboard. Score wallboard through face paper by cutting along a straightedge with a utility knife.

**27.** Place the scored wallboard over a table edge or a 2 x 4, bend or snap core away from scored side with the palm of your hand. Slice through back paper with a utility knife. Smooth cut edges with a sureform, rasp, or coarse sandpaper.

Mark stud location lightly on floor and interior sill. Lift wallboard into place. Snap chalklines to locate center of studs, and nail wallboard into place. Use pairs of sheetrock nails 2" apart and at 1' intervals.

Drive nails flush, then dimple the surface with the last hammer blow. Don't strike hard enough to break the paper.

Cut and nail the remaining wallboard in place.

**28.** Apply a thick layer of joint compound to wallboard seams and spread with 6" putty knife. Center perforated tape over length of joint. With the putty knife, press the tape into the compound.

Feather the joint, spreading the compound to either side. Apply compound over any nail heads between seams.

When the first coat has dried, apply a thick second coat with a 10" taping knife, and feather edges.

Add a very thin third coat, feathering it out 12" to 14". When the joint compound is thoroughly dry, sand the surface until smooth.

## H. Interior Trim

**29.** Cut the interior stool (or sill) to length. It will sit flush against the bottom rail of the window sash and should be long enough to extend at least beyond the interior side casings which will be added over the jambs.

To notch the stool at either side, hold it level with the sill and mark the position of the side jambs. Also mark a line on the face where it will fit against the wall surface. Make the necessary cuts and set in place. With casing nails, nail the back edge of the stool into the rough sill.

**30.** Check window detail in the rest of your house for the type of casing and the method of installation. Casing is used to finish the room side of a window. Depending on the window detail in your house, set a piece of side casing in position on the stool running it along the side of the window jamb, or set it back $\frac{3}{16}$" from the inside of the

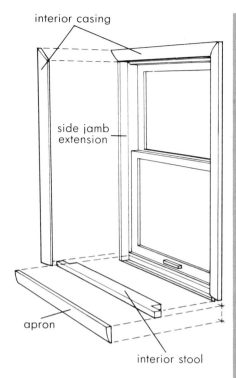

interior casing

side jamb
extension

apron

interior stool

jamb. This will give a reveal along the inside edge of the window. Mark the position of the miter (an angled cut of 45 degrees). Cut the miter and nail casing in place so that the inner edge is flush with or set back from the inner face of the jambs. Cut head and second side casing to length and nail in place.

**31.** Cut the apron to the distance between the outside edges of the side casing. It will fit below the stool to cover the joint between the window and wallboard. Nail to 2 x 4 rough sill and through stool into apron.

**32.** Replace ceiling molding, baseboard, base cap, and base shoe. Countersink all nail heads and fill with wood putty.

Attach window lock and sash lift.

# Bay Window

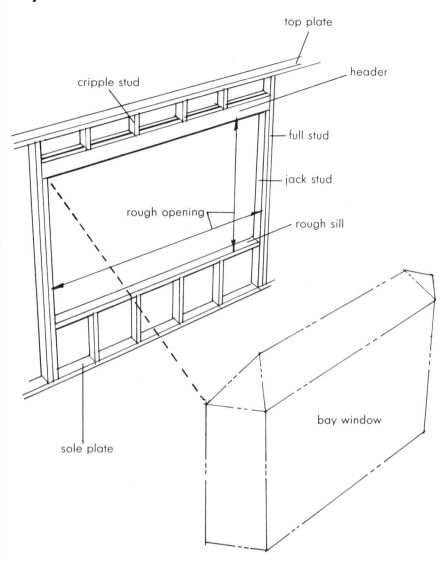

top plate

cripple stud

header

full stud

jack stud

rough opening

rough sill

sole plate

bay window

*Installing a bay window*

**What it does:** Bay windows will actually flood a room with light; they are not only larger than double-hung windows, but they gather more sunlight because they project beyond the house.

Bay windows also provide the additional space of a window seat, and overhead space for hanging window plants.

**Tips:** Usually bay windows have a fixed center set of windows which runs parallel to the exterior house wall, and windows at either side which are set at an angle. The units come in 5′ to 9′ widths, in 1′ increments.

When a bay window is purchased, the kit includes the window, head or ceiling board, window seat, and sometimes an insulating panel below the seat. Other units also include the drip cap, a roof kit of plywood sheathing cut to fit, as well as hip, end, and intermediate rafters.

## How to build:

## A. Setting the Window

**1.** Prepare the rough opening as explained in Steps 1-14 (pp. 60-61 under "Double-hung Window").

Read carefully the manufacturer's instructions which come with the unit; some bay windows rest against the siding rather than the sheathing.

**2.** Tilt the window into place; you will need helpers to steady the unit. Rest the bottom on the rough sill, and slowly tip window into opening until the exterior window casing is flush against the sheathing.

Center the unit between the jack studs, and hold it in position with sawhorses.

**3.** From inside, level the seat board to find which side is higher. Nail that side into the rough sill, 2" in from the side jamb.

**4.** Shim up the other side between the window unit and the rough sill until it reads level. Nail into rough sill.

**5.** Plumb the side jambs with a level. With a helper on the outside of the house to adjust the tilt of the window, install shims 1' apart between the side jambs and the jack studs, and nail in place.

**6.** Wedge shims between the top of the window unit (headboard) and header. Nail through headboard and shims into header.

Fill the gaps between the window jambs and studs with plenty of insulation.

**7.** Triangular knee brackets also may come with the unit. They support the window on the outside of the house. These are placed under the two vertical corners (mullions) separating adjoining windows.

Drill holes through the longer leg

of the bracket into the cripple stud in the wall, and fasten with ⅜" lag screws. If there is no cripple stud directly behind the bracket, toenail one in place.

Drill a hole through the shorter leg into the insulating panel below the window seat and screw together with a wood screw.

**8.** Caulk around the bottom of the window and then nail quarter-round molding to cover the joint between the window unit and the house siding.

## B. The Roof

**9.** If your unit doesn't come with pre-cut roof pieces, they will have to be cut.

Above the window trim, nail the manufacturer's drip cap.

There are three pre-cut pieces of roof sheathing. Place these temporarily against the drip cap so that they rest against the house siding.

Draw a line around the edge of the window roof to indicate how much of the house siding must be removed. Saw along the outline, and remove siding.

**10.** Lag screw a length of perforated metal strapping into the cripple stud behind the house sheathing about 10" above the headboard of the window unit. Lag screw the other end into the mullion post at the angled corner of the

window. Do the same at the other corner.

**11.** The two thicker rafters in the kit span the distance between the mullion and the house sheathing. These hip rafters should be nailed to the sheathing, leaving a space the thickness of the roof sheathing between the rafter and the house siding. Nail other rafter end into mullion post and headboard.

**12.** The end rafter will rest flat against the house and perpendicular to the hip rafter. Nail it into the sheathing and hip rafter, leaving room for the roof sheathing. Do the other corner. Then nail the intervening rafters in place, spacing them equally along the window. Each will be nailed into the headboard and the house sheathing.

**13.** Begin at one end and butt one of the triangular pieces of roof sheathing against the house sheathing. It will extend to the hip rafter. Nail into place at 6" intervals.

**14.** Above the headboard, lay down plenty of insulation.

**15.** Add the center section of roof sheathing. Nail in place. Then nail the triangular piece at the other end.

**16.** With roofing nails, attach the metal drip edge to the bottom edge of the roof sheathing.

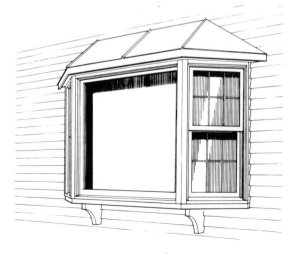

Staple roofing felt to the sheathing, working up from the drip edge.

## C. Flashing

**17.** Flashing will be needed between the house siding and the shingled roof of the window.

Loosen the nails of the siding along both end rafters. Work right-angled pieces of flashing up between the house siding and sheathing. The other angled end is nailed to the sheathing of the bay window. Use one roofing nail in the top corner and nail into window sheathing. Then apply a row of roofing shingles which will cover the first piece of step flashing.

**18.** Slide the next piece of flashing under the house siding far enough up the bay roof sheathing so that it will be covered by the next row of shingles. Finish shingling and flashing triangular section of roof.

**19.** Shingle rest of roof.

**20.** Cut a piece of flashing 8" longer than the length of the center section of the roof. Notch the corners at either end so that the flashing will slide under the siding.

Bend the flashing to 90 degrees. Loosen the house siding. Spread roofing cement on top of the window asphalt shingling. Slide flashing into place and press into the tar.

Bend tabs around hips, and seal all edges with roofing cement.

**21.** Renail loosened siding.

**22.** Cut 12" x 36" shingles in thirds. Nail shingles to hips, working from bottom to top. Be sure nails are covered by the next shingle. Coat any nail heads with roofing tar.

**23.** Caulk on both sides between window and house siding.

# Sliding Patio Doors

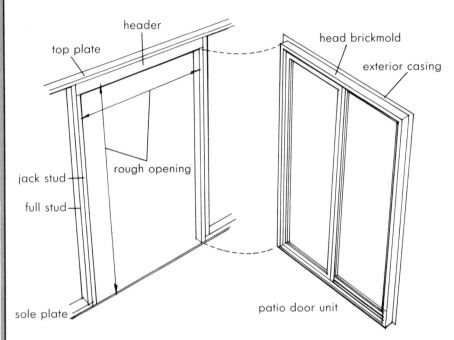

*Installing sliding patio doors*

**What they do:** Patio, or sliding glass doors, offer the advantages of windows (light, ventilation, heat gain, if they are located on a south-facing wall), and the convenience of doors. And because of the slide-by panels, these units don't require the space of hinged doors.

Sliding patio doors brighten up and visually enlarge any space. If located between the house and backyard, they serve to "bring the outdoors inside."

**Tips:** The standard patio door kits are available in 80" heights and 5-, 6- and 8- foot widths. The kits include the two door panels, the frame (wood, aluminum, or steel), and all the necessary hardware.

The unit can easily be installed by two people.

The doors will alter the light, ventilation, privacy, and traffic patterns of your interior space; doors that face directly into the prevailing winds will lose more heat than those on more sheltered sides of the house, or those protected by walls, fences, or outdoor planting. Keep these things in mind when locating the unit.

Pay special attention when buying the lumber; framing for the unit must be straight. Also square and plumb the metal frame carefully or the doors will stick.

Be sure you know whether or not you are cutting into a load-bearing wall. (See p. 58.)

Before removing the existing studs, you may want to add bracing to carry the weight of the roof and floors above. The braces can be removed once the wall has been modified.

Check p. 61 for the header size; it should correspond to the span of your opening.

Install the unit when the weather is favorable, and start early in the day; until the doors are in place, there will be a sizable hole in your house wall.

## How to build:

## A. Fastening the Frame

**1.** Cut and frame the rough opening according to Steps 1-14 (pp. 60-61). Follow manufacturer's instructions for the exact size of the rough opening. Usually the opening is ½" wider and ⅜" higher than the unit.

**2.** Assemble the frame. Run parallel beads of caulking along the subfloor. Set the frame in place from the outside, and center it in the opening. Press down at the threshold to spread the caulking.

**3.** You will need at least one helper to hold the frame against the opening while you nail the interior edge of the threshold to the sill every 12".

**4.** Tack through the exterior casing (brickmold) into the framing 4" above the sill and 4" down from the head brickmold. Check the entire unit for squareness.

**5.** Continue to plumb and level the frame by hammering in wedges between the frame and jack stud on both sides.

**6.** Hammer in three shims between header and the frame, frequently checking for level. Secure frame temporarily with screws. Recheck that the unit is square and plumb.

**7.** Adjust the frame if necessary. Screw to jack studs and header through predrilled holes in the frame.

**8.** Finish nailing the brickmold.

**9.** Install drip cap (Steps 15-16, p. 61) over the exterior head brickmold.

**10.** Cut a strip of wood to the width and thickness of the exterior threshold overhang. Set in place and nail into the house sheathing.

## B. The Panels

**11.** Apply a small amount of caulking to the channel that will hold the stationary panel. From outdoors, lift the stationary panel into the outside overhead track. Bring the bottom of the panel over the floor sill and lower it into the proper track. It should slide into the side jamb of the frame. If it doesn't slide flush against the side jamb, force it by pressing down on a 2 x 4, angled between the door panel and the opposite side jamb. Then secure angle brackets, top and bottom, to the threshold and head jamb. (They are provided with the door unit.)

**12.** Screw the parting strip into the stationary panel; it will separate the stationary from the movable panel.

**13.** Turn the movable panel so that the latch will be against the jamb on the inside when in closed position.
   Set rollers into the inside channel. Angle the top of the movable panel into the channel at the top behind the head stop. Swing the bottom of the panel towards the channel and set on the rollers.

**14.** Close the movable door. If it is not plumb against the side jamb, pry off the plastic guard caps in the bottom rail of the frame. Turn the height-adjustment screws which will raise or lower the door on the rollers until the door meets the side jamb squarely.

**15.** Check lock connection. Door should operate with a slight drag.

**16.** After interior wall finish is added, trim out the door with interior casing molding.

# Solar Glassed-in Porch

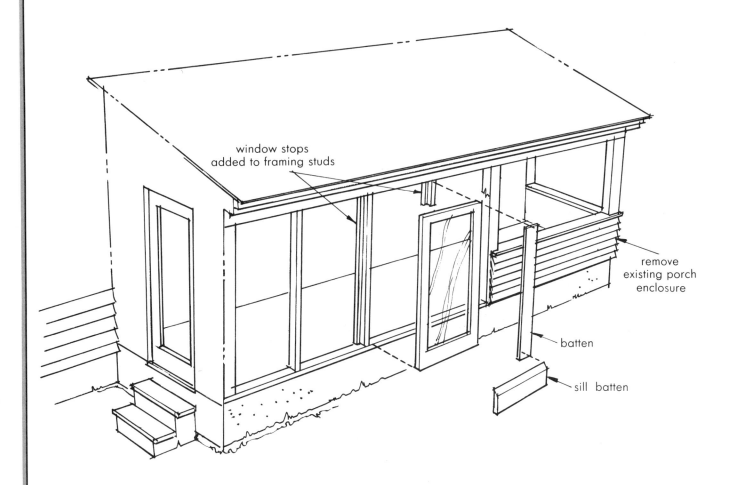

window stops
added to framing studs

remove
existing porch
enclosure

batten

sill batten

**What it does:** If you already have a structurally sound porch with good solar exposure, it is relatively simple to turn it into a glassed-in solar porch. Once the framing is in for the glass, only the trim and flashing need to be added.

Because of the expanse of south-facing glass, the porch becomes an effective solar collector during sunny periods as well as adding extra year-round space to your home. Doors and windows also can be incorporated into your design where exits and ventilation are needed. And plants will love the sunlight.

**How it works:** Glass is highly transparent to solar radiation; when the sun is out, the porch will warm up quickly. By noon on a sunny day there will be excess heat which can be vented into the house by opening the adjoining door. As the warm air circulates, temperatures in the house will rise steadily; temperatures in the porch will remain relatively stable. When outdoor temperatures begin to dip, and at night, the adjoining door should be closed to retain the house heat; closing thermal shades or shutters along the porch glazing will further decrease heat loss along the south wall of the house.

Temperatures inside the porch will fluctuate with outdoor temperatures, but will consistently remain 10 to 40 degrees F. above outdoor temperatures.

If you want to use the porch for plants, excess heat can be stored for nighttime use. Heat is already being stored in the floor and adjoining wall as well as in the porch furnishings. Even more can be stored if you choose materials with high heat storage capacities. Concrete, tiles, bricks, and slate, for example, will store more heat than wooden floors, and should be of medium to dark colors for best heat absorption. Of all the inexpensive possibilities, water stores the most heat in the smallest volume. Specially made water storage tubes, 55-gallon drums, or even plastic milk containers filled with water can be stacked against the north wall. Be sure the floor can support the weight (water weighs 8.4 pounds per gallon). The water will absorb excess heat during the day and re-radiate this into the porch space at night. Do not use these if tempera-tures will drop below freezing.

For the storing of heat to be ef-fective, it is essential that the glass be fitted with some kind of night-time insulation.

**Advantages:**
1. Uses house's existing poten-tial.
2. Puts an under-used room into solar use.
3. Is cheaper and less complex than building a solar collector or greenhouse.
4. Frequently the thermal storage mass already exists (i.e., brick or concrete floors and/or walls).
5. In some climates, may be used year-round as greenhouse be-cause temperatures in solar porch never go below freezing–ideal environment for many hardy crops.
6. Construction materials for solar porch are readily avail-able and moderately priced.

**Disadvantages:**
1. Privacy.
2. Annoying glare, and this may cause furniture to fade.

**Tips:** Replacement glass for patio doors comes in standard sizes of 28″ x 76″; 34″ x 76″; 46″ x 76″, and is made of two layers of sealed, tempered glass with a ¾″ dead air space between the layers. The units are prefabricated, so they are cheaper per square foot than hav-ing the windows custom-made.

Check with your glass dealer for the sizes of replacement patio door units, and prehung sliding glass doors if you want an exit. Decide whether you want operable win-dows. Windows located low on one wall, high on the opposite wall will allow the porch to be easily venti-lated.

Draw a plan of your porch, with the sizes and placement of the units. Allow ¼″ tolerance on all sides of glass panels. If necessary, additional framing can be added and glass can be cut-to-fit for the non-standard openings. Or the awkward sized openings can be in-sulated and covered with siding.

Any of the rigid plastics also may be used. Some are of double wall construction to increase their insu-lating value.

Most solar experts still prefer glass for its durability, aesthetics, and high percentage of solar trans-mittance; while many homeowners prefer the plastics because they are light, flexible, easy to install, and shatterproof.

The plastics can be cut to any size or shape, and they vary from semi-opaque colors to solar tints to translucent and transparent sur-faces. The translucent panels offer privacy and provide diffuse light which is ideal for plant growth.

The thickness of framing mem-bers (sill, head stops, jambs) will vary according to your specific situ-ation and needs. Consult a car-pentry text before beginning construction.

The lumber should be rot-resis-tant; use cedar, redwood, or pressure-treated wood.

The porch should face south, or slightly east of south for the early morning sunlight.

Temperatures in the solar porch will rise rapidly on a sunny day. Don't leave children or pets un-tended in the porch.

Check with your local building inspector; you may need a building permit.

## How to build:

## A. Preparing the Porch

**1.** Strip down the porch to the basics of roof, supporting posts, and floor. Take out the porch ceil-ing and trim so that you can insu-late between the joists; then replace the ceiling. Leave fascia and soffit boards in place. (You also will want to insulate between the floor joists, keeping the vapor barrier toward the warm side. And if there are any walls to be left without glass, be sure they too are insulated.)

**2.** Within the porch area, expose the sheathing by removing the wood or aluminum siding if you wish the porch to match the interior house decor; furring strips to hold wallboard can be nailed into brick or flat stucco walls.

**3.** Check that vertical supports are in good condition. If the structure isn't sound, the glass may crack. Before replacing a structural mem-ber, provide temporary support to either side until the new one is in-stalled.

## B. The Framing

**4.** Cut a sill to go around the out-side edge of the porch or between the posts. Caulk before setting the sill, and lag screw or bolt it in place.

**5.** Add the framing members. Be sure the framing is square and plumb.

**6.** Cut window stops to the proper length and width from 1-by stock. They should be the width of the framing member minus the thickness of the glass, minus ¼″ for caulking.

**7.** Snap chalklines to be sure the stops will be plumb, then glue and nail them to the vertical members.

**8.** Prime or stain all framing members.

Fill in any gaps with insulation and sheathing. Caulk all seams.

## C. The Glazing

**9.** Hang operable windows and doors first.

**10.** Cut to length 1" x 3" vertical battens. (After each piece of glass has been installed, the battens will be screwed on the outside into the vertical framing members and should extend ¾" onto the glass on either side.)

**11.** Horizontal battens to run along the bottom of the glazing will sit flush with the bottom of the sill and extend ¾" onto the glass. Cut them to length and bevel one edge so that they will shed water. Set aside.

**12.** Place butyl glazing tape around each frame against the inside window stops.

Set three neoprene setting blocks on the bottom of the frame. Lift the thermopane glass onto the blocks, center the pane in the opening, and tilt slowly into the frame so that the glass presses against the sticky glazing tape.

Run tape around the exterior perimeter of the glass while a second person holds the pane in place.

**13.** Screw the battens into the framing members to hold the glass tightly in place. Before bottom battens are screwed in, place and nail flashing to the sill plate.

**14.** Run caulking around all seams to seal the glass. Most silicones can't be painted. Use white silicone if you are going to paint the wood white, or use clear caulking if the wood will be stained.

# Solar Skylight:

- Installing a Prefabricated Unit
- Building Your Own Glazing Unit

**Skills required:** Moderate. (Directions do not include constructing a light shaft. This is more complicated, but will have to be built unless the skylight is set into a flat roof or roof/ceiling.)

**Cost:** Probably over $100, but cost depends on the kind and size of prefabricated skylight; if you build your own glass or Plexiglas unit, expenses can be as low as $25 to $35.

**Amount of heat gain:** Minimal heat gain if located on south-sloping roof—even less heat gain than through south-facing vertical glazing of the same size because the warmest room air will collect around the skylight opening. The amount of light gain is substantial, dependent on the orientation and size of the skylight. On a bright but cloudy day, a 2′ x 2′ unit will provide the light equivalent of three 100-watt light bulbs.

**What it does:** Skylights brighten interior rooms in a way that no artificial light source can. Even on cloudy days, they offer a surprising amount of illumination. Skylights are ideal to illuminate dark stairways, bathrooms, and kitchens. In humid areas such as bathrooms and kitchens, however, water will condense on the interior glazing.

Skylights are an easy way to get light into living spaces when the windows are shaded by nearby buildings or trees. In attic bedrooms, they are especially attractive because they give the illusion of greater space.

An operable window for ventilation is often chosen.

Skylights can be installed in tin, copper, aluminum, wood, and asphalt shingle roofs. Installations in tile and slate roofs aren't recommended for homeowners because they are more difficult. Skylights also can be installed in any roof pitch; flat roofs are the simplest.

**How it works:** On sunny days, skylights increase the amount of heat absorbed by the interior of the house. As the outdoor temperatures cool, this heat is re-radiated, thereby moderating temperature swings in the room.

To maximize the effectiveness of the skylight as a solar collector, the inside of the light shaft should be painted a light color or gloss white or even lined with reflective foil. In addition, louvered slats, insulated roller shades, sliding panels, or rigid foam panels are recommended to insulate the glazing at night or during cloudy periods.

**Advantages:**
1. Cheerful.
2. May add to the direct heat gain of the house.
3. Improves the character and apparent space of the room.
4. Low cost in terms of visual impact, and very reasonably priced if it's a do-it-yourself project.
5. Captures the sun's warmth on sunny winter days; if the window is operable, the skylight will help cool the house in summer.

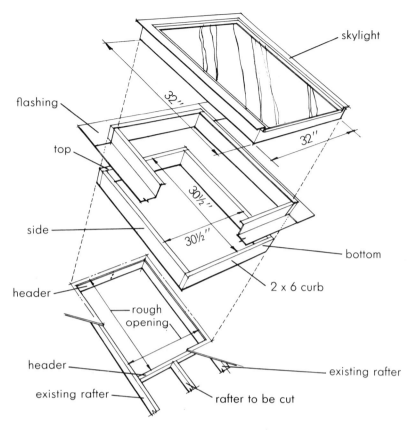

skylight

flashing

top

side

header

header

existing rafter

32"

32"

30½"

30½"

bottom

2 x 6 curb

rough opening

existing rafter

rafter to be cut

6. Provides even, diffuse light—pleasing quality to light as it shifts during the day and over the year.
7. Can be located to frame view of trees, hills, etc.
8. Lets in sunlight while maintaining privacy. You can use translucent or diffuse glazing panels, if you don't want the view.
9. Unlike windows, adds light while maintaining house security.
10. Reduces the chance of solar blockage by trees or buildings.
11. Good for plants.

**Disadvantages:**
1. Needs movable insulation to minimize heat loss.
2. Excessive heat in summer unless unit can be opened for ventilation.
3. Water leakage may be a problem unless unit has been carefully sealed.
4. Are worse than windows for heat loss, unless there is good thermal insulation.

**Materials:**

| Amount | Size | Item |
|---|---|---|
| 1 | 2″ x 6″ x 12′ | Pine, fir, or spruce |
| 2 | Same dimension lumber as existing rafters x 30½″ | Headers |
| 1 | 9″ x 13′ | Aluminum flashing |
| 1 gal. | | Roofing cement |
| 1 | | Two-part epoxy cement (PC-7) |
| ½ lb. | 16d | Common nails |
| ½ lb. | 12d | Common nails |
| ⅕ lb. | 8d | Common nails |
| 1 lb. | 1″ | Galvanized roofing nails |
| 20 | 1″ | Aluminum nails |
| | | Staples |
| | | Scrap lumber |

**Tools:**

Tape measure
Carpenter's square
Chalkline
Hammer
Keyhole saw or saber saw
Circular saw
Tin snips

Ladders and roof jacks (if steep roof)
Pry bar
Utility knife
Rafter square
Level
Old gloves

# How to build:

*Directions are given for installing a 32" x 32" skylight in a flat roof or roof/ceiling. For this unit and those smaller, there should be no need to double up the rafters on each side of the opening even though one rafter is cut. For larger units, where three or more rafters will have to be cut, check a carpentry text; additional supports will be necessary.*

## A. Cutting Away the Interior Wall

**1.** From the inside, determine the top line of the skylight opening with a level. You may wish to make a template of the skylight opening to decide where you want to place the unit.

**2.** Locate the rafters on each side. Use a nail for a probe until you locate the inside edge of one of the rafters. From this point measure horizontally 30½".

Locate the second rafter with a nail probe.

**3.** Mark the sides with a rafter square. They will run along the inside edge of each rafter and be 33½" long (the height of the unit plus 1½" for each of the headers which will be added later; the headers will bridge the space be-tween the rafters and rough in the opening).

Draw the bottom line (30½") with the level. Check that all corners are square.

**4.** Drill pilot holes in one corner until you can insert a keyhole saw or saber saw, and cut out the opening in the interior wall covering. Remove it.

## B. Building the Curb

**5.** From the 2 x 6, cut two side pieces to 30½" and two end pieces (top and bottom) to 33½". Nail through the ends into the sides with three 12d common nails.

**6.** With 6d or 8d nails, nail temporary diagonal cross braces to keep the curb square. Use any size of lumber; the cross braces will be removed after the curb has been nailed in place. Don't set the nails; you will remove them later.

---

Skylights come in many different sizes, but their measurements are limited to the normal rafter spacings of 16" and 24" on center or exact multiples thereof (i.e., skylights are typically available in sizes of 16" x 24", 16" x 48", 24" x 24", 24" x 48", 32" x 32", 32" x 48", and 48" x 48"). For the larger sizes (those wider than 24"), one or two rafters will have to be cut.

If the skylight will be installed over a trafficked area and there is any fear of breakage, use a shatterproof plastic, not glass.

Prefabricated kits are available in dome, square, or rectangular shapes. Some are installed directly onto the roof decking; others require that a curb be built to which the unit is attached. (Curbs are simply boxes nailed over the sheathing to which the skylight is then attached.) Follow the manufacturer's instructions.

The advantage of the curb is that it raises the critical seams above the roof. This reduces the possibility that wind will drive water past the flashing and into the home.

In purchasing a unit, check that it is double glazed, and that the layers of glazing are separated by an air space. The outer layer should be vented to the outside by a series of weep holes. Check the aluminum frame and flashing; they should be rigid and welded at the corners to prevent leakage.

It is important that the 2 x 6 lumber for the curb be free of all but the smallest knots. Choose pieces that are not warped or bowed.

Before buying a unit, check the rafter spacing in your attic. If the spacing is 16" on center, for example, a 32" model will fit within two rafter bays and necessitate cutting only one rafter.

## C. The Roof

**7.** As a precaution, nail a 2 x 4 above and one below the location where the rafter will be cut. These will support the cut rafter when you work later from the roof. If there is an interior finish on the attic ceiling, make a T-shaped brace to run between the rafters at either side of the opening. Wedge it against the interior wall covering above the opening. This will prevent the cut rafter from sagging and cracking the finished ceiling.

**8.** Cut through and remove the section of the middle rafter (33½") which runs through the skylight opening. This is a 90 degree cut. Do not cut through the roof sheathing yet.

**9.** On the underside of the roof sheathing, mark the rough opening for the skylight. Its width will be to the inside edge of the adjacent rafters; its height will be that of the opening in the interior wall minus 3" (1½" less on top and bottom for the headers to be added later), or an opening of 30½" x 30½".

**10.** Drive four 16d nails through the roof to mark the corners of this new opening.

**11.** The opening can be cut from inside, but it is more easily done from the roof.

Go up on the roof with the 2 x 6 curb, power saw, chalkline, pry bar, utility knife, and hammer. On a steep roof, you may need to use roof jacks or a second ladder hooked over the ridge. If it is a tin roof, you also will need tin snips.

**12.** Place the curb so the four protruding nails fit inside it. Using the chalkline, snap a line around the outside of the curb. This line indicates the extent of roofing material to be removed. Set curb aside.

Cut away roofing materials with the utility knife. (The curb will butt against the roofing paper.) Save the undamaged shingles in case you need them later for patching.

Loosen and remove the shingle nails within 4" of the opening with the end of the pry bar.

**13.** Lay curb back in place, now on top of the bare sheathing, and trace a line inside the curb. Remove curb and along the line you have just drawn cut the opening in the roof with a circular, saber, or reciprocating saw.

## D. The Flashing

**14.** With the aluminum flashing, flash the curb to prevent any chance of water leakage. Cut flashing with tin snips or heavy scissors. Cut four pieces, each 9" by 39".

Cut and bend the flashing to the following diagram. Notice that there will be a 3" overlap under the roof.

The solid lines are where the flashing should be cut; the dotted lines indicate where the flashing should be bent to a 90 degree angle.

**15.** Use the curb as a form around which to bend the flashing. Bend the bottom flashing, then sides and top. Mark the pieces so that they can be easily reassembled, and remove them from the curb.

## E. Setting the Curb in Place

**16.** You will need the gallon of roofing cement, a pair of old gloves, and a piece of scrap lumber with which to apply the tar.

Within 4" of the roof opening, apply roofing cement on top of the roof tarpaper. Apply also to both sides of flashing flange. Begin with the bottom piece of flashing. After the tar has been applied, slide the

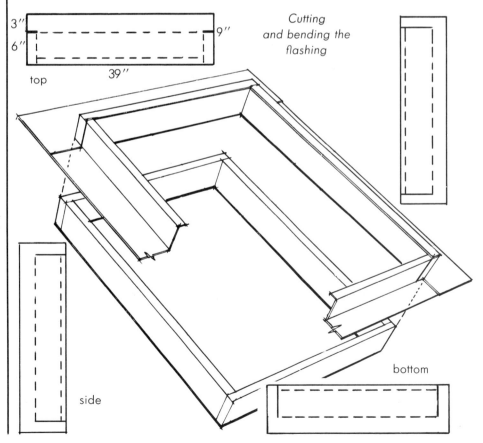

Cutting and bending the flashing

flange under the shingles. Press the shingles back in place with the bottom flashing bent slightly away from the opening.

Tar the two sides; slip the tarred flanges into position. Do the top strip last. Be sure the flashing overlaps as shown, and that the four pieces are bent back from the opening so that they won't interfere with setting the curb.

**17.** Place the curb in position on the sheathing. Toenail through the inside edge of the curb into the roof rafter with 8d common nails. Along the top and bottom, nail up through the sheathing with 16d common nails into the curb.

**18.** Bend the flashing up against the curb, and nail around the top edge of the curb with 1″ aluminum nails every 12″. Begin with the bottom flashing, then sides, and lastly the top flashing.

Nail flashing overlaps at the corners to curb, and cover the corners with a coat of epoxy (PC-7), following the directions on the can.

**19.** Renail the roof shingles up to, but not into, the flashing; cover the nail heads with roofing cement.

**20.** Apply roofing cement around the edges between the roofing material and the flashing.

## F. The Headers

**21.** Cut two headers using the same dimension lumber as the existing rafters, and each 30½″ long.

Toenail top and bottom headers into rafters using 12d common nails. Endnail through the headers into the cut rafters.

For smaller units where no rafters will need cutting, install cross blocks below and above the unit between the two adjacent rafters.

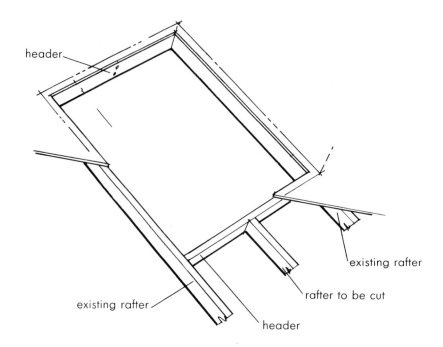

header

existing rafter

existing rafter

rafter to be cut

header

## G. Attaching the Skylight

**22.** Lift the skylight from the outside into the opening and fasten it into position according to the manufacturer's instructions. You may want to run a bead of silicone caulking around the top edge of the curb. This will bond the curb and frame of the skylight.

Screws are provided by the manufacturer to attach the skylight to the curb.

## H. Skylights without Curbs

**23.** If you install a skylight without a curb, you will need a larger opening in the roof shingles. Remove the shingles 10″ beyond where sides and top edge of the skylight opening will be, and only 2″ beyond the bottom edge. It is better to remove whole shingles than to cut along the chalkline.

**24.** Once the headers are in place, attach a 1 x 4 cleat to the top header so that at least 1″ of it protrudes above the roof decking. The cleat is used later to align the top

and sides of the skylight with the roof opening.

**25.** Spread roofing mastic in a 4″ wide swath about ⅛″ to ¼″ thick around the perimeter of the opening as a bed for the skylight flange.

**26.** Lift the skylight into position. Rest the interior top edge on the cleat. Shift the skylight laterally until the interior sides line up with the edges of the opening.

**27.** Secure the unit by nailing through the flange with roofing nails. The bottom edge of the flange should rest over the existing roofing.

**28.** Cut new shingles (from those you've removed without damaging) to fit around the top and sides of the skylight. Work from the bottom of the unit to the top, staggering slots and tabs to match the original courses of shingles. Secure the shingles with roofing cement and roofing nails.

The shingles also should overlap the top of the unit and be secured with roofing nails and roofing cement.

## I. Inside

**29.** Before beginning any interior work, check that the skylight won't leak. Douse the unit with water or wait until it rains. Look for leaks between the roofing material and the flashing. You may need to apply additional roofing tar.

**30.** If the ceiling is already finished, you won't need additional framing; for units installed in roofs which aren't ceilings, a light shaft will have to be built and a hole cut in the attic floor so that light will penetrate to the floor below. This hole will be cut and framed as you did the one in the roof.

Between the two openings, add framing, then insulation, interior wall finish and trim.

**31.** The four sides of the shaft may be built plumb, or one or more of the sides may be angled to increase the amount of sunlight which enters the room. If the walls flare out, sunlight will be more widely distributed. The walls should be painted white, or the same color as the ceiling.

Skylights are installed to gain light and/or heat. If lighting is the primary concern, the skylight can face any direction; in studios they usually face north for the preferred softer light. When added to the south pitch of a roof, skylights provide light as well as heat. In summer, this may cause problems of excessive heating and glare which can be solved by installing movable insulation.

Check outside your house. If there are deciduous trees, these may shade the skylight sufficiently in summer; but if you have evergreens, the skylight may be shaded year-round. Also check other buildings or parts of your house that might cast unwanted shadows.

# Solar Skylight:
# Building Your Own Glazing Unit

*To avoid the expense of purchasing a prefabricated skylight unit, you can build your own glazed roof.*

**Materials:**

The amount and size of materials will depend on the size of the skylight you build.

#8 wood screws
Faucet washers
Plexiglas or plate glass
2″ aluminum angle
Quarter-round trim

1 cartridge of silicone caulking
Sandpaper
Battens
4d common nails

**Tools:**

Hammer
¼″ electric drill with bits and countersink

Caulking gun
Handsaw
Clamps

Building your own glazing unit

## How to build:

### A. Single Glazed

**1.** Build a curb from 2 x 6s to whatever dimensions you wish following the earlier directions. Check to be sure the top edges of the curb are even; sand or plane down any unevenness.

**2.** With 4d nails, attach battens along the outside edge and on top of the curb. The battens should be ¾" wide and twice the thickness of the glazing material.

**3.** Cut the aluminum angle to the outside dimensions of the curb.

Drill countersunk holes along one side of the angle, ½" from the edge and every 12".

**4.** Lay a bead of silicone caulking ½" from the inside top edge of the curb on all sides.

**5.** Cut the Plexiglas to size. It will rest ¼" in from the battens, so should be ½" shorter than the measurements inside the battens.

Before cutting the Plexiglas, clamp a straightedge to your work surface so that it sandwiches the Plexiglas. Cut with a circular saw and plywood blade. If you have a saber saw, use a blade with 14 teeth per inch. Do not remove the protective covering before cutting.

**6.** After the Plexiglas is cut to size, peel off the protective paper from the underside and set the sheet over the curb. Press it into place. There should be ¼" tolerance on all sides.

Take the protective paper off the top.

**7.** Add a second bead of caulking around the edge of the Plexiglas. This bead should be higher than the batten so that when the aluminum angle is set in place it will form a seal with the silicone.

Before installing a skylight primarily for heat, consider your roof pitch and orientation. The south roof should be no more than 30 degrees east or west of south, and the optimum tilt of the skylight should be equal to your latitude plus 10 to 15 degrees. In parts of the country above 40 degrees latitude, this means an optimum angle of 50 to 60 degrees; however, most roof pitches are 0 to 30 degrees. The result is that in winter when heat gain is important, the skylight is as much as 40 percent less efficient than it could be. And in summer when the sun is directly overhead, the skylight may be collecting too much heat.

When a unit is sized for heat, it must be larger than one sized for light; it also must be fitted with movable nighttime insulation. (Double glazing or thermopane glass isn't enough to cut heat losses adequately.) This, of course, adds to the expense.

For these reasons, it may be advisable to install smaller units primarily for additional light. As a rule of thumb, skylights should equal at least ten percent of the floor area of the room.

Consider also the distance from the skylight opening to the house floor. If this distance is greater than 14', much of the light will be dissipated; for better distribution, install two or three smaller units rather than one large one.

**8.** Set the aluminum angles in place. Slip the #8 wood screws into the faucet washers and screw the aluminum angle into the curb.

Coat all seams of the aluminum angle and all exposed screw heads with silicone caulking.

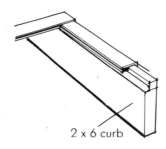

2 x 6 curb

### B. Double Glazed

**9.** For double glazed skylights, nail 1 x 1 spacers around the inside and flush with the top edge of the curb. These will create a ¾" dead air space.

Measure down the thickness of the glazing material, and nail a strip of quarter-round molding to the curb along the length of one side.

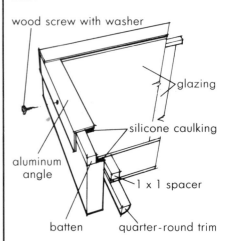

wood screw with washer

glazing

silicone caulking

aluminum angle

1 x 1 spacer

batten

quarter-round trim

**10.** Cut the glazing ⅛" narrower on all sides (¼" for Plexiglas) than the inner dimensions of the curb.

Tip the glazing into place. Add quarter-round strips for the other three sides.

### Other design possibilities

**The Light Shaft.** The light shaft can be built with all four walls plumb, or one or more of the sides can be angled to increase the amount of sunlight that enters the room. If the walls flare out, the sunlight will be more widely distributed.

Depending on your situation, there are other configurations which may better direct the light into the living space.

**Fans.** Heat will collect around the skylight. Install a fan to push the hot air down so that it won't be lost through the glazing.

**Size.** Skylights can be as large as a shed-type greenhouse added above a flat roof. In such applications, you will need a fan and duct system to move the collected air down into the living space below. These additions may be extensive enough to require some kind of thermal storage to moderate temperature swings.

# Window Collector

**Skills required:** Moderate.

**Cost:** $40 to $90. This collector was built for $84 with all new materials; costs can be cut using ¾″ insulation or recycled building materials such as used storm windows and scrap lumber.

**Amount of heat gain:** During sunny days, the window collector supplies enough extra heat to warm a moderately sized room. This averages out to be one gallon of fuel oil saved per heating season per square foot of collector area.

**What it does:** Window collectors are appropriate for winter space heating in factories, warehouses, and office buildings as well as homes. They are most easily used with double-hung windows and can be adapted to fit any size, south-facing window opening. They can be vented into windows on any story of a building. In some cases, you may be able to use an eave, first-floor porch or other parts of existing roofs for support of a second-story collector.

Window collectors require no building alteration, and can be removed for summer.

If properly sited, these collectors will provide free heat on a sunny day for seven hours. However, it is necessary to use the heat directly as produced; there is no storage. This means the collectors are especially well suited to buildings that need only daytime heating.

**How it works:** The greenhouse effect is the operating principle of the window collector. Sunlight passes through the glazing, is changed into heat, most of which is trapped within the collector. This heat, now trapped in the dead air space between the glazing and absorber plate, is quickly conducted through the aluminum. As the hot metal heats the air around it, the air becomes lighter and rises. The heated air automatically begins moving up between the absorber and the divider. As this happens, cooler air is pulled into the collector from the house. The air then circulates by natural convection out of and into

the building, recycling itself through the solar collector. The curved baffles lessen the flow resistance into the collector and around the bottom "U."

At night, cold air will fill the back channel and the bottom of the collector, causing the air flow to stagnate, but as the air temperature rises during the day, the collector will reactivate itself. Insulation keeps the back side of the collector cooler than the top side; without it, the back side could become warm enough to cause a reverse flow in the collector.

Sufficient insulation and caulking, the keys to insuring the self-activating, self-damping principle of the collector, eliminate the need for any moving parts.

Proper air flow in the collector is also important; too little flow during the day causes the collector to overheat which in turn causes heat loss through the glazing. For the collector to heat efficiently, there must be an air flow of 2 to 4 cubic feet per minute per square foot of glazing.

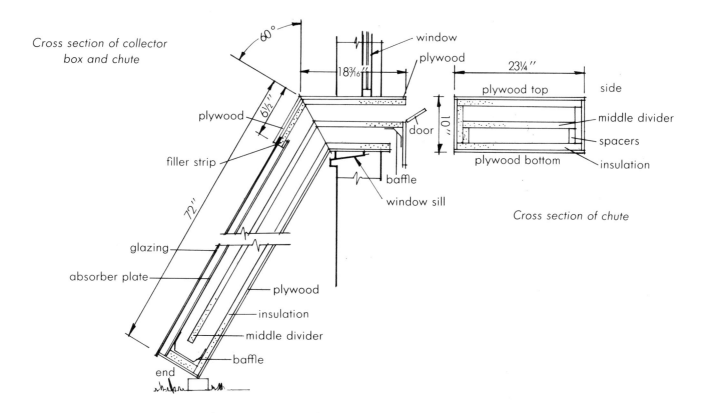

Cross section of collector box and chute

60°

window
plywood
18³⁄₁₆″
6½″
plywood
filler strip
door
10″
23¼″
plywood top — side
middle divider
spacers
plywood bottom — insulation

Cross section of chute

72″

glazing
absorber plate
plywood
insulation
middle divider
baffle
end

window sill
baffle

## Materials:

| Amount | Size | Item |
|---|---|---|
| 1 | ⅜″ x 4′ x 8′ | CDX exterior plywood |
| 2 | 1″ x 4′ x 8′ | Thermax (insulation) |
| 1 | 1″ x 10″ x 6′ | #2 pine |
| 1 | 1″ x 10″ x 12′ | #2 pine |
| 1 | 1″ x 2″ x 2′ | #2 pine (or scrap lumber) |
| 1 tube | | Silicone caulking |
| 1 can | | Derusto flat black spray paint |
| 1 roll | | Aluminum foil duct tape |
| 1 | 10″ x 39½″ | Aluminum flashing |
| 1 | 19½″ x 65″ | Corrugated aluminum roofing |
| 1 | | Form-fit neoprene gasket for aluminum roofing |
| 1 | 23¼″ x 67½″ | Kalwall Sunlite Premium II .040 |
| 1 tube | | DAP Foamboard and Panel Adhesive |
| 2 sets | 1″ | Utility hinges |
| 1 | 2′ x 6′ | Polyethylene plastic |
| 1 lb. | 1″ | Drywall screws |
| 1 lb. | 2″ | Drywall screws |
| 16 | 1″ | Flathead wood screws |
| 35 | | Neoprene washers |
| 35 | ¾″ | Aluminum or stainless steel screws |
| 1 | | Hook and latch |
| 2 | 6″ | Mending plates |
| | 3′ | Weatherstripping |
| 1 batt | | Fiberglass insulation |

## Tools:

Power drill with ⅛″ and ³⁄₁₆″ bits
Circular saw
#8 Screwmate
Phillips head screwdriver
Slotted head screwdriver
Caulking gun
Metal straightedge
Carpenter's square
Tape measure
2 C-clamps
Try square
Utility knife
Staple gun and staples
Tin snips

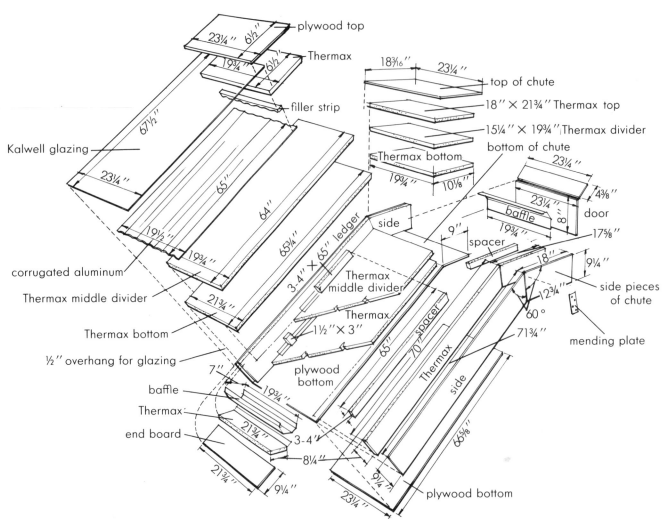

## Advantages:

1. Cost is minimal if left-over materials are used.
2. Collector can be removed in summer.
3. No house alterations are necessary.
4. Significant increase in heat-absorbing area of house.
5. Portable; if you rent, can take it with you when you move.
6. Will still work even if installation is a little east or west of true south.
7. The simplest and most economical retrofit for many building situations, especially when it isn't vented through a masonry wall.
8. When properly designed and built, will deliver heat as efficiently as most active air systems.
9. Because collector is isolated from heated space, does not become a source of heat loss at night.
10. Possibility of adding heat storage unit.
11. Ideal retrofit because easy to add on.
12. No dampers or moving parts (i.e., fans, pumps, controls, etc.) needed; stagnant cold night air prevents reverse air flow.
13. Some of collector costs may be deductible from state and federal income tax.

## Disadvantages:

1. If glass is used, it may break should anything fall on it.
2. Air seal between house and window may mean some loss of collector-heated air.
3. Cold air infiltration can be major problem if joints and wall and window openings are not tightly sealed.
4. Appearance.
5. Performance is limited because only daytime heating is possible, and only limited storage option.
6. Collector isn't much good in poorly insulated house. It's cheaper to save energy than to produce it, even with collectors.
7. Window and collector of equal size receive same amount of daily solar radiation; if you cover the window with night-time insulation, it may be as efficient as adding collector.

**Tips:** Before beginning construction, determine the optimum angle for your collector. This angle is related to your geographic location and your intended seasonal use of the system. Most people install the collector for heat gain in the winter. Since the winter sun is so much lower in the sky, the collector has to be sharply tilted and accurately sited for maximum efficiency.

To determine the correct collector angle, add 10 to 15 degrees to your local latitude. For example, Miami is on a latitude of 26 degrees. Adding 10 degrees to this means that the collector should be at a 36 degree tilt. Lexington, Kentucky, is 38 degrees, plus 10 degrees, or a collector tilt of 48 degrees. Portland, Maine, is 43 degrees, plus 10 degrees, or a collector tilt of 53 degrees. These figures don't have to be exact, but should be close.

The collector in these instructions is built for a 60 degree tilt. For the angled cuts in the following directions, substitute the collector angle appropriate for your location.

This angle positions your collector perpendicular to the winter sun to maximize winter heat gain. If necessary, however, collectors can be tilted 20 to 30 degrees off the optimum angle and still intercept 90 percent of the daily solar radiation.

Choose a window for the collector that has good southern exposure, preferably one that directly faces south. However, collectors oriented up to 30 degrees east or west of south will receive 90 percent of the possible solar radiation.

Examine your house and yard carefully to be sure the collector can be mounted at the proper angle with an unobstructed southern exposure. Insure that the collector won't be shaded by evergreens, chimneys, other buildings, or jutting portions of the house, such as an ell or garage. Deciduous trees are usually no problem since they shed their foliage in winter.

## How to build:

*The overall dimensions of the unit are 9⅝″ x 23¼″ x 6′ for the collector box which is attached to another 10″ x 23¼″ x 18³⁄₁₆″ box which is the chute. The chute connects the collector with a house room through a partially opened house window.*

*Dimensions for the following collector are given for a double-hung window with a distance between the window jambs of 27¼″; this measurement was decreased to 23½″ because of the aluminum combination storm window frame, and again to 23¼″ to allow an ⅛″ tolerance on either side of the collector.*

*You will have to adjust the measurements given here to suit your window. The collector can easily be made narrower or wider; above all, when installed, it should fit tightly inside your south-facing opening.*

*The length of the collector (which is 6′ in these instructions) can be decreased or increased. However, don't build the collector so long that it has to rest on the ground. Dampness will eventually rot the wood.*

*Ideally, the collector should rest on bricks, concrete blocks, or a wooden support; in cold climates, it should be raised sufficiently so that snow build-up is no problem.*

*Most collectors are 4′ to 8′ in length.*

## A. The Three-sided Collector Box

**1.** From the 1″ x 10″ x 12′ board, cut the end piece of the collector to 21¾″.

**2.** Cut the two sides of the collector to the dimensions shown.

**3.** From the 4′ x 8′ sheet of ⅜″ CDX plywood, cut a piece for the collector bottom to the dimensions shown. The angle of the beveled edge should duplicate that of the side pieces. If you are using a circular saw, set the base plate to 30 degrees.

**4.** The box can now be assembled. Clamp a scrap piece of lumber to the edge of the work surface to give you something to push against. Rest the end piece on edge against, but perpendicular to, the stop. At right angles, position one of the sides. Align with try or rafter square. Drill four equidistant screw holes through the side into the end with a #8 Screwmate. Before screwing together, run a bead of carpenter's wood glue along surfaces that will join. Spread bead with a scrap of wood so that glue is evenly applied.

Again align end and side pieces so they are square, and screw together with 2″ drywall screws.

Flip over so that side now rests along stop. Position the second side, being sure that the side cuts both angle in the same direction. Drill holes, glue, and screw together, frequently checking that both corners remain square.

**5.** Turn frame over and position plywood bottom. Its beveled edge should match the angle of the sides. Predrill holes ⅜″ in from edge of plywood. You may wish to drill holes at the four corners of the plywood and partially set screws to keep the side pieces from moving.

Then finish predrilling holes. Holes should be at 6" intervals.

Remove plywood. Run a bead of carpenter's wood glue around edge of plywood, then spread to a width of ¾". Apply glue to edge of three-sided frame. Set plywood in place and screw together with 1" drywall screws.

**6.** Lay box on plywood bottom and caulk all seams with silicone rubber caulking.

## B. Thermax Insulation

**7.** From the 4' x 8' sheet of Thermax, cut two side pieces to 8¼" x 70" with one end cut at a 60 degree angle to match the wooden side pieces; one bottom piece to 21¾" x 65¾"; and one end piece to 8¼" x 21¾". Cut with knife, utility knife, or linoleum cutter, and straightedge.

The bottom piece of Thermax will need a beveled edge to correspond with the angle of the sides. Mark and remove a 30 degree triangular scrap along one of the 21¾" edges.

**8.** Slide bottom into box so it rests against the end and sides. Slide end, then side insulation, into place. Carefully tape all joints with aluminum foil duct tape.

**9.** There will be a middle divider placed 4" from the end and parallel to, but 3" above, the bottom insulation of the box. From the second sheet of Thermax, cut divider to 19¾" x 64" and bevel one edge of the shorter dimension.

**10.** From the scraps of the first sheet of Thermax, cut supports to 1½" x 3" to hold the divider in place. The supports should be spaced every 12". Use DAP Foamboard and Panel Adhesive to hold them upright against the Thermax sides. Rest divider on top. Tape all seams with aluminum foil duct tape.

## C. Chute

**11.** From the scrap 1" x 10" pine, cut two pieces to the dimensions shown. The smaller of the two dimensions (12¾") is crucial. The difference, after subtracting 3" from the distance, should be at least equal to the distance from the inner lip of your window sill to the outermost projection of your house window—be it the window frame or aluminum storm window frame. In houses with large sills, it may be necessary to increase this length so that the collector will reach into the room sufficiently. If length adjustments are needed, be sure to retain the same angled cut.

**12.** For top and bottom, cut two pieces from the remaining plywood. Cut the top to 18³⁄₁₆" x 23¼", with a 60 degree bevel along one edge of the longer dimension; cut the bottom to 9" x 23¼", with a 60 degree bevel along one edge of the longer dimension. Set top piece of plywood aside until Thermax has been added to chute.

**13.** Position the 1 x 10s so that they are on edge, with the longer length resting on the work surface. Place the plywood bottom piece so that the bevel of the plywood aligns with the angle of the sides. Be sure the edges are flush. With a #8 Screwmate, predrill holes ⅜" in from the edges of the plywood at 6" intervals. Remove plywood, apply glue to all surfaces; replace plywood, and screw together with 1" drywall screws. Before screwing in all screws, check that adjoining surfaces are square.

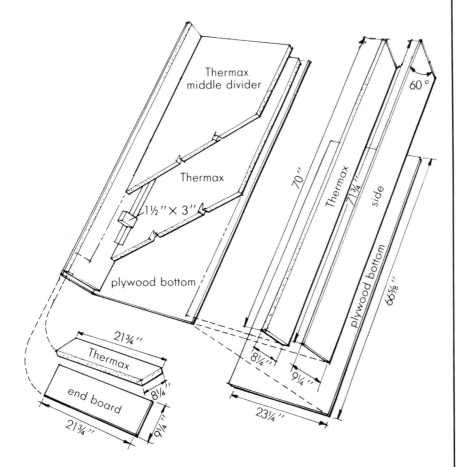

**14.** From the second sheet of Thermax, cut the following pieces: one top 18" x 21¾" with one end of the longer dimensions beveled at a 60 degree angle; two sides to 8¼" x 17⅝" and angled; one bottom to 10⅛" x 19¾" with one beveled longer edge; and one divider cut to 15¼" x 19¾" with one beveled longer edge.

Turn the chute over. Caulk joints with silicone. Position side pieces of Thermax in place so that they are flush against the 1 x 10 sides. Add bottom insulation. Tape the joints, being sure that the beveled edges are aligned.

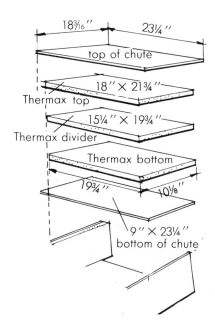

**15.** Add 1½" x 3" spacer blocks, two per side. Glue to side insulation with DAP Foamboard and Panel Adhesive. The middle divider, which will be added later, will rest on these spacers.

**16.** Set top piece of Thermax (18" x 21¾") on top of side insulation, being sure the beveled edge aligns with the angle of the chute.

Add top plywood piece, again with its beveled edge matching that of the sides. Predrill, glue, and screw plywood top into the 1 x 10 sides. Tape joints between top and side insulation.

**17.** Cut a piece of plywood to 8" x 23¼". The top edge of the plywood will be flush with the top of the middle divider and will extend below the chute. Be sure sides are flush with 1 x 10 sides. Predrill two screw holes per side, glue and screw together.

## D. Door (optional)

**18.** Cut a second piece of plywood to 4⅜" x 23¼". Hinge this to the first piece with a pair of 1" utility hinges.

**19.** The door will be tighter if it closes against weatherstripping. Staple felt weatherstripping around the door opening.

**20.** Mount a hook and eye. Center the eye in the end grain of the plywood door, with the hook screwed into the plywood top.

## E. Baffles

**21.** Two baffles will be needed to facilitate air flow. From the aluminum flashing, cut a strip to 6¼" x 19¾". Make two bends along the long edge, one bend 1" from the edge; the other 2" from the edge. Do the same to the other side so that after the four bends, the aluminum makes a semi-circle.

**22.** With the chute resting on its top, slip in the aluminum baffle to insure it fits. Remove and replace when the finished unit has been installed in the window.

**23.** A baffle also is needed for the collector. Cut a second piece of flashing to 10" x 19¾". Along the longer dimension and 4½" from the edge, bend the aluminum towards the center. Make a second set of bends 1" from each edge. The aluminum will form a semi-circle. Insert in the bottom of the collector and secure in place with silicone caulking. The baffle will ease the movement of air from bottom to top air channel.

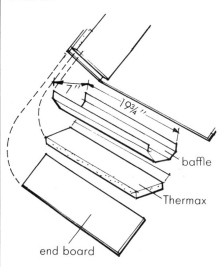

## F. Absorber Plate

**24.** Use tin snips or a circular saw with a metal cutting blade to cut the sheet of corrugated aluminum roofing to 19½" x 65". When cutting lengthwise, score the sheet with a utility knife and bend along scored line. Be sure lengthwise cuts are symmetrical by trimming both sides so that the edges will rest evenly on ledger strips.

**25.** From the Thermax, cut 3" to 4" x 65" ledger strips; these will support the absorber plate.

Ideally the peaks of the corrugated roofing should be 1" below the edge of the collector box. If your lengthwise cuts along the absorber were through the peaks, you may want to use 4" ledgers to raise the absorber plate to within 1" of the edge of the collector box. Conversely, use 3" ledgers if your cuts were along the valleys.

Glue strips to Thermax sides with DAP Foamboard and Panel Adhesive.

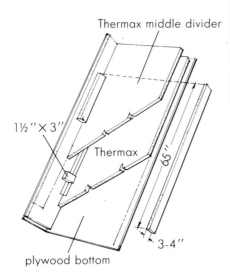

Thermax middle divider

1½" X 3"

Thermax

65"

3-4"

plywood bottom

**26.** Lift absorber plate into place to check the fit. The absorber will rest against the bottom insulation and on the ledger strips with ⅛" tolerance on both sides. Remove, and in a well-ventilated place, spray paint both sides of absorber with Derusto flat black paint. Let dry 24 hours. Thurmalox paint, a selective surface paint, can be used instead. It has higher solar absorbtance/lower solar emittance percentages than Derusto, but is more expensive. Install absorber plate in collector.

**27.** Before completing assembly, collector should be baked in the sun. This is an important step because the paint when heated may leave a film on the glazing which will reduce light transmittance.

Put the collector in the direct sun for a few days. Cover it with polyethylene, stapled to the collector. The excessive heat will drive out any moisture and residue paint vapors in the collector. Then proceed with assembly.

## G. Assembly

**28.** Remove polyethylene.

Measure the overall width of your box. If it is even slightly larger than 23¼" at the top (open end), it will be difficult to attach the chute. To hold the box to its proper width, use a pipe clamp or a stick cut to approximately 26" in length. Into the stick, drive two 8d nails, 23¼" apart. Press the sides of the box together until you can slip the jig over. Double check the collector width. You may have to adjust the jig.

**29.** To attach chute to collector box, apply glue to adjoining edges. Have a helper align and hold chute in place against collector.

Clean off excess glue with damp rag. Then apply silicone caulking to the two outside joints. Predrill and screw mending plate to collector and chute so that it is centered over the joint. Screw mending plate to opposite side with 1" wood screws.

**30.** With chute now in place, tape joints between bottom and side pieces of Thermax in chute. Add Thermax middle divider (see Step 14), and tape along edges in chute and between divider of collector and chute.

**31.** Set form fit neoprene gasket on top of the corrugated aluminum absorber plate and cut to fit if necessary; it should rest snugly in the peaks and valleys of the corrugations to prevent air leaks. Remove.

**32.** Cut a piece of Thermax to 6½" x 19¾" with a 60 degree bevel along one of the 19¾" lengths.

On your work surface, lay the Thermax on its 6½" width. Lengthwise along the square edge, align the neoprene gasket with flat side of end seal down and glue it to the Thermax. Also run a bead of sili-

cone caulking along the top edge of the absorber plate.

Turn Thermax over and set in place so that closure strip meets caulking on absorber plate, Thermax should butt against side insulation of collector box and top insulation of chute. The top of the Thermax should be flush with the top edge of collector box.

## H. Glazing

**33.** If you bought a 2' x 6' sheet of plastic glazing, cut it to 23¼" x 67½" with ordinary kitchen shears.

Lift glazing onto collector box. Align side edges. Leave a ½" lip at the bottom edge so run-off water doesn't sit on wood. (The glazing will not reach the full length of the collector box; its top edge should rest on the 6½" wide Thermax strip installed in previous Step.) Predrill ³⁄₁₆" holes through the glazing only, every 6" and ⅜" in from the edge. Then predrill into the wood with an ⅛" bit. You may want to set screws loosely at each corner to keep glazing flat.

**34.** Remove glazing, run a bead of silicone caulking along the edge of the 1 x 10s and Thermax piece installed in Step 32 where it will meet the glazing. Use plenty of caulking. Then replace glazing and screw to 1 x 10s with ¾" screws and neoprene washers.

**35.** Cut a piece of plywood 6½" x 23¼" with a 60 degree bevel. This will fit on top of the 1 x 10 side pieces and overlap the upper lip of the glazing by 1½". The bevel should match that of the chute.

**36.** Predrill plywood edges to be screwed into 1 x 10s. Turn plywood over. Apply glue to both edges and DAP Panel and Foamboard Adhesive to center of plywood piece. Also apply adhesive to Thermax piece just installed.

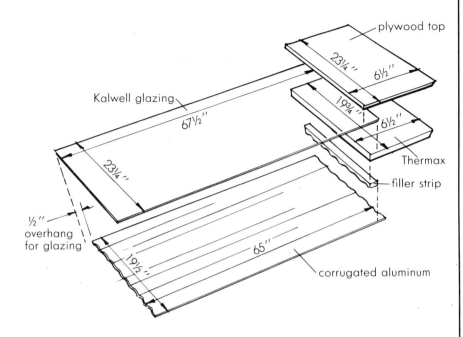

plywood top

23¼ "

6½ "

Kalwell glazing

67½ "

19¾ "

6½ "

23¼ "

Thermax

filler strip

½ " overhang for glazing

19½ "

65 "

corrugated aluminum

**37.** Apply glue to 1 x 10s. Turn plywood over and screw into place.

Press Thermax to plywood by reaching through door of chute. If you can't reach it, make a "T" of scrap lumber which you can use to push gently against the insulation.

**38.** Apply bead of silicone caulking to joint between glazing and plywood. Caulk also where the top pieces of plywood meet.

Turn the collector over and caulk the joint between the bottom pieces of collector and chute.

Go over collector carefully with caulking compound. Smear it over all countersunk screw holes, all exterior seams, and along all exposed end grain.

**39.** Paint all wood flat black with the exception of the door and inside lip. These you can paint any color to match your room. Let paint dry 24 hours.

## I. Installation

**40.** Before installing collector, assemble necessary ground support. Concrete blocks are ideal.

**41.** Open the house window. Lay fiberglass insulation on sill. Lift chute through the window. Set collector box on support to hold it at the proper angle.

If you have aluminum combination storms, staple weatherstripping to top of collector where it will meet the storm.

You may wish to staple a third storm of plastic on the outside of the house around the window and window collector to insure that the snow doesn't blow in through the cracks.

From the inside, apply adhesive-backed foam, or felt weatherstripping to collector where it will meet house window. Then stuff fiberglass around both sides of the collector

between sides of box and window jambs. You may even want to stuff some insulation between the aluminum storm and the house window.

Because both the storm and house windows must remain open to accept the collector, it is vitally important that all spaces around the collector be well weatherized (see Wind Plug, p. 86).

**42.** Insert baffle (made in Step 22) into chute and secure if necessary with beads of silicone caulking along the edges.

### Other design possibilities

**Glazing.** Fiber-reinforced plastics are translucent, lightweight, easy to handle, shatterproof and can be cut with shears; but be sure you choose a brand which has been tested for use with solar collectors. Some plastics become brittle with age, or yellow, which reduces light transmission.

Glass is the best glazing material if there's no danger of breakage. Single-strength glass is too fragile; double-strength is preferable. If your window opening is large enough, patio replacement doors, which are double glazed, are ideal.

Used storm window sashes in good condition can be used for the glazing. They are attractive and will greatly reduce the expense.

These collectors generally need only one layer of glazing. In very cold climates, a second layer may be justified with a ¾" to 1" dead air space between. Solar films such as Teflon are particularly suitable for the inner layer. They have high light transmittance and excellent weatherability.

Cut the film to the size of the collector plus 2" per side. Fold over film along edges. Staple to collector, and reinforce with duct tape.

**Box.** The collector box must be weathertight and durable enough to withstand outdoor conditions. It can be built of wood, exterior plywood or sheet metal.

**Absorber.** Instead of the aluminum absorber plate, five to six layers of slit-and-expanded metal lath (used for plaster work) wired together, can be used behind the glazing. The mesh is fastened diagonally the length of the flow channel. Air filters through the mesh, is heated by the sun, and rises.

An alternate design includes cutting strips of the metal mesh and installing them at regular intervals diagonally across the flow channel.

In place of mesh, wire screening or slit-and-expanded aluminum (used for grease filters) can be used. Excessively dense meshes, however, will impede the flow of air. Also before purchasing, be sure the metal can be painted.

Using meshes allows dust to collect on the glazing which can severely reduce light transmission. If meshes are used, attach glazing to the collector box so that it can be easily removed for cleaning. With a solid absorber plate (similar to that used in these directions), the interior of the glazing is protected from collecting dust, but heat transfer is not as good as with the meshes.

Another variation allows air to circulate around both sides of the absorber. With this design, heat transfer is good, especially if corrugated metal roofing is used; the glazing, however, will get dirty.

Avoid using an absorber plate of plywood that has been painted black. Plywood swells at high temperatures. It also absorbs and releases heat more slowly than the aluminum.

**Insulation.** One-inch Thermax or Celotex is recommended; it can be reduced to ¾". This type of insulation is a rigid, foil-faced isocyanurate foam which can withstand collector temperatures. (Stagnant air in the collector may reach 300 degrees F.) Do not use polystyrene.

The depth of the collector will have to be adjusted for collectors longer or shorter than 6' because the depth of the air channels should be 1/20 of the collector length. For a 5' collector, the depth of each channel should be 3"; for an 8' collector, it is 4.8".

If the house window opening is too small and the window sill too close to the ground to permit a collector of any appreciable size, install the collector on a second-floor window.

Remember that if the collector is vented into the room with the furnace thermostat, the furnace will start up less frequently, causing the rest of the house to be colder.

It expands and melts at about 180 degrees F.

**Size.** Collectors are usually built to the size of the window opening, but it is possible to construct them wider. However, undersized vents (i.e., vents smaller than the width of the collector and the depth of the flow channel) are the usual cause of poorly functioning collectors. In collectors wider than the vent, warmed air gets caught and stagnates at either side of the opening. This stagnation can be alleviated somewhat by adding baffles to direct the air flow. Increasing the depth of the collector beyond that of the vent allows convection currents to develop within the channels; this too reduces the collector's performance.

**Seasonal Flap.** For collectors that can't or won't be removed for summer, add a hinged flap on the top side of the chute. In summer, close the interior door and open the seasonal flap to keep the solar heated air outdoors.

**Wind Plug.** Wind can easily enter the house between the collector and the window frame. In addition to the insulation and weatherstripping, you may wish to design a panel to fit around the collector. Use 1" lumber or plywood. Weatherstrip and secure with wood screws to interior window trim.

**Fans.** It is possible to install a fan, although it won't add appreciably to the efficiency of the collector. The fan can be pre-set so that when the interior temperature of the collector reaches 120 degrees F., the fan is automatically switched on, and at 80 degrees F. is automatically switched off.

**Chute-less Collectors.** Collectors can be built without the chute. These are easier to construct, and the flow is better because air doesn't have to change direction. However, more window space is sacrificed. (Remember, windows are also solar collectors.)

**Large Window Collectors.** Window collectors can be constructed to connect two or more windows. In such cases, you may want to add baffles to the chute in both channels to guide the flow of air. Otherwise air will stagnate between the windows.

**Wall-mounted Window Collectors.** Wall-mounted collectors are a variation of window collectors and TAPs (see p. 88). They should be used only where there is a drop below the space to be heated, so that the collector will be low enough in the wall to effectively heat the whole room.

These are especially well-adapted to second-story windows where the support system necessary to achieve the appropriate angle may be cumbersome.

The collector is constructed as described earlier except that it is mounted directly against the south-facing wall with brackets. To facilitate air flow, curved baffles should be added wherever there is a 90 degree turn, or the collector can be angled.

The collector may become a more integral part of the wall by using the exterior house sheathing as the back. In this case, the house siding (aluminum, wood shingles, etc.) is removed to the width of the collector and 2 x 2s or 2 x 4s added to the sheathing. The collector is then nailed to these.

It is simpler but less efficient to add the rigid insulation directly to the exterior wall. To create an effective seal, the side pieces of the collector will need to be scribed to fit over the siding, and the joints well caulked to create a tight seal.

Collectors may be vented through windows; they can be vented through an exterior wall. Design the collector so that it can be vented between the wall studs. (See TAP for instructions on cutting through exterior walls, pp. 92-93.)

Collectors can even be vented through concrete block walls, with every other block left in place for support, and reinforcement steel added to the wall if necessary.

Such units should be vented 6" to 8" above the floor to prevent dust and lint from being drawn into the collector and clouding the glazing.

**Window Collectors with Storage.**
To window collectors, a heat storage unit, either of water containers or phase change material, can be added. With two adjustable dampers, the collector can store or deliver heat.

# Thermosyphoning Air Panel (TAP)

**Skills required:** Moderate.

**Cost:** $225.

**Amount of heat gain:** On a clear sunny day, there will be a temperature rise of 20 to 50 degrees F. between the air entering and that leaving the TAP, or an increase of 75,000 to 100,000 BTUs during the heating season for every square foot of glazing. This means a savings of approximately $25 a year.

**What it does:** The thermosyphoning air panel is a low-cost totally passive heating system permanently mounted on the exterior sheathing of an unobstructed south wall. The panel has a return-air top vent and a supply-air bottom vent. Within the panel, air moves by natural convection behind a black absorber plate which in turn is heated by sunlight passing through an exterior layer of glazing.

Air flow is controlled by the occupant who must open the top vent for winter heating; in summer, the top vent is closed and remains shut until heat is again needed.

The TAP provides solar heat only during daylight hours. At night, reverse thermosyphoning of cold air from the TAP into the house is automatically prevented by a flap which is attached to the inside of the lower vent grille.

TAPs are ideal in cold climates where daytime heating is necessary.

**How it works:** As sunlight strikes the glazing of the collector, some of the solar radiation is reflected while the greater portion is captured within the collector. The absorber plate picks up this light and converts it to thermal energy (heat) which cannot be easily transmitted back through the glazing.

The black paint, by minimizing the amount of energy that is reflected, maximizes the collector's absorbability. Temperatures on the collector surface can easily reach 120 degrees F.

As the heat builds up, it is gradually conducted through the absorber plate to the air gap behind. Here it is trapped because the reflective surface of the Thermoply prevents it from being absorbed by the house wall. Trapped, the heated air begins to rise and exit through the upper register into the room.

This creates a thermosyphoning effect within the air space behind the absorber plate. The syphon pulls cooler room air into the TAP through the bottom register. This air is in turn heated by the collector plate. It rises, and is vented through the top room register. As long as the sun shines, the process continues, but comes to a halt once the collector temperature falls below that of the adjoining room. At that point the cool air falls to the bottom of the TAP. This causes the backdraft flap to shut and keeps cool air from entering the house through the bottom vent. Without the flap cold air would exit through the lower register, drawing warmer room air after it into the TAP.

In summer, when the heat is not wanted, the convective flow can be stopped by closing the top register.

The placement of the vents ensures that the air flows over as large an area as possible to make maximum contact with all parts of the absorber plate. The corrugations in the aluminum increase the surface area to pick up light and transform it into heat; they also create turbulence in the air stream behind the absorber plate. This activity is important because it maximizes the transference of heat from the absorber plate to the passing air.

**Advantages:**

1. Simple, low-cost addition to home; takes one to two days to install.
2. Can be built from locally available materials.
3. Requires no backing of insulation because house already has this.
4. If funds are limited, you can build additional modules later.
5. Can be added to most homes with south wall exposed to the sun.
6. Little maintenance, and is easily accessible for repairs, recaulking, and repainting.
7. Operates even under hazy conditions when radiation is more diffused.
8. Blends well with pre-existing structures.
9. Fits where you might not want windows because of lack of privacy.
10. May qualify for federal and state energy tax credits.
11. Gains from snow-reflected solar energy; reflects away summer sun.
12. No ducting necessary if it is adjacent to area to be heated.
13. Is at its best when sun is low in the sky, and this is when weather is usually the coldest.

**Disadvantages:**

1. Trees that shade collector in winter will have to be trimmed or cut down.
2. Do-it-yourself units may not be as efficient as commercial collectors.
3. Damper will have to be carefully watched because it controls the air movement from collector to house.

**Materials:**

| Amount | Size | Item |
|---|---|---|
| 2 | 2″ x 6″ x 10′ | Fir or spruce |
| 1 | 2″ x 4″ x 8′ | Fir or spruce |
| 2 | 1″ x 3″ x 10′ | Fir or spruce |
| 2 | 1″ x 2″ x 10′ | Fir or spruce |
| 1 | 34″ x 76″ | Sliding glass door replacement unit |
| 1 | 4′ x 8′ | Thermoply |
| 1 | 3′ x 7′ | Corrugated aluminum |
| 2 | 8″ x 14″ | Vent boots |
| 1 | 8½″ x 14″ | Closable register cover |
| 1 | 8½″ x 14″ | Register cover |
| 1 | 5″ x 4′ | Aluminum drip edge |
| 1 | 8″ x 4′ | Aluminum flashing |
| 3 tubes | | Silicone caulking |
| 2 tubes | | Silicone latex caulking |
| 6 | 3″ x 3″ | Metal angle brackets |
| 2 | 1″ x 3″ x 8′ | Furring strips |
| 1 | 14′ | Felt weatherstripping |
| 2 | | Form-fit neoprene gaskets for aluminum |
| 2 | ¼″ x ⅝″ x 2″ | 80-90 Shore A Durometer neoprene setting blocks |
| 20 | ½″ x ⅛″ x 3″ | 30-40 Shore A Durometer neoprene spacers |
| 1 lb. | 1″ | Aluminum roofing nails |
| 36 | 3″ x #10 | Flat head wood screws |
| 1 lb. | 8d | Galvanized nails |
| 1 lb. | 6d | Galvanized nails |
| 24 | 1½″ x #8 | Brass or stainless steel wood screws |
| 6 | ⅜″ x 4″ | Lag bolts |
| 2 qts. | | White shellac sealer |
| 2 spray cans | | High-temperature flat black paint |
| 3 | ½″ x ½″ | Pieces of screening |
| 1 | ⅓ yard | Rip-stop nylon |
| 1 | 3″ x 3′ | Rip-stop nylon tape |
| | | Resorcinol glue |

**Tools:**

| | |
|---|---|
| Handsaw | Utility knife |
| Circular saw | Flat bar |
| Jigsaw or keyhole saw | Chalkline |
| Electric drill with ¼″ and ⁵⁄₁₆″ bits | Tape measure |
| Countersink bit | Caulking gun |
| Wood and metal cutting blades for circular saw | Straightedge |
| | Plumb bob |
| Try square | Ratchet and socket set |
| Combination square | 2 C-clamps |
| Rafter square | Safety glasses |
| Hammer | Paint brush |
| Level | Paint thinner |
| Tin snips | Stepladder |
| Screwdriver | |

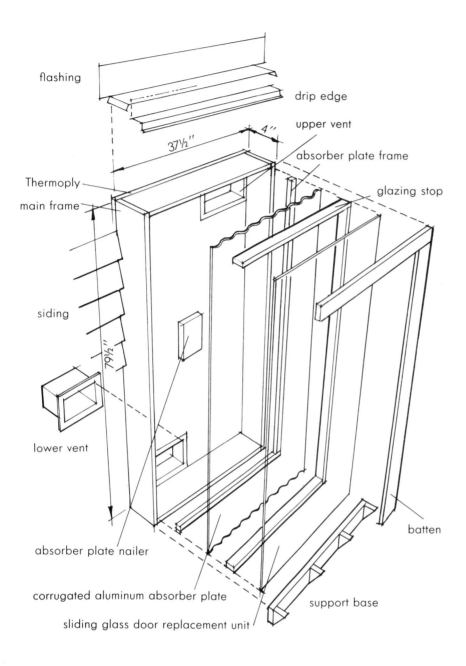

flashing

drip edge

upper vent

37½"

4"

absorber plate frame

Thermoply

glazing stop

main frame

79½"

siding

lower vent

batten

absorber plate nailer

corrugated aluminum absorber plate

support base

sliding glass door replacement unit

**Tips:** Before installing a TAP, be sure your house is already well insulated, fitted with storm windows, caulked, and weatherstripped. It is foolish to spend money to build heating devices that can't be used efficiently. The payback period is much faster on money spent to weatherize a house—a payback usually of less than a year—than for the addition of solar devices.

TAPs are primarily for houses of wood frame construction, although they can be installed on brick walls if masonry anchors are used and a plywood back is added to the frame.

The directions given here for cutting the vent openings are based on studs spaced 16″ on center. If your stud cavities are smaller, you may have to cut a stud. If so, frame in the vent opening with 2 x 4s, top

and bottom, and secure them to the nearest studs.

TAPs should not be constructed on walls containing flammable insulation; the collector will raise the adjoining house wall to higher-than-normal temperatures. This could create a fire hazard.

Construct the TAP on a flat wall that is no more than 15 degrees east or west of south. Because the panel should receive 6 to 8 hours of direct sun a day, check for objects that might shade the collector, such as nearby buildings or a wing of the house, evergreens, chimneys, doors, and windows. Never block existing windows; with movable nighttime insulation, they are more effective collectors of solar energy than TAPs.

Since the TAP can heat only the space directly behind it and only during the day, it should be installed on an outside wall of a room with frequent daytime use in the winter, such as a kitchen, den, or living room. Avoid bedrooms, storage areas, closets, and guest rooms. If this is unavoidable, heat from the TAP can be ducted. However, the shorter the ductwork the better, because the thermosyphoning action of the panel is weak and may not be able to overcome the flow resistance of long runs of piping.

If necessary, you can direct heated air a greater distance by mounting a small fan in the upper outlet with a thermostatic control. The fan also increases flexibility in locating the panel, but will add an ongoing expense.

The directions that follow make use of sliding glass door replacement panels for the glazing. Because they are a manufactured item, they are low in cost (approximately $60 a panel). In addition, they are better adapted than plastics to the daily temperatures of the TAP, which can vary by 100 degrees F. Under such conditions, glass expands and contracts 1/10″;

the plastics can vary by as much as ½″, which makes it more difficult to retain an airtight seal.

The sliding glass units are available in sizes of 34″ x 76″ and 34″ x 96″. To determine which size you should buy, measure from floor to ceiling on the interior house wall where you intend to vent the TAP. For rooms of less than 9' in height, use the 34″ x 76″ size.

On the interior wall, consider the location of the top and bottom vents (at diagonally opposite ends of the panel). Their placement should avoid obstructions such as cabinets, electrical outlets and wiring, appliances, furniture, plumbing, heating ducts, and radiators. Avoid locations near wood stoves or furnace hot air registers which may interfere with the proper operation of the TAP vents.

Examine your exterior wall as well. Use an existing window sill as a reference point. From inside, measure from the sill to the floor, and from the sill to the ceiling. Open the window and mark the height of the sill on the house exterior. Working from outside, measure from this point to transfer the floor and ceiling heights to the outside of the house. Relocate the panel if it will interfere with chimneys, outdoor spigots, utility meters, dryer vents, drains, outdoor wiring, oil tank filler pipes, or anything else that will make it difficult to cut through the house siding.

If possible, group TAPs in modules of two, three, or four units mounted either in horizontal or upright position.

TAPs require minimal maintenance. Periodically and especially before every heating season, the glazing should be washed. During the winter, snow may have to be cleared if it has drifted against the panel, but leave any snow accumulation on the ground in front of the unit. Light will be reflected off the snow to the absorber plate.

# How to build:

*A 37½″ x 83″ TAP will need a cutout in the siding of the south wall of 37¾″ x 83½″. This assumes that a sliding glass door replacement panel of ⅝″ x 34″ x 76″ will be used. If the 34″ x 96″ panel is used, measurements will have to be adjusted accordingly.*

*Lumber is given in nominal sizes; actual sizes are smaller. Whenever the sizes differ, the actual sizes are given in parentheses after the nominal dimensions.*

# A. The Main Frame and Absorber Plate Frame

1. Attach the edge guide to the circular saw, and cut the two 2″ x 6″ x 10′ boards (1½″ x 5½″ x 10′ actual) lengthwise into two pieces. One piece will be 4″ wide; the other 1⅜″ wide; ⅛″ will be lost in the saw kerf. Cut the 4″ wide strips into two lengths of 79½″ and two of 34½″.

Cut a length of 34½″ from each of the 1⅜″ strips. Save the remaining two lengths to be cut to length when the absorber plate frame is assembled.

2. Glue and nail with five 8d galvanized nails the 1½″ x 1⅜″ x 34½″ pieces flush with the bottom of the face of the 1½″ x 4″ x 34½″ pieces to form a ledge. The ledges will hold the top and bottom of the absorber plate frame. The cut surfaces of the 1⅜″ strips should face the center of the frame; the cut surfaces of the 4″ pieces should face the wall of the house.

3. Clamp a stop to your work surface against which you can push. Place one of the pieces which you have just nailed together, ledger strip down, on your work surface with one end resting against the stop. Position one of the 1½″ x 4″ x 79½″ pieces perpendicular to this so that the boards form a corner.

Drill and countersink three holes through the long piece into the end of the 34½″ piece. The holes should be equally spaced. Glue the corner, check for square, then screw together with three 3″ x #10 wood screws.

Repeat this procedure for the remaining three corners. Be sure the top and bottom ledgers face the center of the frame.

When the frame is assembled, measure the length of the diagonals at opposite corners. When they are equal, nail two temporary cross braces to stabilize the frame during mounting.

**4.** Measure the length between the top and bottom absorber-plate frame members. Cut the 1½″ x 1⅜″ x 85½″ pieces to these lengths (approximately 73¾″). The pieces should fit snugly. Glue and nail with the fresh-cut edge toward the center. They should butt against the top and bottom ledger strips, and be flush with the edge of the 79½″ framing member. Nail with seven 8d galvanized nails. Do not let the corners loosen when nailing.

## B. The Support Base

**5.** Square one end of the 2″ x 4″ x 8′ (1½″ x 3½″ x 8′). Cut off a piece 37½″ long. From the remaining piece of the 2″ x 4″ x 8′, cut four triangles with perpendicular sides of 3½″ x 2½″.

Evenly space the four triangles on the 3½″ face. Mark their locations. Turn the support base over. Mark the same locations for the triangular pieces. Drill two countersunk holes for each triangle from the rear and part way into each triangle. Glue and screw together using eight 3″ x #10 wood screws.

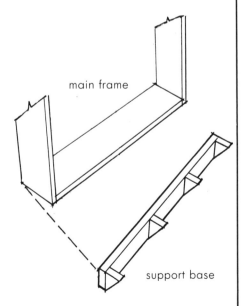

main frame

support base

## C. Wood Sealer

**6.** Apply two coats of white shellac sealer to all wood pieces.

## D. Insulation

**7.** Cut the Thermoply to 37½″ x 79½″. Measure the diagonals to be sure the sheet is square.

## E. The Absorber Plate

**8.** With the metal cutting blade, cut the aluminum absorber plate to 34″ x 75½″. Be sure the lengthwise cuts are symmetrical so that each side will have a flat edge to rest on the absorber plate frame.

Clean any grease or factory oils from the corrugated aluminum plate with cleanser (Spic and Span), if the plate has not been pre-painted. If these oils are left, the paint won't bond well. Rinse and wash with one cup of vinegar to one gallon of water. Rinse in lots of water to remove the etching solution, and let dry.

Spray both sides with two coats of high-temperature flat black paint, and let dry for two days before installing in panel. If a selective surface is desired, paint the outside surface with Dampney Thurmalox flat black paint and the inside with Rustoleum matte black.

## F. Vent Openings

**9.** Locate the vent openings on the inside of the house. To establish the location of the lower vent, cut a fist-sized hole with a utility knife about 6″ above the floor. This should place the hole above the baseboard and bottom plate of the wall. *Because there may be wiring behind the wall, throw the circuit breaker or remove the fuse to turn off power to the area where you will be working.* The hole should be at approxi-

mately the center of the 8″ x 14″ opening for the vent. Remove any insulation. Feel inside the stud cavity for electrical wires, pipes, ducts or other obstructions. Any wiring running through this area will have to be rerouted above the collector area.

Locate the studs at either side of the hole. You may be able to find them by looking for a vertical line of nails in the interior wall finish. Otherwise estimate their location by feeling through the hole which you have just cut.

One side of the vent hole should be flush with an adjacent stud so that you can later nail the metal boot of the vent to it.

To cut the vent opening, draw a line parallel with but 1″ above the baseboard. Using the square, lay out a 8″ x 14″ rectangle. The 14″ side should fall between adjacent studs. With the utility knife and square, jigsaw, or keyhole saw, cut the 8″ x 14″ hole through the interior wall finish.

**10.** To locate the upper vent opening, measure 55½″ above the top outside edge of the lower vent. Then, using the level, draw a horizontal line 30½″ long. Draw a parallel line 8″ above the first and 14″ long.

Make a hole in the interior wall finish approximately in the center of the rectangle that you have just drawn. Check for wires, pipes, ducts, etc. Mark the location of the studs. Cut out vent opening so that one side of the opening will be flush with an adjacent stud.

## G. The Outside Wall

**11.** At the lower outer corner of the bottom vent and at the upper outer corner of the top vent, drill holes through the siding and sheathing from the inside to the outside. Use the electric drill and ¼″ bit.

Go to the outside of the house. Double check their locations. They should be separated by 71½" vertically and 30½" horizontally. If these numbers are fairly accurate, establish the exact location for the TAP.

**12.** Lay out a vertical center line on the house siding between the corner holes drilled through the vent openings. Then measure 18⅞" to either side of the center line, and draw two vertical lines.

*Marking cutout in house siding*

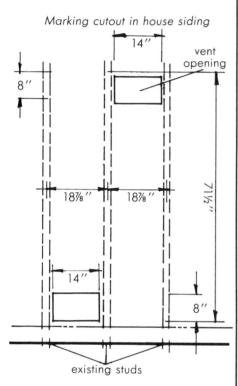

existing studs

From the lower drilled hole through the vent opening, measure down 6". Draw a horizontal line through that point which will intersect the two vertical lines. From this bottom line, measure up 83½" and draw another horizontal line using the level. This will leave a 37¾" x 83½" rectangle for the TAP. Check that it is square and plumb; the bottom line should be above the sill plate, the top should be below the ceiling. The sides will be 2⅞" from the center of the right and left wall studs.

To double check that you have the correct location of the wall studs on the exterior of the house, examine the nailing pattern on the

exterior siding. Nails should be located every 16". If you are unable to find the nails as will be the case with shingles, clapboards, board and batten siding, etc., strip off part of the siding in the center of your TAP location. Once the center stud is located, measure to either side 16", from center to center, to locate the adjacent studs.

**13.** Remove all nails in the siding where the cuts will be made, or wear goggles and use a saw blade you are willing to sacrifice to any nails.

To cut away the siding, nail two 1" x 3" x 8' furring strips ½" to either side of the lines where the cuts are to be made. The base of the circular saw will ride on one strip; the other will be used for the edge of the saw base to rest upon and for the edge guide to ride against, thus ensuring a straight cut.

Adjust the depth of the blade so that it will saw through the siding, and cut out the rectangle for the TAP.

**14.** To cut through the sheathing for the vents, outline the 8" x 14" rectangles on the exposed sheathing, working from the holes which were drilled earlier. Be sure the layout is square and plumb. Cut through the sheathing for the two 8" x 14" vent openings.

## H. Installing the Support Base

**15.** Align the assembled support base on the studs at the bottom of the TAP hole which has been cut in the siding. Level the unit, drill two holes with a ⁵⁄₁₆" bit through the support and into each stud. There will be three pairs of holes through the face of the support base and into each stud. Secure to the wall using six ⅜" x 4" lag bolts.

## I. Attaching the Thermoply

**16.** Rest Thermoply against sheathing on the support base assembly. You will need a helper to lift the TAP frame into place against the Thermoply. Be sure the frame is aligned squarely with the Thermoply.

Have a helper outline the vent openings on the Thermoply from inside the house. Remove the frame. Cut out vent openings in the Thermoply with a straightedge and utility knife.

Place the TAP frame on a flat surface with the cut side of the frame up. (Absorber plate frame will also be up.) Apply glue to TAP frame and plate frame, and in a 2⅞" border around the Thermoply. Turn Thermoply over and center it on frame. Nail with twenty aluminum roofing nails, nailing every 12" through the Thermoply into the sides of the 4" wide members of the TAP.

**17.** Caulk back edge of Thermoply and corresponding location on sheathing. Rest TAP frame again on support assembly. Press Thermoply against sheathing and caulking. Drill twelve countersunk holes through the 1½" x 1⅜" frame into the wall studs. The holes should be 12" apart. Screw the absorber plate frame to the wall with 3" x #10 wood screws.

Attach the angle brackets at the top of the TAP frame and to the house. Nail bottom of frame to wall support base. Remove cross braces. Check that the frame is square and plumb.

Run a bead of silicone caulking to further seal edge between Thermoply and TAP frame.

## J. Installing the Vents

**18.** Slide both vent boots through the TAP and wall opening until the flanges rest against the Thermoply. The boots will seal in air passing to and from the back of the absorber plate and house, thus preventing it from entering the wall cavity.

Go inside. Mark the part of the vent boots that extends beyond the inner house wall. From the outside, remove the boots, and cut where marked, using the saw with a metal cutting blade.

Reinsert vent boot from outside. Nail outside flanges through Thermoply into sheathing or abutting studs with aluminum roofing nails.

These boots can be factory-made or site-made with aluminum flashing. You may prefer to make them out of leftover Thermoply and aluminum duct tape.

Install the upper and lower vent registers on the inside wall. Place the register with the movable louvers in the upper vent opening. If necessary, use foam or felt weatherstripping to make an airtight seal between the back of the lower register and the interior wall surface.

## K. Absorber Plate Nailer

**19.** In the center of the Thermoply, glue and nail the 1½ x 3½" x 6" absorber plate nailer to the sheathing with four 8d galvanized nails.

## L. Absorber Plate

**20.** Apply silicone caulking to the groove of the form-fit neoprene gaskets and fit them over the top and bottom edges of the corrugated aluminum sheet. These closure strips will prevent air leaks.

**21.** Rest the bottom of the absorber plate on a ½" shim and center within TAP frame, leaving ¼" tolerance on each side. Then drill ¼" holes every 4" to 6" through the edge of the aluminum. Remove absorber plate and caulk perimeter of the vertical surfaces of the absorber with silicone. Reposition plate and nail to frame with aluminum nails.

Use one aluminum roofing nail to attach the sheet to the center support.

Remove the shim and with the silicone, caulk all nail holes. If necessary, touch up the absorber plate with paint.

## M. Frame for Glazing

**22.** Cut the two 1" x 3" x 10' boards (¾" x 2½" x 10') for the battens into lengths which correspond with the outer edges of the TAP frame.

Bevel the bottom batten of the frame to shed water. Cut a 45 degree bevel and plane the top pointed edge of the bevel to a flat surface, ⅛" wide to later hold the caulking.

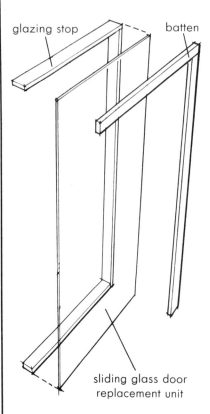

glazing stop        batten

sliding glass door replacement unit

**23.** The glazing stops will be cut from the 1" x 2" x 10' boards (¾" x 1½" x 10'). The glass will rest between the stops and the battens.

Cut the vertical stops into lengths

of 76½". Trim the width of the 76½" (or vertical) strips lengthwise to 1⁷⁄₁₆" for a ⅝" thick glass panel, to 1⁵⁄₁₆" for ¾" glass, and to 1³⁄₁₆" for ⅞" glass.

Cut the horizontal stops to 33" (top and bottom) or· to a dimension that will keep pressure on the aluminum absorber plate while remaining flush with the vertical glazing stops you have just trimmed.

Paint the four glazing stops with two coats of white shellac sealer to avoid outgasing.

Prime and paint the outside of the TAP frame and the battens with your trim or house color. Let dry.

## N. Weep Holes

**24.** In the bottom (1½" x 4") piece of the frame, cut three channels with the drill and ¼" bit to allow moisture that accumulates beneath the glass to evaporate. To the underside of the bottom, attach ½" squares of screening with staples or caulking to keep out bugs and insects.

## O. Installing the Glazing Frame

**25.** Press the ¾" surface of the top and bottom glazing stops against the aluminum absorber plate. Nail them to the TAP frame with the 6d galvanized nails every 12". Fit the side pieces into place and nail. Be sure the outer faces are flush with each other to provide a smooth surface against which the glass will rest.

**26.** Space the neoprene spacers along the glazing stops, three on each vertical side (one-fourth the distance from each edge of the glass) and two on each horizontal side (one-third the distance from each edge of the glass). Adhere the ½" side of the spacers in place with silicone caulking.

Again using the silicone caulking, adhere the two neoprene setting blocks to the frame, flat side down and one-third the distance from each edge of the glass; they should abut against the two bottom spacers. If necessary, cut the setting blocks to match the thickness of your glass if it is less than 5/8" thick.

## P. Installing the Glass

**27.** Clean the glass with window cleaner. You will need three people to lift the glass into place—two persons wearing gloves will lift the glass, and a third person on the ladder will guide and hold the glass until it has been temporarily secured.

The glass should be set carefully onto the neoprene blocks. With one person holding the glass firmly in place, a second person should set the ten remaining neoprene spacers opposite the first set against which the glass is now resting. Secure with caulking. Caulk also between the TAP frame and the glass.

With someone still holding the glass, drill and screw a vertical batten in place. Use seven 1½" x #8 brass or stainless steel screws, equally spaced. Then screw in the top and bottom battens with five screws each. Finally, install the last vertical batten.

Caulk between the battens and the glass to form a double seal.

## Q. The Drip Edge

**28.** Using the tin snips, cut the drip edge to 37¾". Center drip edge. Nail with four roofing nails to the top of the TAP.

To prevent water seepage from between the collector and the house, flash under the clapboards above the TAP.

Cut the 8" x 4' aluminum flashing to 37¾". Fold the flashing in half and bend it lengthwise to 90 degrees. Pry up the clapboards or

shingles. Slip flashing underneath house siding and nail in place through the siding with five 6d galvanized nails.

Caulk the joint between the flashing and the drip edge. Nail through the flashing and drip edge into the TAP with five aluminum roofing nails. Nail far enough from the edge of the flashing so as not to disturb the caulking.

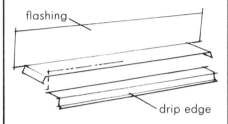

flashing

drip edge

**29.** Caulk between the TAP frame and the house siding with silicone latex caulking.

## R. The Vents

**30.** The lower, non-operable register is the only moving part of the TAP. It controls air movement into the collector. The flap will open to allow air to circulate into the room when there is heat in the collector, and will close to prevent cold air in the collector from flowing into the house at night. During the day the flap must be able to move freely within the vent boot without having its edges catch on the sides of the boot, and at night it must form an airtight seal.

To install the flap, cover the rough edges of the register with rip-stop nylon tape. The tape should extend ½" over the sides and bottom of the register opening and provide a flat surface for the nylon to seal against.

Tape one of the 4" x 13¾" rip-stop nylon pieces to the top of the inside of the vent register to make a flap; be sure the flap is centered on the inside of the vent register to permit free air movement.

**31.** Slip the registers into the openings provided by the vent boots.

The register with the operable louvers goes into the top opening.

Using the attachment holes on the side flanges of the registers as a guide, drill ⅛" holes into the studs; with the screws supplied with each register, screw the registers to the wall.

### Other design possibilities

**Frame.** The 1½" x 4" frame can be built of "E" channel instead of wood to make a lighter, longer-lasting frame. Metal, however, lacks the insulating value of wood; for increased insulating value, add a layer of high-density fiberglass.

TAPs can be constructed with a ⅜" exterior plywood back if you don't want to cut through your house siding, or if your south wall is of brick or masonry. The unit is attached to the siding/sheathing/studs with metal corner braces or to a brick wall with masonry anchors.

**Size.** TAPs can be of any size as long as their length is 6" less than the height of the room in order to keep the lower vent above the floor.

Top and bottom vents should always be of the same dimensions, and a damper in the lower vent is essential for the correct functioning of the panel.

The width of the gap between the house wall and the absorber will vary depending upon the length of the run—the distance that the air moves from inlet to outlet. This gap should be ½" for runs up to 8'; ¾" for runs up to 16'; and 1½" for runs up to 32'. As the run increases, so too must the gap to overcome the flow resistance. If the gap is properly sized, the air flow will be sufficient to keep the collector cool yet provide outlet air from the collector which is comfortably warm.

On a sunny day, check the efficiency of the panel by blowing smoke in the bottom vent. In four seconds it should travel from vent to vent. If not, check that the vents are free of obstructions and dust. It is essential that as much air as possible move through the collector; restrictions will cause the collector to overheat, with most of the heat being lost through the glazing.

At night, check that the one-way vent flap remains tight against the back of the register. The flap may become bent and have to be replaced.

Routinely check the panel for missing paint and caulking. The caulking is especially important because it is very inefficient to lose 100 degrees F. air to infiltration leaks. The caulking around the glazing should be replaced every 10 years, if not sooner. After the panel has been recaulked, repaint the exterior frame.

If you use Kalwall fiberglass for the glazing, apply a thin coating of Kal-lac or its equivalent to the glazing every five years, according to the manufacturer's instructions.

If the aluminum absorber plate begins peeling, remove the glass and repaint the aluminum.

Choose the two 2″ x 6″ x 10′ boards carefully. They must be straight and true so that the glass will fit. They should be spruce or fir, not pine, to minimize the condensation of outgases on the glazing. Also do not use pine for the glazing stops.

**Thermoply.** The purpose of the foil-faced cardboard is to prevent the heat trapped behind the absorber plate from being conducted into the house wall where it would be wasted; the foil reflects the heat back into the air channel. As an inexpensive alternative, use a heavy-grade aluminum foil to cover the sheathing.

**The Absorber.** The absorber plate should be 0.02″ thick for the rapid transfer of heat, and be painted flat black for maximum collector efficiency. Don't use paints that contain lead or any other toxic compound. The high temperatures of the collector release the noxious elements as gases which will be picked up in the air flow.

It is important to use a high-temperature spray paint such as Rustoleum flat black, and to apply it as evenly and thinly as possible; if applied thickly, the paint will act as an insulator and reduce heat transfer through the metal. It is also more likely to peel.

Aluminum is the best choice for the absorber plate, although galvanized steel may be more easily available.

It is difficult to get paint to adhere to galvanized steel. Before painting, etch with a weak solution of water and muriatic acid. Wear gloves and don't let the acid solution touch your skin. Wash off metal sheets in lots of water. Let dry before painting.

Sherwin Williams carries Galvaprep which also can be used to etch the galvanized metal. Add a galvanized metal primer before painting.

There are pre-painted aluminum absorber plates which eliminate the risk of peeling paint, and some corrugated galvanized metal sheets are available with baked-on enamel finishes. They are more expensive but ensure good paint bonding. The glossiness of the enamel will have to be sanded to a dull finish before the paint is applied. Allow paint to dry two days before installing the panel.

Printer's aluminum press plates can be used, but they are neither corrugated nor rigid. Cut to size and rivet together. Clean with steel wool, then with white spirits. Let dry before spray painting.

**Glazing.** Of the various options, glass is the most attractive and longest lasting of the glazings. However, it is difficult to work with, heavy, and breakable.

Instead of glass, rigid plastics such as Kalwall Sunlite Premium II can be substituted. These plastics are convenient, easy to install, and have almost the same percentage of transmissivity as glass.

Old storm windows are usually plentiful, but the dimensions of the panel will have to be adjusted so that the window frames just cover the front of the TAP frame. Check the glass and frames carefully. The frames should be sturdy and freshly painted. The glass may need to be recaulked. Replace any missing or broken panes.

If you want to double-glaze the collector, do not use polyethylene; it will melt because of the high temperatures of the TAP.

**Blower.** Blowers will increase the natural convective flow by moving air faster and farther. For TAP applications, squirrel cage blowers are preferable because the motor is located out of the air stream; this prevents the motor from overheating.

A blower should move approximately 3 to 5 cubic feet of air per minute for every square foot of collector glazing, and be installed in the upper vent. Fans moving 2.5 to 3 cfm create slow enough air movement to permit maximum absorption of heat, while those which move 4 to 5 cfm allow less heat loss through the glazing, but use more electricity.

The blower system can be further upgraded with a thermostat mounted on top of the collector in the air passage, and a manual override mounted at some convenient point of access in the room. The thermostat can then be set to turn the blower on between 90 and

155 degrees F. and off below 90 degrees F., which will make the operation of the blower totally automatic. Even with a blower, don't count on long runs of duct-work.

**Flow Patterns.** Many different panel patterns can be devised for moving the heated air. The TAP design previously described is the easiest and cheapest. It simply draws air over a large area from bottom to top, and because there are no obstructions (baffles), there is little resistance to this upward flow. Air, however, does stagnate in the two corners where there are no vents.

To eliminate these hot spots, a serpentine flow can be established by inserting 2" x 2" baffles to direct the air. The baffles ensure that the air circulates in such a pattern that it comes into maximum contact with all portions of the absorber plate.

The serpentine design, however, creates greater static pressure because there are so many turns of air in the narrow passageways, and because of the increased distance the air must travel. This results in a hotter collector—therefore more heat loss and decreased collector efficiency.

A third design moves the air in straight, horizontal runs from a series of inlets matched by an equivalent number of outlets. This method eliminates curves and hot spots. However, the design requires more construction time and cost.

**Reflective Shutters.** A reflective shutter can be hinged to the bottom of the TAP. It will reduce heat loss in winter, as well as at night and during cloudy periods. When opened, it will increase solar reflection from the snow, and in summer it will protect the panel from damage and the house from overheating.

Build the shutter to the size of the

TAP. See p. 54 for construction details. Be sure it closes firmly against the panel so that wind or snow won't get trapped behind the shutter and decrease its effectiveness.

Paint the outside of the shutter to match the house or collector panel box.

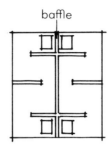 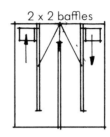

Serpentine flow pattern

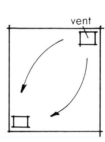 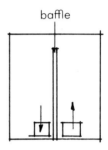

Simplest flow pattern

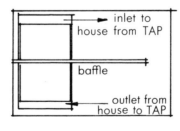 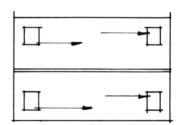

Horizontal flow pattern

*Various TAP designs to alter air flow patterns*

# Batch Water Heater

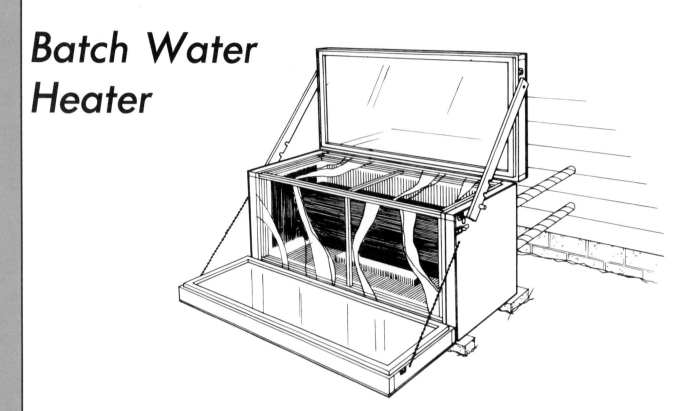

**Skills required:** Moderate carpentry and plumbing skills required.

**Cost:** $300 to $400. Of the total cost, approximately $50 will be for plumbing supplies, $150 for lumber and glazing materials, and $130 for a 30-gallon water tank. Cost figures can be reduced by obtaining a used water tank in good condition, and by building the insulated heater box of recycled lumber.

**Amount of heat gain:** The batch heater will save as much as 25 percent of water heating costs, which will be a saving of approximately $75 per year. This saving can be increased by using two 30-gallon tanks.

On a sunny day, the batch heater can heat 30 gallons of cold groundwater (about 47 degrees F.) to 110 to 130 degrees F.

**What it does:** The batch water heater is a 30-gallon water tank (size can vary), mounted in a double- or triple-glazed box fitted with insulated reflective covers. During the day, the covers are opened to let the sun's rays hit the black surface of the tank and heat the water within; at night the shutters are closed to conserve this heat. (The insulating covers usually reduce the temperature drop at night by 10 to 25 degrees F.) The covers, because they are foil-faced, also reflect additional solar radiation.

The insulating shutters are optional in mild climates, but essential where freezing is a danger.

The heater is controlled by adjusting three valves. These automatically direct incoming cold water from the main line into the bottom of the water tank, using the existing water pressure of the home

plumbing system. In the tank, the "batch" of water is heated by the sun. When there is demand on the house water supply, warmed water is drawn off from the top of the tank. It then is fed either directly to the house faucets or into the existing hot water tank where if necessary it is boosted to the desired temperature.

The design must allow the batch heater to be by-passed by the existing hot water system, and it must be drainable to prevent winter freeze-up.

During cloudy periods, the batch heater will heat the water to 50 to 80 degrees F. However, if more than two-thirds of the month is cloudy, there may be a net heat loss. If such is the case, by-pass the batch heater until days are sunny again.

The heater is designed to work in

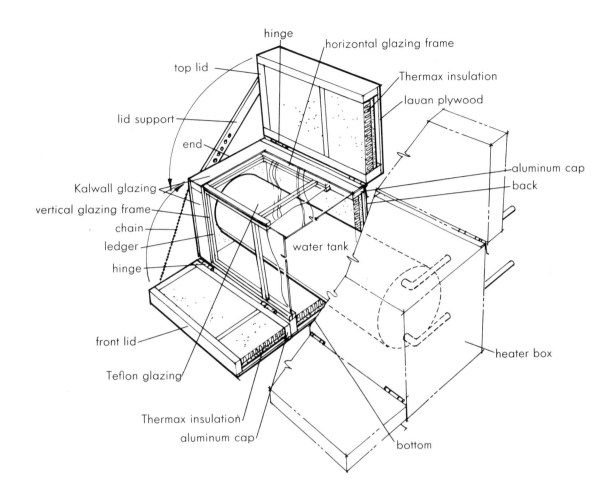

hinge

horizontal glazing frame

top lid

Thermax insulation

lauan plywood

lid support

end

aluminum cap

back

Kalwall glazing

vertical glazing frame

chain

ledger

water tank

hinge

front lid

heater box

Teflon glazing

Thermax insulation

aluminum cap

bottom

above-freezing temperatures, usually from April to October. When temperatures go below freezing, the system will have to be drained and disconnected. This means relying on your conventional hot water tank in the winter.

On an annual basis, the batch heater cannot supply all household water needs, and therefore must be used in conjunction with a conventional system. However, when the weather is clear and hot water demand low and confined to daytime use, the batch heater should be able to meet household demands. When demand is high or the weather is cloudy, more than one preheater tank installed in series will be needed or the conventional system must be used.

**Timing is important**

To obtain maximum benefit from the batch heater, all washing

should be done in late afternoon when the water is hottest. By early morning and early evening, when hot water demand is usually the greatest, the tank water is cooler.

The potential for year-round use of the batch heater, especially in New England or in cold climate areas of the United States, can be increased if the unit is placed within a tempered, weatherproof environment such as a greenhouse or sunspace.

**How it works:** Some sunlight hits the batch water tank directly; other rays bounce off the aluminum-faced Thermax of the top and front lids before passing through the glazing. (For these lids to function for maximum collector efficiency, their reflective surfaces must be angled to bounce solar rays into the box.) The sunlight is absorbed by

the black heater tank and, because of the layers of glazing, is prevented from easily escaping.

The sunlight, now converted to heat, warms the cold water which has passed from the house main to the heater tank. The solar-heated water rises in the tank, creating a relatively stationary layer at the top. This water is especially hot during the summer when the sun is high.

When there is a hot water demand in the house, hot water from the batch heater is drawn off from the top of the tank, and is replaced at the bottom with cold. Mixing of hot and cold water is minimized by the location of inlet/outlet pipes: cold enters at the bottom, hot exits at the top. The curved hot water pipe and drooler for the cold also minimize the mixing of hot with the incoming cold.

**Materials:**

| Amount | Size | Item |
|---|---|---|
| 7 | 2″ x 4″ x 10′ | Pressure-treated pine, fir, or spruce |
| 1 | 2″ x 4″ x 8′ | Pressure-treated pine, fir, or spruce |
| 1 | 2″ x 3″ x 8′ | Fir or spruce |
| 1 | 2″ x 3″ x 4′ | Fir or spruce |
| 1 | 1″ x 4″ x 8′ | #2 pine |
| 1 | 1″ x 3″ x 4′ | #2 pine |
| 1 | 1″ x 2″ x 8′ | #2 pine |
| 3 | ¼″ x 4′ x 8′ | Lauan plywood |
| 3 | ½″ x 4′ x 8′ | Thermax rigid insulation |
| 2 | 2″ x 4′ x 8′ | Thermax rigid insulation |
| 1 | 54¼″ x 43¼″ | .001 Teflon glazing |
| 4 | | Luggage catches |
| 2 sets | 3½″ | Butt hinges |
| 1 roll | 2½″ wide | Aluminum foil duct tape |
| 1 tube | | DAP Foamboard and Panel Adhesive |
| | | Carpenter's wood glue |
| 1 tin | | Soldering flux |
| 1 roll | | Solder wire 50/50 |
| 1 roll | | Teflon plumbing tape |
| 1 tube | | Silicone caulking |
| 1 tube | | Clear silicone caulking |
| 1 | ½″ x 2′ | Hardwood dowel (optional) |
| — | 2′ | Small-link chain |
| 1 | 4′ x 5′ | Kalwall Sunlite Premium II |
| 1 | 1″ x 1½″ x 26′ | Adhesive-backed neoprene weatherstripping |
| 1 | 14″ x 5′ | .025 sheet aluminum |
| 1 pint | | Primer |
| 1 pint | | Flat black paint or 1 can flat black spray paint (Rustoleum Matte Black or Dampney Thurmalox) |
| 1 | 30 gallon | Water tank |
| — | ¾″ | Galvanized plugs as necessary |
| — | | Tubular foam insulation as needed |
| 2 | ¾″ | Copper bushings |
| 2 | ¾″ | Brass nipples |
| 2 | ¾″ | 90 degree elbows |
| 1 | ½″ x 2′ | Copper pipe, Type L, plus enough to reach into the house plumbing for the hot and cold water lines |
| 2 | ¾″ | Tees |
| 2 | ¾″ | "Stop and waste" valves |
| 1 | ½″ x 2′ | Copper pipe |
| — | | Staples |
| 2¼ lbs. | 16d | Galvanized common nails |
| ⅛ lb. | 4d | Galvanized finishing nails |
| 6 oz. | 1″ | Brads |
| 40 | ¾″ | Aluminum screws |
| 40 | | Neoprene washers |
| 20 | #8 | Flathead sheet metal screws |

**Tools:**

Circular saw or table saw
Hammer
Combination square
Tape measure
Caulking gun
Utility knife
Sureform
Straightedge
Electric drill and bits
Propane torch
Steel wool
Old toothbrush or flux brush
Staple gun
Tin snips
Screwdriver
Level
Pipe cutter
Hacksaw
Paint brush
Sandpaper, medium grade
Pipe wrenches, if using a recycled tank

To maintain tank temperatures, it is important that the hot water lines be insulated.

A well-caulked, well-insulated heater box, reduces heat lost to the outside air. Most of the heat loss will occur through the glazing, making it essential to create as tight a seal as possible when the lids are closed.

An hour or so after sundown, the top hottest layer will have given up much of its heat by conduction to the cooler water below. This means water in the tank is at its warmest in the early to mid-afternoon.

The efficiency and water storage capacity of this system can be increased by using multiple tanks plumbed in series. In multiple tank arrangements, the cold water enters the bottom of one tank, is heated, rises, and passes from the top of this tank to the bottom of a second tank. Here it is further heated. Water can even pass on to a third tank. House water is drawn from the top of the hottest of the tanks. Plumbing the tanks in series reduces the mixing of hot and cold, and slows the arrival of any cold water at the last tank.

The vertical rather than horizontal positioning of the water tank increases the stratification within the tank; because less mixing occurs, the outlet water temperature is higher.

In most climates the batch heater has to be used in conjunction with a conventional heater where hot water is either maintained or boosted to the desired temperature.

## Advantages:

1. Cheapest and simplest of all solar hot water systems. Costs much less than half of a conventional flat plate domestic hot water system, and is the most straightforward, i.e., a tank in the sun.
2. Of the domestic hot water heating systems, the batch heater is the easiest to construct, the least expensive to install, and the most cost-effective.
3. No pumps; no separate heat transfer fluids; no controls; no other moving parts, antifreeze, or electric wiring.
4. Uses readily available materials and conventional construction techniques.
5. May qualify for state tax credits.
6. Architecturally flexible; with a sunny wall, you can integrate heater into home's siding to give built-in appearance. If home faces the wrong way, you can build a freestanding version.
7. Can cut water-heating costs by one-fourth.
8. Extremely reliable.

## Disadvantages:

1. Requires human attention at least twice a day to open and close lids. Also depends on human interaction for efficient cloudy daytime operation.
2. Unlike collectors, requires large tank area, plus nighttime insulation for heat loss reduction.
3. Must be drained when the temperatures are below freezing.
4. A month averaging 1,000 degree days is too cold for the batch heater to be useful.

**Tips:** The heating of water is the second greatest home energy consumer. Before spending time and money on a batch water heater, examine ways to reduce the expense of your hot water system.

Turn down the setting of your water heater to 110 to 120 degrees F.; the water will still be quite hot.

Insulate the water heater with a 6″ fiberglass jacket and insulate the hot water pipes so that they will retain more heat.

Some communities now have off-peak rates. If you have an electric heater, this means your tank will operate at a lower cost during those times when the company has power to spare.

Water consumption also can be reduced by using low-flow shower heads and faucet aerators, and by taking showers (not baths), washing full loads in the washing machine or dishwasher, and fixing dripping faucets.

Compare energy-efficiency ratings before buying new appliances.

## Installation.

The batch heater should face as close to solar south as possible, and be in full sun year-round between 9 a.m. and 3 p.m. It also should be located as close to the existing hot water tank as possible; long pipe runs increase the costs. They also increase heat loss which will decrease the efficiency of your batch heater. Keep plumbing lines less than 30' long (or as short as possible).

The batch heater can be placed on the ground, on a platform, or mounted on an existing roof, patio, deck, or carport. If it is placed on a roof, structural reinforcement may be necessary unless the heater is part of a new addition. When full, a single tank weighs 450 pounds.

Usually the ground is the most practical location; it makes installation and shuttering easier. Also the tank is more accessible should repairs or draining of the system be necessary.

Theoretically, any tank of any size can be used. However, the greater the surface-to-volume ratio, the faster the water temperature will rise. Therefore hot water tanks, because they are long and narrow, are recommended.

There are three suitable types: stainless steel tanks, range boilers, and glass-lined tanks. The stainless steel tanks are durable, resistant to corrosion, last 20 years (whereas the galvanized steel tanks last only 10 years), but they are not widely used and are expensive.

Range boilers are made of galvanized steel, and are available in many sizes. Their cost is almost that of a glass-lined tank, but they won't last very long unless the water never becomes very hot and the steel is quite thick to prevent the action of corrosive elements. They should be used as the last resort.

Glass-lined tanks are the most readily available, are long-lived, and are manufactured for use as gas-fired or electric units. They are made from galvanized steel, and because hot water rusts steel more rapidly than cold, these tanks are lined to form a smooth surface that resists corrosion.

Especially adapted for use as a batch heater are mobile home tanks, because they are long and thin. The 20-gallon Sears model #153321210 is widely available, and has a relatively large surface-to-volume ratio. However, if galvanized tanks are used with copper pipe, make sure the metals are separated with a dielectric fitting to prevent accelerated corrosion.

Unfortunately, it is difficult to buy these tanks without buying a complete water tank unit (including insulation, controls, and steel jacket, all of which will have to be removed).

### Fear of freezing

In many climates, frozen water pipes are a constant worry. This fear can be diminished by increasing the size of the tank, but the greater volume of water will heat up more slowly. Other safety measures include leaving in the heating elements on electric heaters to use as a back-up. The thermostat will then have to be set quite low so that the elements operate only for freeze protection. Otherwise on cloudy days with the shutters open, you could be wasting expensive heat.

Heat tapes can be used around the heater and attached with epoxy, and heat tapes can be

## Old Tanks

To reduce the expense, old hot water tanks can be used. Some risk is involved (they may leak), but they are usually available through plumbing supply houses for little or nothing. Use them only for on-the-ground installations in case leaks should occur.

If you plan to salvage a gas or electric heater, strip down the tank. Save the insulation; if in good condition, it can be used in the box walls. Clean the outside carefully, looking for leaks (one in three tanks usually is usable). Pay special attention to the welded seams; they are the first to fail. Electric tanks also may leak around the element mountings.

Mark hot and cold inlets (they are indicated on the jacket). If you can't read the labeling, look for the dip tube which carries the cold water down to the bottom of the tank. This pipe extends into the tank to minimize the immediate mixing of incoming cold with the tank's stored hot water.

Use penetrating oil to remove the plumbing fittings, if necessary. With the fittings off, check the tank by tilting it so that you can see the glass lining through one of the openings. Rotate the tank until you have seen the entire inner lining. Reject the tank if the lining isn't intact.

Rinse out the tank with a detergent to remove mineral deposits, rust, and salts. Pressure-test the tank for leaks by blocking all but one of the holes with plugs. Test with an air compressor or have this done by a gas station or radiator shop. The pressure load for recycled tanks should not exceed 65 percent of the new tank pressure rating.

Leaks can be patched with epoxy. Use J.B. Weld epoxy steel mender ($3.50/can). If the tank is already painted, sand down the metal before patching. Or attach a garden hose with the hose nipple fitted in the last hole. Turn on water and run under pressure through the tank, checking for leaks.

### Remove anode

Remove the sacrificial anode, another fitting at the top of the tank. This rod keeps the steel walls from rusting; should the glass lining crack, the rod will corrode first since substances such as chlorine and hardwater are attracted to it. Inspect the anode. If more than half of it is gone (the rod is originally ¾″ thick), replace it with a new anode. Tanks protected with a sacrificial anode should last 10 years.

Leave in the temperature/pressure valve; it releases the pressure when the tank temperature builds to high levels.

The drain can still be used to empty the tank if fitted with a length of pipe and removable plug, or it can be used as the cold water inlet.

Wirebrush the tank exterior and let dry. Then paint tank with a metal primer and one coat of a flat-black paint such as Rustoleum Matte Black. Better but more expensive is Dampney's Thurmalox. This selective surface paint has higher solar absorptance/lower solar emittance percentages than the Rustoleum. Instead of paint, a selective, self-adhesive foil such as Berry Solar Strip can be applied to reduce radiant heat loss from the tank.

wrapped around the inlet/outlet water pipes. Many of these plastic-enclosed heating ribbons include a thermostat set to turn on the element when a certain temperature is reached. One end of the tape must be plugged into an outlet.

Or leave a faucet dripping. It too will prevent frozen pipes.

Or you can drain the tank.

# How to build:

The batch heater box with lids will measure 31½" (height) x 28" (width) x 61¼" (length) with an ⅛" overlap of the top lid on three sides of the box. The box will hold a tank no larger than 18" in diameter and 50" in length (including the two 90 degree elbows necessary at the top of the tank for water inlet and outlet pipes).

## A. The BACK of the Box

**1.** From the 2" x 4" x 8' lengths, cut two uprights to 21" and two crosspieces to 53¾". Cut two additional uprights from the 2 x 3s to 21".

Lay the crosspieces flat and align their ends. From one end, measure in 16½". Mark a squared line with the combination square on both 2 x 4s. Place an "X" on the side of the line toward the center.

Measure in from the other end 16½". Draw a squared line with an "X" on the side of the line toward the center of the board.

**2.** With a sturdy surface to nail against, position one of the 2 x 4 uprights on edge. It should be perpendicular to one end of the crosspiece. Check for square, then nail through the crosspiece into the upright with two 16d nails.

Position the 2 x 3 uprights so that each covers an "X" and is aligned with one outside edge of the crosspiece. Nail together with two 16d nails for each connection.

Through the other end of the crosspiece, nail into the second 2 x 4 upright.

**3.** Rotate the BACK so that the crosspiece rests against the nailing surface. Butt the second crosspiece against the ends of the four uprights and nail together. Be sure the 2 x 3 uprights align with the same outside edge of the crosspiece, and are flush with the square lines. Set aside.

## B. BOTTOM of the Box

**4.** From the 2 x 4 stock, cut four pieces to 21" and two pieces to 53¾". Assemble in the same manner as the BACK.

## C. The Two ENDs of the Box

**5.** Cut four lengths of 2 x 4 to 24½" and four lengths to 24". With a sturdy surface to nail against, position a 24½" board on edge and

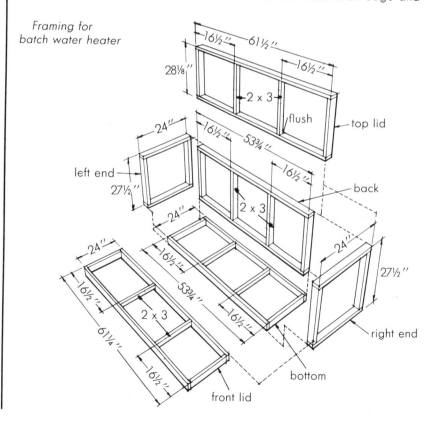

*Framing for batch water heater*

left end

right end

front lid

bottom

back

top lid

flush

perpendicular to one of the 24" lengths so that the edges are flush. Nail through the 24" board with two 16d nails. Then nail through the other end of the 24" piece into the second 24½" length.

Rotate so that the 24" length rests against the nailing surface. Nail through the second 24" piece into the ends of the two 24½" pieces. Check for square.

Make a second rectangle in the same fashion.

## D. The LIDs

**6.** The box will have TOP and FRONT LIDs. For the TOP LID, cut two 2" x 4" x 25⅛" and two 2" x 4" x 61½" pieces. Also cut from the 2 x 3s, two lengths of 25⅛". Assemble following the same procedure as for the BACK of the box. Label and set aside.

**7.** For the FRONT LID, cut two uprights from the 2 x 4s to 21" and two crosspieces to 61¼". From the 2 x 3 stock, cut two uprights to 21". Assemble as for BACK of box.

## E. GLAZING FRAMES

**8.** Two glazing frames will be cut from the 1" x 4" x 8' board.

Rip the board into four strips, each ¾" square and 8' long. Use a circular saw with an edge guide or rip the board on a table saw.

**9.** Cut one of the strips into three pieces; two should be 18¼" long and a third 53¾". From the second strip, cut one length to 53¾" and a second to 18¼". These will be used to construct the HORIZONTAL GLAZING FRAME.

To assemble the frame, nail through the longer strips into the shorter ones at both ends. Use 4d finishing nails. A support is centered between the two end pieces. Mark its position and nail. Set frame aside.

**10.** From the remaining ¾" strips, cut three lengths of 21" and two of 53¾" for the VERTICAL GLAZING FRAME. Nail together as explained above, and set frame aside.

## F. Insulation

**11.** It is important that the insulation fit as tightly as possible to prevent air leaks. Consequently each piece should be measured, cut and fitted separately. Edges can be trimmed if necessary with a utility knife or sureform.

Lay the FRONT LID of the box face down on a flat surface. (All uprights should touch the work surface.) From the ½" Thermax, cut a piece to fit between the two end uprights. This piece should measure 21" x 58¼". Put the insulation in place; it will rest on top of the 2 x 3s. Center and press down strips of the aluminum foil duct tape over the joints between the insulation and the wood frame. (There will be a ½" space between the insulation and the outside of the 2 x 4 uprights. This too can be filled with insulation, but it will add to the expense of building the box.)

**12.** Cut six ½" x 1" x 2" Thermax spacers. Spread adhesive on both sides of the spacers and center them along the edge of the insulation.

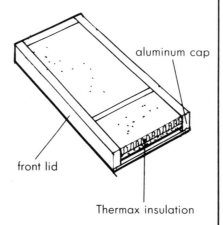

aluminum cap

front lid

Thermax insulation

**13.** Cut a piece of plywood to 24" x 61¼". Lay the plywood over the Thermax spacers so that it rests on the 2 x 4 frame. Apply glue to adjoining surfaces and nail into 2 x 4 frame with 1" brads spaced every 6". Turn over lid and tape all Thermax-to-wood joints.

**14.** To fill remainder of space in this lid, cut insulation to fit the recesses (two pieces cut to 15" x 21" and one to 25¼" x 21" of both 2" and ½" insulation; for each recess this means there will be a piece of ½" and a piece of 2" insulation). Put Thermax in place and tape all joints.

**15.** Lay TOP LID on a flat surface with all the uprights touching the work surface. Cut a piece of ½" Thermax to fit (25⅛" x 58½"). Tape the joints. Apply adhesive to ½" spacers and position on insulation. Cut a piece of plywood to 28⅛" x 61½", glue and nail into place. Turn LID over and tape all joints.

Using pieces of ½" and 2" insulation, fill the 2½" recesses and tape joints.

**16.** Lay one of the ENDs on edge on a flat surface. Cut a plywood rectangle to 24" x 27½". Add glue and nail into the 2 x 4s, spacing the 1" brads every 6" and nailing them ¾" in from the edges.

Turn END over. Cut four spacers. Apply adhesive and center them along each side of the plywood. Cut Thermax to fit opening (3" x 21" x 24½"). Place insulation in END and tape all joints.

Follow the same procedure for the other END.

**17.** Butt one of the ENDs against the BOTTOM so that it aligns front and back. Nail along BOTTOM into END ¾" from the bottom edge, spacing the 16d nails every 6". Nail other END into BOTTOM.

**18.** Turn over box so that the top crosspieces of the ENDs rest on a flat surface. From the plywood, cut a 24″ x 61¼″ rectangle from the scrap of the first two sheets of plywood. This means cutting two pieces, one piece to 24″ x 21″ and a second to 24″ x 40¼″. The pieces should butt along one of the 2 x 4 supports of the BOTTOM and extend a ¼″ beyond each END. Nail plywood pieces to 2 x 4 frame of BOTTOM and ENDs with 1″ brads, spaced every 6″. Turn BOTTOM over so that it rests on the plywood.

**19.** Cut twelve ½″ x 1″ x 2″ spacers. Spread adhesive on both sides of the 1″ x 2″ faces, and center them along each side in the recesses on the BOTTOM. Then cut 3″ of Thermax to fill BOTTOM cavities. Two of the cavities will measure 15″ x 21″ and one will measure 17¾″ x 21″. (Use one piece of 2″ Thermax and two pieces of ½″ for each recess.) Set in place and seal edges with duct tape.

**20.** Set BACK on top of BOTTOM so that BACK fits between the ENDs and is flush with the outside edge of the BOTTOM. The BACK should be positioned so that the flush surface of the 2 x 3 uprights faces the center of the box.

Measure in ¾″ from the outside edge of the BACK crosspiece which rests on the BOTTOM, and drive 16d nails into the BOTTOM along this line. Space them every 16″. Check all corners for square. Then nail the front lip of the BACK bottom crosspiece to the middle 2 x 4s of the BOTTOM. Check again for square.

Nail through the BACK uprights into each of the two END pieces ¾″ in from the outside edge. Check again for square.

**21.** Tip the box over so that it rests on the front uprights of the ENDs. Measure the inside dimensions between the 2 x 4s of the BACK (21″ x

50¾″). Cut a piece of ½″ Thermax to these measurements and set in place against the 2 x 3s. Center and press into place strips of duct tape to cover the joints between the insulation and wood frame. Cut six ½″ x 1″ x 2″ spacers. Apply adhesive to both sides and space them equally around perimeter of insulation.

From the third sheet of plywood, cut a piece to 27¾″ x 61¼″. The plywood will extend ¼″ beyond each END. Glue and nail into END and BACK 2 x 4s with 1″ brads spaced every 6″.

Tip box again so that it rests on plywood BACK. Cut insulation to fill the three 2½″ cavities—two pieces to 2½″ x 15″ x 21″ and one to 2½″ x 17¾″ x 21″. Seal with duct tape along all edges.

**22.** Apply generous amounts of caulking to all wood joints.

**23.** To make sure the plywood lasts, cover it with two to three coats of resin-epoxy. Auto body and marine product suppliers can provide colored resins that give an excellent finish.

## G. The Water Tank

**24.** You should have a tank, whether new or recycled, that will not leak.

Wirebrush the tank exterior, degrease, wash again, and let the tank dry. Paint with a primer followed by two coats of a flat-black paint. Or apply a selective, self-adhesive black foil.

**25.** If you are using a recycled tank, remove the current fittings. Plan where the new fittings will be—when the tank is laid on its side, the hot water outlet should be near the top, the cold water inlet directly below, with the drain at the bottom. (The position of the drain is important if you plan to empty the tank in winter.)

Fill all unnecessary holes with ¾″ plugs. (Leave the anode in place, unless it needs to be replaced.) Wrap the threads of the plugs with three to four layers of Teflon plumbing tape to provide a watertight seal.

**26.** You will want to use the same material (i.e., copper or galvanized steel) used in your house plumbing system. If you do change from copper to steel, use a dielectric union to make the connection.

For the cold water inlet, flatten one end of a 12″ piece of ½″ copper piping. Drill ⅜″ holes every inch along one side of the pipe.

**27.** Solder the circular end of the ½″ pipe to one end of a ¾″ bush-

---

### Selective Self-Adhesive Foils

The selective surface coating is designed to absorb large amounts of solar energy while re-radiating very little. The thin sheets of metal foil are protected with a plastic, peel-off backing to make them easy to apply.

Before adhering the foil, be sure the tank is smooth and clean. Use sandpaper to remove any rough spots from the tank's exterior. Then wipe down with de-natured alcohol. Let dry. Paint the top and bottom of the tank only (the concave and convex parts) with black paint. Let dry.

Cut the first sheet of foil long enough to wrap around the tank with a 1″ overlap. Peel the adhesive backing off and press the foil to the tank, beginning at the bottom and working up.

Use a soft rag to press out any air bubbles. If plumbing connections are covered, use a utility knife to cut away the foil. Add sheets as necessary, leaving a 1″ overlap; trim the last sheet to fit.

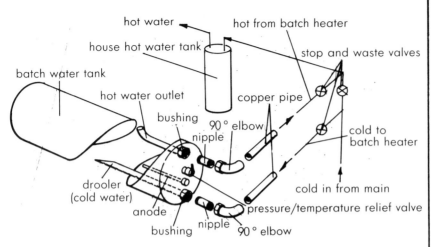

**hot water**
**house hot water tank**
**batch water tank**
**hot water outlet**
**bushing**
**90° elbow**
**nipple**
**drooler (cold water)**
**anode**
**bushing**
**nipple**
**90° elbow**
**hot from batch heater**
**stop and waste valves**
**copper pipe**
**cold to batch heater**
**cold in from main**
**pressure/temperature relief valve**

*Fittings for batch water heater and to tie heater into house plumbing*

ing. Before soldering, make two or three practice joints unless you are experienced.

To solder the joint, clean the end of the pipe with sandpaper, steel wool, or the abrasive cloth used by auto body shops. Shine enough of the pipe for the fitting plus ½″ so that the solder will flow completely around the edge of the fitting. Also clean the inside of the fitting.

**28.** With a toothbrush or small brush made for fluxing, spread soldering flux on the shiny metal on the inside of the fitting and on the outside of the pipe.

Slip the bushing over the pipe; do not force. Heat the metal fitting with the propane torch. The flame will have an outer cone of hot gas surrounding a small, bright blue inner cone. Place the tip of the inner cone (where the torch's highest temperatures are) against the fitting you intend to solder.

When the pipe and fitting are hot enough, hold the solder against the joint. If the joint is sufficiently hot, the tip of the solder wire will suddenly melt and flow into the space between the pipe and the fitting. Capillary action will draw the solder around and into the joint.

Once the solder has hardened, wipe the joint with a clean cloth to remove any excess flux.

**29.** Slip a nipple over the bushing and solder together. Mark the side of the nipple to locate the holes in the end of the copper tube. Wrap Teflon plumbing tape around the threaded end of the nipple and screw into tank cold water inlet. Be sure drooler holes in the copper pipe face the outside of the tank.

**30.** Into the hot water outlet, place a ½″ x 12″ piece of copper pipe, a ¼″ bushing, and a ¾″ nipple. The 12″ copper pipe should be gradually bent to reach from the outlet hole to the side of the tank, a bend of approximately ¾″. Do not flatten the end of the tube. Solder the fittings together and screw into the tank.

**31.** To both pipes, screw on ¾″ 90 degree elbows, then solder a length of copper pipe. The pipe should be long enough to pass through the heater box with sufficient working space to solder on the next length of pipe. (This length will connect with the house plumbing.) Or you may want to do this with one length of pipe.

**32.** With the tank on its side, lift it into the batch water heater box and center it between the ENDs. Be sure tank is positioned so that the

hot water outlet is *on top of* the cold water inlet. The tank will lie on the 2 x 4 supports of the BOTTOM. On the BACK, mark where the two pipes will exit the heater box. Remove the tank and drill through the Thermax and plywood with a ⅞″ drill bit.

If the tank will be drained in winter, you will need plastic fittings and a plug to attach to the tank drain. Also mark where the drain will pass through the heater box, and drill the hole.

**33.** Carry the batch heater box to location. Rest the box on bricks or stones to raise it off the ground. Leave enough space between the house and heater box so that you can solder the next length of pipe (if necessary), drill water pipe holes through the house wall with a ⅞″ bit, and hinge the TOP LID to the BACK. Once these jobs are completed, the box can be moved closer to the house wall where it will benefit from any escaping heat.

With the box on its approximate site, lift the water tank again into place, slipping the copper pipes through the holes in the BACK, and positioning the drain outlet. Cut a length of 2 x 4 to 20¾″ and nail it between the 2 x 4 middle support pieces of the BOTTOM to hold the tank firmly against the BACK uprights.

**34.** Screw on drain fittings.

## H. Installing the Glazing Frames

**35.** With the combination square, measure down ¾″ from the top edge of the ENDs and top crosspiece of the BACK. Mark. Also measure in ¾″ on both sides of the ENDs. And in from the outside edge of the front crosspiece of the BOTTOM. Mark.

Rip the 1" x 2" x 8' board in half. Cut each ¾" strip into three ledgers, measuring 53¾", 19" and 21¾" in length. For the ledger along the top crosspiece of the BACK, align one of the 53¾" strips below the ¾" line, and nail into crosspiece with 4d finishing nails spaced every 6".

Position one of the 19" ledgers to butt against the BACK ledger and be flush with the ¾" mark along the END. Tack in place.

Follow the same process for the second horizontal ledger.

**36.** Tack the second 53¾" piece into place; it will run along the BOTTOM ¾" in from the edge. Perpendicular to and at either end of this ledger, add the two 21¾" strips. These will fit along the END uprights.

**37.** For the VERTICAL GLAZING FRAME, cut a piece of Teflon glazing to 23" x 54¼". Align the 54¼" edge along the top face of the FRAME crossrail, leaving a ¼" overlap on four sides. Begin in the center. Fold the ¼" overlap under and staple Teflon to rail. Work along crossrail towards end rails, being sure plastic film is taut before stapling.

Work from the center along other crossrail. Fold under ¼" overlap. Pull plastic taut, then staple. Do end rails.

**38.** For the HORIZONTAL GLAZING FRAME, cut a piece of Teflon glazing to 20¼" x 54¼". Align the 54¼" edge along edge of crossrail, leaving a ¼" overlap. Staple down as for VERTICAL GLAZING FRAME. Set aside.

**39.** Set VERTICAL GLAZING FRAME against END and BOTTOM ledgers with the stapled Teflon side facing the water tank. Nail to ledgers with brads. Lift HORIZONTAL GLAZING FRAME into place with the stapled Teflon side facing the

water tank. Its front edge should be flush with the outside top edge of the VERTICAL FRAME. Nail into ledgers and VERTICAL FRAME.

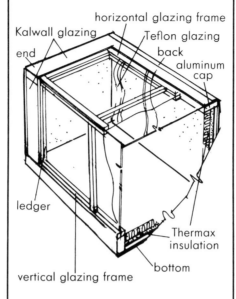

horizontal glazing frame
Kalwall glazing end
Teflon glazing
back
aluminum cap
ledger
Thermax insulation
vertical glazing frame
bottom

## I. Acrylic Glazing

**40.** From the 4' x 5' piece of Kalwall glazing, cut two pieces: one cut to 22¼" x 55½" for the top of the box, and a second cut to 25¾" x 55½" for the front. Cut with shears or tin snips.

Center top piece on ENDs with the front edge of the plastic flush with the front edge of the ENDs. Drill ³⁄₁₆" holes through the glazing only, every 6", and ⅜" in from the edge. Then drill into the wood with an ⅛" bit. You may want to screw in each corner to keep the glazing flat.

Remove the glazing, run a perimeter bead of silicone caulking along the adjoining edges of the 2 x 4s. Use plenty of caulking. Then replace glazing and screw in with ¾" aluminum screws and neoprene washers.

Center front piece of acrylic with top edge of plastic flush with top edge of ENDs. Drill, caulk, and screw into ENDs and BOTTOM.

Run a bead of clear silicone sealant along the adjoining edges at the front of the box.

## J. Aluminum Cap

**41.** From the sheet aluminum or from 26 gauge galvanized metal, cut a strip 9" x 55¾". Measure in and bend the aluminum in half lengthwise to a 90 degree angle. Make a second bend of 45 degrees lengthwise of the sheet and in the opposite direction of the first bend to leave a 1" lip.

Use the #8 flathead, self-tapping screws to secure the aluminum cap over the top crosspiece of the BACK and to the ENDs. Center cap and screw every 6". The 1" lip will be on the outside of the BACK.

**42.** Cut a second aluminum strip to 4⅝" x 55¾". Center and screw it into the BOTTOM crosspiece along the front, leaving a ⅛" lip along the bottom.

Run beads of silicone caulking to seal the edge between the aluminum and glazing.

## K. Weatherstripping

**43.** Along the outside edges of the inside of the FRONT and TOP LIDs, mount the 1" x 1½" adhesive-backed weatherstripping.

## L. Butt Hinges

**44.** Lay the FRONT LID on the ground. It should rest on its plywood face. Butt the crosspiece against the END uprights of the batch heater box. Screw one leaf of each hinge into the flat side at either outside edge of the FRONT LID crosspiece. Screw the other leaf of each hinge into the END uprights.

**45.** Rest the TOP LID on the box so that its back edge is flush with the outside edge of the BACK. Mount the two hinges along the back of the box. Before tightening all screws, be sure the lids will close tightly, and that they will open all the way.

## M. Lid Supports

**46.** Cut the 1" x 3" x 4' piece of lumber in half. In one end of each piece, drill a ¼" hole. In the other end at 4" intervals, notch ½" holes along the edge.

At the top front corner of each END, drill a ½" hole. Apply glue and tap a piece of ½" doweling into the hole. Or drive in a 16d nail.

Along the sides of the TOP LID, nail the supports into the 2 x 4s through the hole. If properly positioned, the 1 x 3 lid support should hook over the dowel (or nail) and be used to adjust the angle of the lid.

**47.** Mount the chain for the BOTTOM LID by nailing it into the lid and into the ENDs.

**48.** Screw the four luggage catches into place, one on each end of each lid. Be sure they won't interfere with the 1 x 3 support poles.

## N. Tie-in with House Plumbing

**49.** Solder the batch heater water pipes to lengths of piping which will reach into the house. Readjust the placement of the heater box, if necessary.

**50.** With silicone, seal around the pipes where they leave the heater box and where they enter the house, and around the drain pipe.

**51.** Shut off the house water main and turn off the electricity to the house hot water tank. Open hot and cold water house faucets to reduce the pressure in the water lines.

Decide where you will tap into the house cold water line. Make the first cut with a pipe cutter approximately 6" above the house water tank. (This should be above the tank's insulated jacket.) Then make another cut 1' to 2' above this in the cold water line and remove the section of pipe.

Be sure the pipe and fittings you use are of the same diameter as those in your house water line. For each joint, put in enough solder to form a thin, continuous bead around the neck of the fitting.

**52.** Solder a ¾" tee to the short section of pipe leading to the hot water tank. To the horizontal side of the tee, attach a 6" stub of copper piping, a ¾" "stop and waste" valve, and a 3" length of copper pipe. To the vertical side of the tee, attach a 3" stub, a ¾" "stop and waste" valve and another 3" stub.

Above this, solder a second ¾" tee, and from the horizontal side of this tee, attach a 3" stub, a ¾" "stop and waste" valve and a 3" stub. To the vertical end of the tee, solder whatever length of piping is needed to reconnect into your existing cold water line.

Tilt the water lines slightly so that it will be easy to drain the system.

**53.** Insulate the pipes with tubular foam insulation between the batch heater box and the house water tank.

**54.** To operate the system, adjust valves as shown in the illustration.

| O=open<br>C=closed | V1 | V2 | V3 |
|---|---|---|---|
| Using solar | C | O | O |
| Electric only | O | C | C |

**55.** Should you discover any leaks in the system, drain out the water, reheat the joint to soldering temperature, and flow in more solder.

**56.** To maintain the system, check for leaks, and every two years, check the anode. If it is nearly gone, it should be replaced.

**57.** To make best use of the batch water heater, be sure to open the lids when there is heat to be gained, and to close them at night and during cloudy or adverse weather.

## Other design possibilities

**Insulation.** Insulating materials are assessed by comparing their R-values. The R-value measures the thermal resistance of a material to heat transmission. The higher the R-value, the better the insulation. The batch heater box could be insulated with 3½" of fiberglass, but fiberglass has only an R-value of 3 per inch, whereas Thermax has an R-value of 7.2 per inch. Thermax, therefore, retains the heat much better, which in northern climates is very important.

**Reflectors.** The reflective surfaces are important to raising the collector's efficiency. The dull, aluminum surface of Thermax will scatter a good deal of light into the heater box. If you want to increase the reflection still further, use 0.005" aluminum (or aluminum foil which is cheaper). Apply with silicone sealant to inside surfaces of TOP and FRONT LIDs.

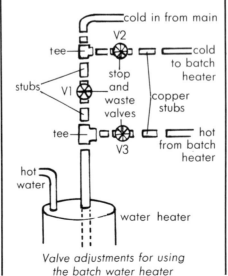

*Valve adjustments for using the batch water heater*

Other reflective materials include white paint, used newspaper printing plates, or polished aluminum sheet metal.

**Glazing.** At least two layers of glazing are recommended in all climates. A third layer provides maximum heat retention.

Glass can be used instead of Teflon and Kalwall. However, if the unit is mounted on the ground, the glass may be inadvertently broken.

**Water Tanks.** In sizing the batch heater and tank, you want sufficient water storage to provide a reasonable amount of hot water (the average person uses 20 to 40 gallons of water per day), but the tank should not be so large as to require an impossible number of hours of solar heating before reaching temperatures of 110 to 120 degrees F. To increase the efficiency and water storage capacity of your system, add more tanks rather than use a larger tank.

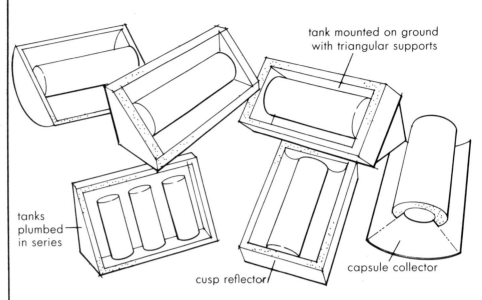

*Other batch water heater designs*

tank mounted on ground with triangular supports

tanks plumbed in series

cusp reflector

capsule collector

**Designs.** There are many different designs for batch heater installations. Some of them are illustrated here.

The tank also can be attached directly to the house. Or it can be built into the roof. Or it can be installed near the peak of a greenhouse roof to take advantage of the warm indoor environment.

# Solar for the Homestead

# Solar Firewood Dryer

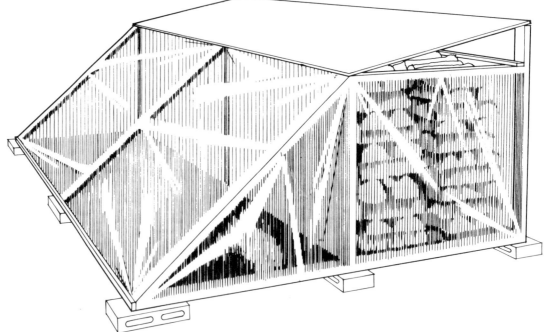

**Skills required:** Slight.

**Cost:** $60 or less.

**Amount of heat gain:** 5,000,000 BTUs/cord more heat than burning a cord of green wood, or a saving of approximately $20/cord for 6 to 8 weeks of drying time.

**What it does:** Wood can be as much as 65 percent moisture, which means that some of the heat of combustion is sacrificed in turning this water into steam. However, the less moisture in the wood, the more recoverable heat for the house.

To decrease moisture content, wood should be air-dried 9 months to 2 years; if the solar firewood dryer is used, these times can be reduced to 6 to 8 weeks. Wood cut in October, for example, can be burned by Christmas.

**How it works:** Solar energy passes through the clear polyethylene plastic along the sloped, south-facing wall. It is absorbed by the black plastic ground cover or by the black painted screening, and is retained within the dryer as heat. Because warm air is lighter than cool air, it rises through the woodpile to the top of the dryer, and is vented out the side and north openings. As the air rises, it pulls in cold air from below the pile, which in turn is heated and vented.

This natural cycle hastens the drying process because warm air can hold more moisture than cool air; as a result moisture is picked up and vented. If the entire pile were covered with plastic, this moisture would be trapped within the dryer and quickly reabsorbed by the wood.

To ensure efficient drying, it is important that nothing interrupt the air flow. Be sure that the wood is not directly touching the plastic; moisture can condense on the plastic and be reabsorbed by splits that touch the plastic.

**Advantages:**
1. Hotter fires.
2. Less creosote.
3. Wood is lighter.
4. Drying times are accelerated.
5. Less wood is needed each season because more heat is recovered.
6. Protects wood from rain and snow.
7. Dryer can be used for starting hardy plants in the spring.

**Tips:** Locate the firewood dryer so that it is convenient, but avoid placing it against the house; the moisture can be destructive. Also the pile may lead to an insect invasion of your home. It is also a fire hazard.

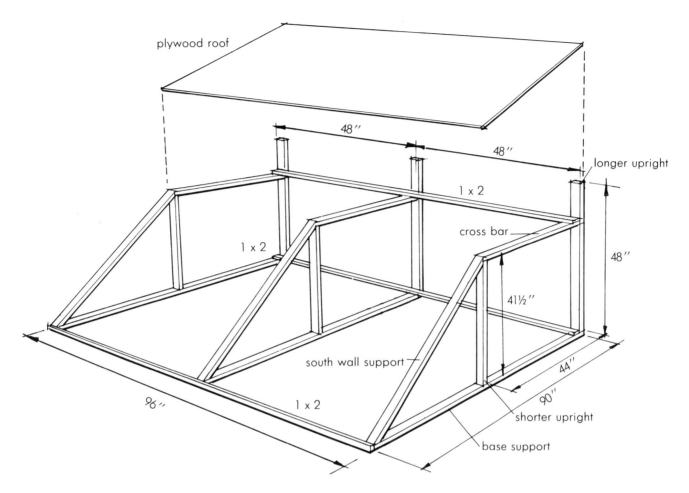

plywood roof

48″

48″

longer upright

1 x 2

cross bar

1 x 2

48″

41½″

south wall support

44″

96″

1 x 2

90″

shorter upright

base support

To hasten the drying process, cut the wood to length, split it (because the bark acts as a vapor barrier), and stack the splits criss-cross on stringers.

The stringers (poles 3″ to 4″ in diameter) should run the length of the pile, and be far enough apart so that the splits will straddle both supports. Bricks, old boards, concrete block, metal pipes, or other improvised supports can be used as long as they raise the pile 4″ off the ground. Never stack wood directly on the bare ground--it will rot because the moisture in the soil will seep into the wood.

Leave space between the rows, and a 2″ to 4″ air space between the wood and plastic. This permits the air to flow freely and prevents any condensate from re-wetting the wood. It also protects the plastic from rubbing on the rough ends of the splits and eventually tearing.

**Materials:**

| Amount | Size | Item |
| --- | --- | --- |
| 11 | 2″ x 4″ x 8′ | Pine, fir, or spruce |
| 1 lb. | 16d | Galvanized nails |
| 6-10 | 6d | Galvanized nails |
| 1 | ⅜″ x 4′ x 8′ | CDX plywood |
| 1 qt. | | White latex exterior paint |
| 1 can | | Black spray paint |
| 1 | 4′ x 8′ | Window screening |
| 1 | 4′ x 8′ | Black polyethylene plastic |
| 1 | 10′ x 16′ | 4 or 6 mil clear polyethylene plastic |
| ¾ lb. | 1″ | Roofing nails |
| 3 | 1″ x 2″ x 8′ | #2 pine |
| | | Cuprinol or wood preservative |

**Tools:**

| | |
| --- | --- |
| Hammer | Paint brush |
| Circular saw or handsaw | Combination square |
| Staple gun | Tape measure |

## How to build:

*The overall dimensions of the solar firewood dryer are 49⅞ inches high by 90¾ inches deep by 8 feet wide, with a slightly sloped roof (8 degrees) and a 45 degree south wall.*

## A. Cutting the 2 x 4s to Length

**1.** The eleven 2 x 4 x 8s should be cut to the following lengths:

| Number | Lengths to cut each 2 x 4 x 8 |
| --- | --- |
| 3 | 90″ (base support) |
| 3 | 1 pc. 48″ (longer upright); 1 pc. 41½″ (shorter upright) |
| 1 | 2 pcs. 44″ (cross bar) |
| 3 | 61″ (outside measurement) with 45 degree bevel cut at each end (south wall support) |
| 1 | 44″ (cross bar) |

## B. The Supports

**2.** Lay one of the longer uprights flat on your work surface. From one end of the 48″ piece, measure in 5″ and make a square line. Place an "X" to the side beyond the square line (the "X" marks the position of the cross bar).

**3.** Now place the longer upright on edge on the floor and parallel to a wall or surface against which you can nail. Align one of the cross bars so that it runs between the wall and the 48″ upright. The cross bar should be flush with the line and cover the "X" which you have just made.

Nail through the upright into the cross bar with three 16d nails. Set aside.

**4.** Lay a base support flat on your work surface. From one end, measure in 44″; draw a square line with the combination square and make an "X" outside the square line.

**5.** Place one of the shorter uprights (41½″) on edge against the wall. Perpendicular to this, position the base support, also on edge.

The upright should cover the "X" which you have just made and be flush with the line. Nail together with three 16d nails.

**6.** To complete the frame, position the longer upright flush with the end of the base support. Nail through the base support into the upright with three 16d nails. (The cross bar should meet the shorter upright to form a rectangle.)

**7.** Tip up the unit so that it rests on the base support.

**8.** Nail through cross bar into shorter upright, using three 16d nails.

**9.** The 61″ section which has a 45 degree cut on both ends will span the distance between the cross bar and the end of the base support. Nail this south wall support in place, using three 16d nails at either end.

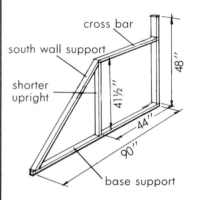

**10.** Make two more supports in the same fashion.

**11.** Paint one side of the plywood white. Paint or apply wood preservative (Cuprinol) to the supports, the 1 x 2s, and the other plywood face. Spray the screening with the black paint. Let dry.

## C. Assembly

**12.** Carry all parts to where the dryer will be located.

Arrange the three supports about 4' apart, with the diagonal ends pointed south.

**13.** With one 1 x 2 lying flat, measure in 46¼" from one end. Make a square line and place an "X" outside this line.

**14.** You will need a helper to steady the supports. Nail through the 1 x 2 into south ends of the 2 x 4 base supports with two 16d nails with one support positioned at each end of the 1 x 2. Be sure to align the center support so that it covers the "X" and is flush with the edge of the square line.

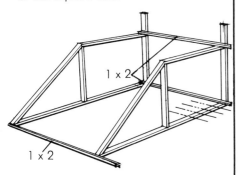

**15.** The second 1 x 2 will support the north side of the solar dryer. It should rest on the base supports and against the taller uprights; nail it into the base supports with 6d nails.

**16.** The remaining 1 x 2 will rest against the taller uprights and lie flat on the cross bars. Nail into cross bars with 6d nails.

**17.** It is advisable to do any further nailing before the plywood roof is added.

Circulation within the woodpile is greatly increased if air can circulate below the pile. You may want to nail stringers to the base supports. Use whatever scrap lumber you have (pieces will need to be at least 4' long and should span the length of the dryer). Spacing between stringers will be determined by the log length you will be storing; stringers should be 3" in from either end of the splits.

**18.** If you don't have scrap lumber, anything will do (rocks, bricks, saplings) as long as it raises the woodpile 4" off the ground. Set these supports in place after the dryer is completed.

**19.** The 4' x 8' sheet of plywood (the roof) will span the distance between the uprights. Nail into uprights with roofing nails, using at least two nails per upright.

**20.** The dryer should be set on bricks or concrete blocks; the bare ground will quickly rot the wood.

Set bricks in place along the base supports. With at least two helpers, lift the solar dryer onto the bricks. They may have to be adjusted to make the dryer level.

Be sure the angled wall of the dryer faces south.

**21.** Staple the blackened screening to the south side of the shorter uprights.

**22.** Cut a 4' x 8' piece of black polyethylene plastic; if you have a 16' roll, cut two pieces 2' x 8'.

Lay the plastic on the ground between the 1 x 2 along the south wall and the vertical black screening. Staple it to the 1 x 2 and base supports; anchor the north side with rocks or scrap pieces of lumber.

## C. The Plastic

**23.** It will be easier to fill the dryer with wood now, before enclosing the structure in plastic. Be sure the wood is stacked above the ground on stringers. Leave space between the stacks for air circulation. If you want the wood to dry as fast as possible, pile the splits crosswise.

**24.** Cut the clear polyethylene plastic to the following diagram. It can be cut with shears, a razor, or utility knife.

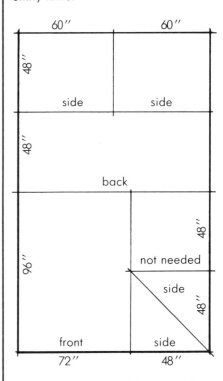

**25.** Wherever possible, wrap the plastic around the 2 x 4s, and fold the plastic a couple of times, then staple through the folds.

Be sure the plastic is well-secured on all sides. You may want to cover the plastic joints with Scotchrap 50 tape before stapling to ensure that the wind won't eventually cause the plastic to rip at the staples. It is best to run furring strips along the joints and to nail through these and the plastic into the 2 x 4s.

**26.** Be sure there is an unobstructed air flow beneath the base supports between the bricks.

**27.** Plastic along the sides should reach up only as far as the cross bars, and up to the 1 x 2 on the north side. Air should be able to flow into and out of the dryer along the top of the back, above the cross bars on either side, and around the bottom of the unit on three sides.

### Other design possibilities

**Angle.** The south wall is tilted at a 45 degree angle; it is the easiest angle to construct. However, it probably isn't the optimum angle for your location.

For greatest efficiency in winter, the angle should be your latitude plus 10 degrees; and 45 degrees during the summer months when the sun is higher in the sky.

**Materials.** Polyethylene plastic comes in 2, 4, and 6 mil thicknesses; the 2 mil, sold for garden mulching and drop cloths, is easily torn; 4 mil is better and not as expensive as the 6 mil. Any of the polyethylene plastics, however, will deteriorate after a few months of exposure to full sunlight. The plastic will last longer if you avoid using the dryer in the hottest part of the summer; you'll have to replace the plastic after one or two seasons.

To make a more permanent structure, clear fiberglass panels, either flat or in corrugated sheets, can be used instead of the polyethylene.

Fiberglass is easy to work with, it is lightweight, and can be cut with a fine-toothed saw or tin snips. It can be drilled, nailed, or screwed with non-rusting fasteners or bolts, as long as protective rubber washers are used around the holes.

The flat fiberglass is strong enough for the vertical spans. However, along the angled south wall, the corrugated panels will offer greater rigidity.

Flat sheets are available in 25" or 49½" to 51½" widths and to any length; the corrugated panels are 26" to 28" wide, which allows for a 1½" to 2" overlap (or a one-corrugation overlap), and are available in 8-, 10-, and 12-foot lengths.

If you use the fiberglass, additional supports on 2' centers will be needed.

Good quality fiberglass should last twenty years. Fiberglass of lesser quality will yellow and may develop a fuzzy texture from the ultra-violet damage. As it discolors, the percentage of light transmitted is reduced and your solar dryer becomes less efficient.

Fiberglass panels will add about $20 to the cost of the solar dryer.

If you want to further increase the durability of the dryer, use a sheet of ⅜" x 4' x 8' CDX plywood for the north wall.

**Size.** By adding additional braces, the dryer can be extended lengthwise in 4' x 4' modules.

# An Inexpensive Solar Firewood Dryer

*The overall dimensions of this dryer are 2 feet deep by 4 feet high by 8 feet long.*

Choose an open, south-facing, sunny location. If located on a hill or knoll, the wood will dry faster because of the increased air currents. Avoid damp places or depressions where water collects after a rainfall.

Wood can be loaded/unloaded from the south or north side. Working from the south side means you will have to roll up the plastic and temporarily store it on top of the plywood. The screen also will have to be removed.

It's easier to work from the north side; there's no screen and less plastic to worry about.

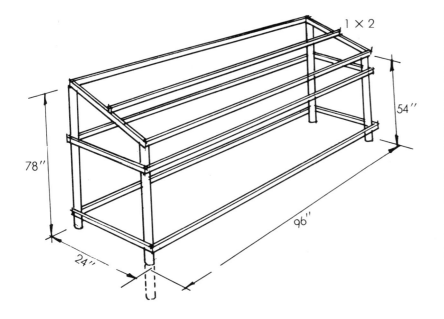

**Materials:**

| Amount | Size | Item |
|---|---|---|
| 2 | 6' | Cedar posts with 4" diameter |
| 2 | 8' | Cedar posts with 4" diameter |
| 1 | 16' x 6' | Clear polyethylene plastic |
| 9 | 1" x 2" x 8' | #2 pine |
| | 3d | Galvanized nails |
| | 8d | Galvanized nails |
| | | Staples |
| | | Cuprinol or wood preservative |

**Tools:**

Hammer        Tape measure

Staple gun      Combination square

Post-hole digger or shovel

# How to build:
## A. The Frame

**1.** Mark out a 2' x 8' rectangular area for the dryer with the 8' dimension oriented east/west. Dig the post holes with the post-hole digger or shovel at the four corners. Holes should be 1½' deep. Set the poles in place with the shorter poles on the south-facing side of the pile, the longer poles to the north.

**2.** Shovel the soil back into the holes, frequently tamping to compact the soil.

**3.** Cut one of the 1 x 2s into four pieces, each 24" in length.
Measure the diagonal between the tops of the two end posts; from another 8' length of 1 x 2, cut two pieces to this distance.

**4.** Treat all 1 x 2s with Cuprinol or wood preservative. Let dry.

**5.** Four inches above the ground, nail an 8' length to the north-facing cedar posts, using 8d nails; nail a second 8' length 4" from the ground between the two south-facing posts. Nail the two 24" lengths on the east and west sides at the same height.

**6.** Four feet above these, nail another four pieces in place around the dryer.

**7.** The 8' piece on the south side should be nailed to the top of the posts. Nail an 8' length between the tops of the two north-facing posts. On the east and west ends and on the inside face of the posts, nail the two diagonals.

**8.** The last 8' section should be centered on the diagonals and nailed to the top edge of the diagonals, using 3d nails.

## B. The Wood Pile

**9.** Lay 8' stringers east and west between the posts and 3" in from the posts toward the center of the pile. If your wood will be cut into 12" lengths, there should be four stringers arranged so that when the splits are piled, they will straddle the stringers. Stringers can be of scrap lumber, saplings, or anything which will raise the wood pile off the ground.
Stack your wood on the stringers until it is as high as the second tier of 1 x 2 bracing.

## C. Plastic

**10.** Cut the plastic to the following dimensions:

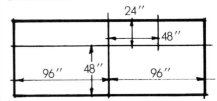

**11.** Staple the plastic to the posts and 1 x 2s. The plastic shouldn't obstruct the passage of air below the pile. Also the vent along the north side and the triangular vents on the east and west sides should be left open. These will allow the heated air to pass through the pile and carry off the excess moisture.

# Solar Food Dryer

**Skills required:** Slight to moderate.

**Cost:** $45 to $50.

**Amount of heat gain:** In sunny weather, dryer temperatures will vary between 95 and 145 degrees F.

**What it does:** The solar food dryer, essentially a solar hot box, is used to dry fruits and vegetables. Once dried, foods take only one-fourth the storage space and have a shelf life that is four to five times greater than that of canned goods.

Easy-to-dry fruits include apples, apricots, cherries, coconut, dates, figs, guavas, nectarines, peaches, pears, plums, and prunes. Easy-to-dry vegetables include shell beans and peas, lentils, soybeans, hot chili peppers, sweet corn, sweet potatoes, and soup mixtures of shredded vegetables, leaves and herbs. Dried vegetables can be used in soups and stews; dried fruits can be used as dessert toppings or as nutritious candy substitutes.

To use the dryer for making fruit leathers, mix the fruit to a creamy consistency in an electric blender. Spread out on glass or waxed paper laid on top of dryer tray. If the glass or cellophane covers too much of the tray screening, it will prevent air circulation. Ten-inch squares of waxed paper are good. The fruit cream should be about ⅜″ thick and will dry down to ⅛″ or less.

Baby foods are easy to make in the solar dryer. Cook fruits or vegetables until tender, run through a strainer or food mill, then dry and package.

Noodles, croutons and breakfast cereals are other easy-to-make products.

With some of the trays removed, the dryer can be used for developing yogurt cultures, leavening bread dough or drying flowers.

**How it works:** Once the food has lost 5 to 25 percent of its original water content, there isn't enough moisture left to support the bacteria or fungi which cause decay. The amount of acceptable moisture will vary with the food; usually more water can be left in fruits (the high acid foods) than in vegetables (the low acid foods).

Since warm air can hold more water than cool air, it is important that dryer temperatures be hotter than outdoor ambient temperatures. This is accomplished by the glazing which lets in sunlight (direct and

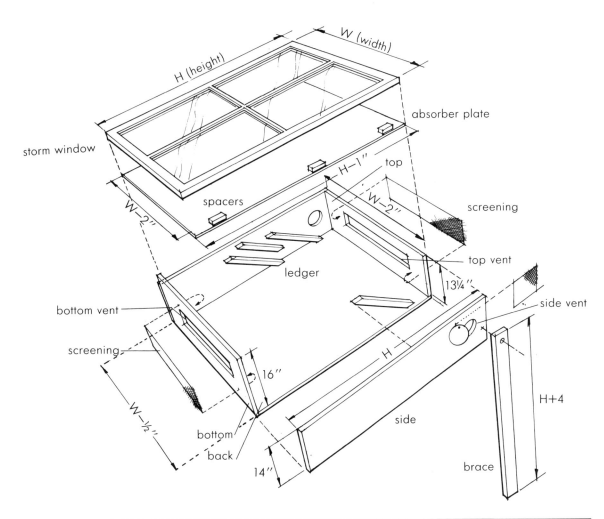

**Materials:**

| Size | Item |
|------|------|
| ¾″ x 4′ x 8′ | CDX plywood |
| 1″ x 3″ | #2 pine |
| 1″ x 2″ | Fir or spruce |
| 1¼″ | Drywall or wood screws |
| 1½″ | Drywall or wood screws |
| 2″ | Hex head bolts with washers and nuts |
| | Food-approved nylon or stainless steel screening |
| | Recycled storm window |
| | Resorcinol or waterproof glue |
| | Aluminum printing plates |
| Spray can | Non-toxic flat black paint |
| | White or silver paint |
| Pint | White spirits |
| | Steel wool |

**Tools:**

Circular saw or handsaw
Electric drill with ⅛″ and ⁵⁄₁₆″ bits
Protractor
Compass
2 C-clamps
Keyhole saw or jigsaw
Brace and 1″ bit
Staple gun and staples
Metal shears
Try square
Pliers or visegrips
Combination square
Pop riveter and rivets
Hammer
Tape measure
Phillips driver or Phillips screw-
    driver or slotted screwdriver
#8 Screwmate (optional)
Thermometer to 140 degrees F.

diffuse), then traps it as heat in a relatively small space. Some of this heat is conducted through the black absorber plate; some of it rises along the glazing.

The staggered shelves of the dryer force the warm air to move in a long circuitous, horizontal path across and under the food. The perforated shelving permits a bottom-to-top air flow. By adjusting the side vents and the tilt of the box, you can hold temperatures in the drying chamber to about 110 degrees F. while allowing sufficient air circulation to carry off moisture released by the food.

As the hotter, moisture-laden air leaves the dryer through the side and top vents, it creates a partial vacuum, thereby drawing in cooler, drier air through the bottom vents—the drying process continues by natural convection. There is always a constant and perceptible air flow over the drying food unless the outside air is too cool or too humid.

The size of the food slices is significant; to remove the moisture in foods, warm dry air should pass over the maximum surface area.

Food can be dried in the open sun, but temperatures are hard to regulate. If they are too hot, the food caramelises because it has dried unevenly and too quickly. This locks in moisture which will cause spoilage.

The blackened interior plate which absorbs solar radiation, also prevents direct exposure of food to sunlight; direct exposure destroys flavor, color, vitamins, minerals, and enzymes.

## Advantages:

1. Simplest, safest, most healthful, and most natural way of food preservation.
2. Costs nothing to operate; freezing and canning are complicated, may involve potentially dangerous procedures, and demand energy for processing (i.e., stoves, pans, pressure gauges, jars, lids, spices, syrups, etc.). Both canning and freezing involve a loss of vitamins.
3. Useful for the outdoor person, vacationer, hiker, camper, fisherman, etc. who want compact food supply.
4. Provides healthful snacks.
5. Good type of food storage for second home or isolated locations where electricity is unavailable, undependable, or infrequently used.
6. Emergency foodstuffs.
7. Will keep indefinitely with airtight packaging.
8. Worry-free product in contrast to canning, because decreased danger of bacterial growth.
9. Taste compares favorably with fresh; nutrient and flavor retention is almost as high.
10. Many flavors improve with dehydration (especially mushrooms, herbs, and spices).
11. Can take advantage of special sales at truckstands or supermarkets.
12. Reduces storage space by at least 25 percent.
13. Convenient.
14. If properly stored, longer shelf life than foods preserved by any other method.
15. Foods can be stored in small quantities and can be used in amounts needed.
16. No chemical preservatives as in commercially dried foods.

## Disadvantages:

1. Weather is a crucial factor.
2. Must adjust dryer 1 to 2 times a day.
3. May need an auxiliary drying method if adverse weather.

**Tips:** Select produce that is in prime condition and absolutely fresh. Vegetables should be slightly immature; fruits should be ripe. Do not use blemished or overripe foods; the dried product will not be as flavorful.

Dry the foods as quickly as possible. However, if dryer temperatures get so hot that the food cooks, the appearance and texture will be spoiled.

Wash, dry, pit, and cut up foods as small and thin as possible—the more exposed surface area, the faster the food will dry. Slices ⅛″ to ¼″ thick are ideal. Because there is more water to be removed from vegetables than from fruits, cut the vegetables thinner; slices should be of uniform size for even drying.

Leave the skins on; much of the mineral content in vegetables such as carrots and turnips is in their skins. The bitter-tasting skins of many vegetables (pumpkin and squash for example) will lose their pungent flavors and become sweet after being dried.

Pre-treatment isn't necessary, although you may want to dip the food in an acid juice (lemon or lime) to help preserve the color.

Blanching in scalding water or sterilizing the food in a 160 to 200 degree F. oven before drying helps arrest enzyme activity and retain color. It also will hasten drying because plant walls will have been softened, allowing the water to escape more readily.

Wait until the weather prediction is for at least two sunny days in a row with low humidity.

Choose a location for the dryer near your house, but avoid drying in smog belts or in places near superhighways or near heavily traveled, dusty secondary roads. Ideally, the site should be sheltered from the north by fences, walls, or other natural windbreaks.

Rest the bottom of the dryer on bricks or concrete blocks for better air circulation below the dryer, and orient the unit for maximum solar exposure (i.e., facing south).

Load the dryer as early as possible in the day with a thin layer of food on each tray; spread so as not to obstruct the air flow. Different foods without strong odors can be dried at the same time.

Slide trays into dryer and lift door into place.

If possible, keep dryer temperatures at about 110 degrees F. Above 120 degrees F. nutrient losses begin, and at temperatures in excess of 140 degrees F., enzyme breakdown, food discoloration and loss of vitamin C occur. On the other hand, at readings in the 90s or below, bacteria and mold may spoil the produce.

Regulate dryer temperatures with the side vents. During the hottest time of day (1 to 2 p.m.) or according to temperatures in the dryer, leave vents wide open (temperatures also can be lowered by tilting the dryer away from the sun). To raise temperatures, close the side vents.

Leave a thermometer in the middle of the top tray where it can be read through one of the vents. Temperatures in the top of the dryer will be 4 degrees F. higher than in the lower part.

Several times a day stir food gently so that the slices dry evenly. You also may want to move the trays to shorten drying times and to keep the food drying at the same speed; food on top trays will dry the fastest.

Readjust the dryer several times a day so that it faces the sun directly. Once the sun is low and temperatures are falling, close the vents or drape a cover over the dryer to prevent rehydration from the morning dew; partially-dried contents need not be removed. If you forget to cover the dryer, the foods will reabsorb water; this will lengthen drying times but will not appreciably change the quality. Remove the covering on the following morning and re-position the dryer so that it receives the early morning sun.

# How to build:

*Directions for building this solar food dryer are based on the recycling of a storm window. Since these windows are available in different sizes, the directions refer only to the width and height of the window. (The height should be the longer of the two window dimensions.) Choose a window with 8 square feet or more—a dryer should have a relatively large capacity so that the food can be processed quickly, efficiently, and without spoilage. Don't begin construction with a tiny window (such as a basement-sized storm).*

*You probably will want a dryer large enough to handle 15 to 30 pounds of produce at one time. Each square foot of tray will hold 1½ to 2½ pounds of produce; a 4' x 2' window will provide space to dry approximately 20 pounds of food on 7 trays in a box 14¾" deep.*

## A. Cutting the Box

1. Cut the plywood BACK to the width of your window minus 2", and to the height of your window.

From the plywood, cut two SIDEs to 14" x the height of the window.

Cut the BOTTOM to the width of the window minus ½" x 16".

Cut the TOP to the width of the BACK x 13¼".

## B. The Ledgers

2. Lay one of the SIDE pieces with the longer edge parallel to the edge of your work surface and with the "D" (less good) side of the plywood up. Label the edge facing you the "back." Label one of the 14" edges the "top" and from it measure down along the "back" edge 4" and mark. Then measure every 3" and mark. With a protractor draw 45 degree lines from the marks along the "back" to the front until the lines no longer reach. Do the same on the opposite SIDE, remembering that the 45 degree lines will go in the opposite direction.

3. Measure the length of these lines. Subtract 5". Cut strips from the leftover plywood to this length and to a width of 1". You will need as many pieces as back-to-front lines. These will be the ledgers on which the drying trays will rest.

Start at the "top" of the first SIDE. Position the first ledger so that it comes up to the line and is 1" from the "back" edge of the SIDE. Stagger the placement of the ledgers so that every other one is 1" from the "back"; the intervening ledgers should be 1" in from the front edge.

Drill, glue adjoining surfaces, clamp ledgers to SIDE with the two C-clamps, and screw together with 1¼" wood or drywall screws spaced every 3". Continue until all ledgers are glued and screwed into place.

## C. Vents

**4.** With the SIDEs ledger-side-up, outline a 4" diameter hole in each one with the compass. The center of the hole should be 7" in from the front edge of the dryer and 4" down from the "top" edge. (Adjust size and placement of circle if it interferes with ledger strips.)

With a brace and bit or an electric drill, drill a pilot hole large enough to insert the blade of a keyhole or jigsaw. Cut the holes in both SIDE pieces.

From scrap plywood, cut two circles with 6" diameters. With the SIDEs ledger-side-down, screw each vent cover to SIDE with one 1¼" screw. You should be able to swivel covers to either side of vent holes.

**5.** Vents will be needed in both the TOP and BOTTOM. Measure in 3" from either end. Mark for the removal of a rectangle 4" wide from the center of each piece. Drill a series of pilot holes until you can fit the blade of a keyhole or jigsaw into the opening. Cut out both rectangles.

If you prefer, TOP and BOTTOM vents can be a series of holes. Measure 4" in from each of the four sides. Draw square lines. Continue filling in the grid, spacing the lines about 6" apart. With a brace and 1" bit, cut ventilation holes wherever the lines intersect.

**6.** Cut two pieces of nylon or stainless steel screening to the length and width of the rectangles (or series of ventilation holes). Add 1" to each dimension.

With the "D" (less good) side of the plywood up, center the screening over the area to be covered. Fold under the edges; then work from the center stapling screening to plywood. Do this for both TOP and BOTTOM vents. Be sure screening is taut.

Do the same for the SIDE ventilation ports.

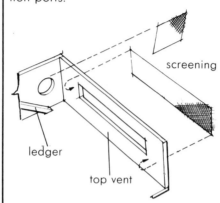

screening

ledger

top vent

## D. Assembly

**7.** Rest the TOP on edge on a flat work surface. Align the top edge of BACK with TOP. (Support under the BACK will be necessary.) With the #8 Screwmate, drill holes ⅜" in from the edge of the BACK at 6" intervals.

Remove BACK. Apply glue to adjoining plywood surfaces. Replace and screw through BACK into TOP with 1½" drywall screws. To save time, use a Phillips driver with an electric drill, or 1½" wood screws and screwdriver. Check for square.

**8.** Tip unit on edge. Position one of the SIDEs on top of, and flush with, TOP and BACK edges. The ledgers should face down and be angled toward the BOTTOM (yet to be put in place). Predrill holes, glue, and screw together. Check for square.

Do the same for the second SIDE and check for square.

**9.** Rest the partially built dryer on its TOP. Position the BOTTOM so that it covers the end grain of the SIDEs and BACK. (The BOTTOM has a lip that extends beyond the SIDEs.)

Drill holes through BOTTOM into SIDEs and BACK every 6". Remove. Apply glue to all adjoining surfaces. Screw BOTTOM into SIDEs and BACK.

## E. Supports

**10.** To the height of the BACK, add 4". From the 1" x 3", cut two boards each to this length for the braces.

Draw a square line on each brace the length of the height of the BACK plus ¾". Align square line with back edge of dryer. Outer edge of brace should be flush with top edge of SIDE. In the remaining 3¼" length of the brace which rests against dryer box, drill a ⁵⁄₁₆" hole. It should pass through brace and SIDE of dryer. Slide a 2" hex head bolt through hole, add washer and nut. Tighten.

Fit second brace to other SIDE in same manner.

## F. Dryer Trays

**11.** To figure approximately the amount of 1 x 2 stock you will need, measure the distance between the inner faces of the SIDEs. Multiply this distance by two; add to it twice the length of the ledgers. Then multiply this figure by the number of trays (i.e., the number of ledgers on one SIDE).

Before cutting the 1 x 2 stock into pieces for the trays, you will have

---

Regulate temperatures on cool or windy days by partially closing the vents.

If the sun is hot enough and the humidity is low, food should dry in two days. However, drying times depend on ambient conditions; and different foods dry at different rates. You may need three days. If the second day of drying is cloudy but followed by a relatively bright day, the food will be fine. If you have a series of cloudy or rainy days, bring the food indoors; it will have to be oven-dried.

Store trays inside during cold night temperatures in early winter; freeze-dried food is acceptable, but is brittle and not as tasty.

to adjust these figures. Cut the side rails to the length of the ledgers, but cut the front and back rails 1¾" less than the distance between the inner faces of the SIDEs.

With the rails on edge, drill through a side rail into a front or back rail. There should be two screw holes equally spaced and ⅜" in from the edge.

Glue adjoining surfaces. Check for square, then screw together with 1½" drywall or wood screws. Assemble rest of frame screwing through the side rails.

Construct rest of trays.

Paint tray frames and outside of dryer box with non-toxic flat black paint; interior walls of dryer should be painted with a reflective silver or white, or covered with aluminum foil.

**12.** Cut food-approved nylon or stainless steel screening to the outer dimensions of tray. Center screening on tray frame. Starting in the center of the back rail, fold under ⅜" of the screening and staple to frame. Do the same on front rail. Work from the center, pulling the screening taut and stapling to frame. Check that tray slides easily in and out along ledger strips.

Staple screening to rest of trays.

## G. Absorber Plate

**13.** On the back side of the window (the puttied panes face outward), measure in 1" on each of the sides and draw a line. From the top, measure down 1" and draw a line. These lines mark the width and height of the absorber plate (plate will be flush with bottom of window).

Make the absorber plate from aluminum printing plates available from any offset printer. If more than one plate is needed, cut them to size, leaving a 3" overlap wherever the sheets meet.

After the sheets have been cut to size, rub them down with steel wool and clean with white spirits.

> To test fruits for dryness, no moisture should appear from a piece when cut. When several pieces are pressed together, they should fall apart once the pressure is released. Slices will be leathery, but pliable. Do not overdry to hardness. Vegetables are dry when they are brittle, or crisp like a chip.
>
> You can weigh produce before and during the drying process; when half the original weight is gone, the food is two-thirds dried.
>
> Store dried produce in sealed jars or coffee cans and where it is safe from insects or animals; do not store in paper or plastic bags. Keep in a cool, dark place. Light will cause a loss of flavor and color (vitamins), and the cooler the storage, the better. With approximately 10 percent moisture, dried produce will keep indefinitely.

Rivet the sheets together by drilling ⅛" holes every 6" along an overlap. With pop rivets and washers, fasten them together with pop riveter. Small bolts and washers can be used instead.

Clean absorber plate. Spray paint both sides with flat black, heat-resistant paint. Let dry.

Also paint storm window frame flat black.

**14.** To mount the absorber on the window, cut 1" x 2" plywood spacers. Align them every 12" inside, but flush with, the penciled perimeter lines on the window. Set absorber plate on top. Drill holes through plate and spacers, then screw to window with 1¼" screws.

Test window in dryer. Window should sit on the BOTTOM; its sides should overlap the SIDEs of the box by ¼", and window should be flush with TOP. If absorber is mounted correctly, its edges shouldn't catch on the plywood SIDEs or TOP.

**15.** Carry dryer to outdoor location. To establish the correct tilt, swing back supports so that they make a 90 degree angle with the dryer. (Supports will be flush with TOP when dryer is correctly angled.)

To load dryer, remove window and rest it against back supports. Slip in trays filled with food. They will rest directly on ledgers. Lift window into place so that it rests on BOTTOM lip.

**16.** If you can see any space between the window and the plywood box, the window should be weatherstripped. Apply adhesive-backed foam or felt weatherstripping to the plywood edge of SIDEs and TOP, and to bottom of window, if necessary.

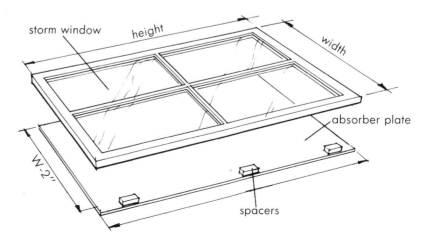

# Solar Oven

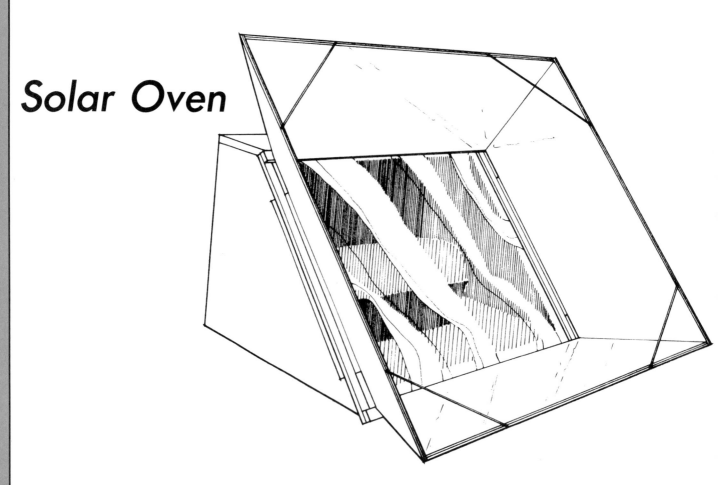

**Skills required:** Moderate.

**Cost:** $40 to $50; inexpensive units can be built of cardboard for less than $25.

**Amount of heat gain:** Without the reflectors, oven temperatures will reach 250 degrees F. on a clear, 65 degree F. day; with the reflectors, oven temperatures will reach 350 to 400 degrees F.

**What it does:** Since most cooking can be done in less than four hours, the solar oven is well-adapted to the sun's schedule; it is ideal for the slow crock-pot type of meal that requires slow cooking at comparatively low temperatures. Turkey, for example, will cook as fast in a solar oven as in an electric one.

**How it works:** The window of the solar oven is another example of the greenhouse effect. Light enters and is turned into longer wavelengths of heat. The insulation is designed to hold in this heat and is painted flat black to increase the heat absorbtiveness of the oven. Convection and conduction losses also are minimized by the caulking.

The reflective panels act like mirrors; when set at the proper angle, they bounce all the light and heat that strikes them into the window opening. This causes a further rise in oven temperature.

**Advantages:**

1. Easy to use.
2. Easy access through the oven door.
3. Lightweight.
4. Fold-up reflectors simplify storage.
5. Construction costs are low.
6. Year-round use is possible.
7. When used at home, may leave oven set up all the time.
8. Cooking is even possible several hours after sundown.
9. Not a fire hazard; campers can cook safely without a fire.
10. Of special interest to those who believe in conservation, the wise use of our natural resources, and the protection of our environment.

**Disadvantages:**

1. Oven temperatures are variable, depending on the sun, and seldom exceed 350 degrees F.

**Tips:** The sides of the oven are cut at an angle. To figure out the angle for your location, add 10 to 15 degrees to your latitude. The sides of the oven in these directions are cut at a 52 degree angle, an ideal angle for use between 37 and 42 degrees latitude.

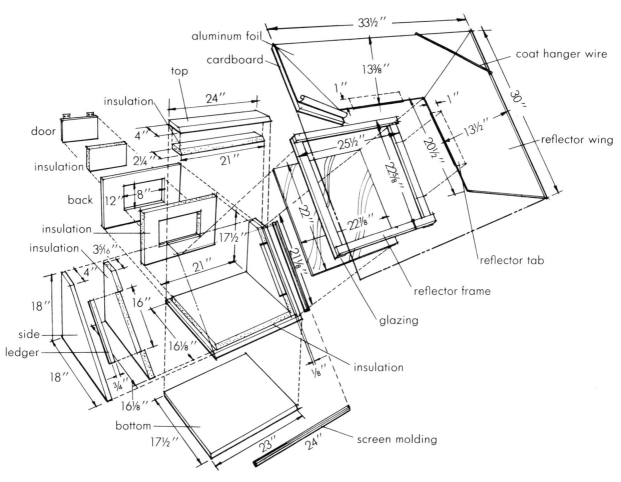

Labels in figure: aluminum foil, cardboard, top, insulation, 33½", 13⅜", 1", coat hanger wire, door, insulation, 24", 30", reflector wing, back, 4", 2¼", 21", 25½", 1", 13½", insulation, 12", 8", 22⅞", 20½", insulation, 22", 22⅞", reflector tab, insulation, 3⁵⁄₁₆", 17½", 22⅞", reflector frame, side, 4", 21", 21⅛", glazing, ledger, 18", 16", 21⅛", insulation, ⅛", 16⅛", ¾", 16⅛", screen molding, bottom, 17½", 23", 24", 18"

| Materials: | | | Tools: |
|---|---|---|---|
| Amount | Size | Item | Handsaw |
| | | | Keyhole saw |
| 1 sheet | ½" x 4' x 8' | CDX exterior plywood | Drill and ⅛" bit |
| 1 tube | | Silicone rubber caulking | #8 Screwmate (optional) |
| 1 roll | | Aluminum foil duct tape | Phillips driver for electric drill (optional) |
| 1 lb. | 1½" | Drywall screws or 1 box 1½" wood screws | Phillips screwdriver |
| 1 lb. | ¾" | Drywall screws or 1 box ¾" wood screws | Slotted head screwdriver |
| 1 tube | | DAP Foamboard and Panel Adhesive | Circular saw with plywood blade |
| 1 | 1" x 4' x 3' | Ductboard | Tape measure |
| 1 | 6' | Screen molding (optional) | Straightedge |
| 1 | 22" x 22⅞" | Double-strength window glass | Try square |
| 1 tube | ¾" | Brads | Utility knife |
| 1 set | 1" | Utility hinges | Cardboard tube or dowel |
| 1 can | | Derusto flat black spray paint | Staple gun |
| 1 roll | 18" | Double strength aluminum foil | Pliers |
| 1 box | ¾" | Staples | C-clamps |
| | | Cardboard (approximately 16½ square feet) | Caulking gun |
| | | Carpenter's wood glue | |
| | | Elmer's white glue | |
| | | Coat hanger wire | |

# How to build:

*The overall dimensions of the oven are 18½ inches high by 18 inches deep by 24 inches wide.*

## A. The Oven Box

**1.** From the plywood, cut the two side pieces to the dimensions shown. Use a fine-toothed handsaw or a plywood blade with a table or circular saw.

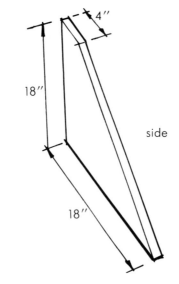

4"

18"

18"

side

**2.** For the bottom of the oven, cut a plywood rectangle 17½" x 23". The edge of one of the 23" sides should be beveled so that it will match the angle (slope) of the sides. This can be done by loosening the wing nut (or blade tilt lock) on a circular saw and adjusting the base plate to the appropriate angle (38 degrees). Or the angle can be marked on the plywood bottom with a protractor (52 degrees) and cut with a hand-saw. Lacking a protractor, duplicate the angle of the sides on a T-bevel; tighten the wing nut and use this to transfer the angle onto the ply-wood.

If you must approximate the angle, draw a line ³⁄₁₆" in from the top edge. Angle the saw in such a way that your cut will remove this triangular scrap.

**3.** Cut a piece of plywood to 4" x 24" for the top of the oven; bevel one of the longer edges to match the angle of the sides.

**4.** For the back of the oven, cut a plywood rectangle 18" x 23". Into this, cut an 8" x 12" door. Mark off the dimensions so that the door will be 3½" up from the bottom edge and centered. With a circular saw, make four pocket cuts by tilting the saw forward and lowering the blade slowly. Cut almost to the end of each line; finish the cuts with a handsaw.

If you have only hand tools, drill a series of holes along one of the sides of the door with a ⅛" drill bit. There should be enough holes to accept the tip of a keyhole saw. To start the saw cut, use vertical strokes, then bring the saw to a 45 degree angle to continue.

Lay the plywood back on your work surface with the "C" (better side) facing up. Mount a pair of l" utility hinges so that the door will swing up and out. Set aside.

**5.** From the remaining ½" plywood, cut two pieces that measure ¾" x 16". These will be the ledger strips on which the glass window will rest.

Lay the right and left sides of the oven on your work surface with the "D" (poorer) side of the plywood up. Position each ledger strip along the angled edge approximately 4" up from the bottom front corner and ³⁄₁₆" in from the edge. Drill these holes through the ledger and into the side panel with a #8 Screwmate. The holes should be 6" apart.

Spread wood glue on the back side of each ledger and on the facing side piece. Clamp each ledger in place with two C-clamps, and

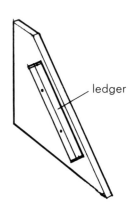

ledger

The directions call for use of an electric drill, a #8 Screwmate, a Phillips head driver, and drywall screws. The Screwmate enables you to drill the pilot hole and countersink in one operation, and since the drywall screws have a Phillips head, they are easily driven with a Phillips head bit. However, twist bits, or a hammer and awl can be used to predrill holes. If you don't have an electric drill, a Phillips screwdriver can be used, and slotted screws work as well as drywall screws.

screw it to the oven side panel using ¾" drywall screws or wood screws.

## B. Assembly of the Oven Box

**6.** Clamp the back of the oven to your work surface with the outside surface facing up and the bottom edge extending beyond the table. Align the back edge of the oven bottom with the edge of the oven back. With this alignment, you will be able to screw through the back into the oven bottom. If the bottom piece does not reach the floor, it will need support. Use a chair, stool, scrap lumber, etc. to raise the bottom piece until it forms a right angle with the back. Drill holes at 6" intervals with a #8 Screwmate. Remove the bottom. Spread glue along both surfaces. Reposition and screw the two together using 1½" drywall screws or wood screws.

Use a try square to check that the adjoining surfaces are square.

**7.** The sides will be screwed into the bottom and back. Remember that the "good" side faces out. Drill holes, then glue and screw. Check all adjoining surfaces for squareness.

**8.** The top will screw into the back and sides. Drill holes (two per side) and every 6" along the back, but do not glue or screw top in place.

**9.** Caulk all interior joints of the oven with silicone rubber caulking. Cut the nozzle of the tube off at a 45 degree angle. Puncture the inner seal at the base of the nozzle with a nail. Insert the cartridge in a caulking gun. Hold the gun at a 45 degree angle and apply caulking by pushing sealant ahead of the nozzle. The caulking compound should adhere to both sides of the joint. To reseal the cartridge, place a nail in the nozzle.

The caulking dries in 24 hours.

## C. Insulating the Oven

**10.** The pressed fiberglass ductboard helps the oven retain heat and should be used instead of the foams (styrofoam or urethane) which will soften, melt, shrink or disintegrate when the oven gets above 200 degrees F.

Ductboard is available from heating and air-conditioning supply houses. It is faced on one side with tough aluminum foil. Plan your cuts so that the aluminum side of the insulation will always be facing into the oven, not toward the plywood walls.

Cut the back piece to 17½" x 21". Cut on the face side, foil side-up, using a jackknife, utility knife or linoleum cutter. Hold the blade at right angles to the ductboard and score by cutting along a heavy straightedge. Remove the straightedge and repeat, cutting through the ductboard. Center the insulation on the back piece, then with a Magic Marker or pencil, mark the lines for the 8" x 12" door opening so that it will correspond with the opening in the plywood.

Cut out the opening for the door. Save the 8" x 12" piece of ductboard; it will be glued to the door later.

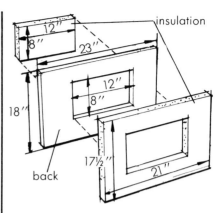

**11.** The dimensions for the side insulation are as illustrated. After one side piece is trimmed to fit, it can be used as a pattern for the other, but make sure to lay them foil- to-foil so that the aluminum of both sides will face into the oven. Accurate insulation cutting and fitting are important to slow conductive and convective heat losses from the oven.

Cut out for the ledger strips. Measure 3" up from the bottom front corner of the side piece of insulation. From there mark off and remove with a utility knife a strip ½" x ¾" x 16".

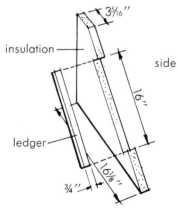

**12.** Cut the bottom insulation to 16⅛" x 21". It will butt up against the sides and back. With the foil side up, bevel the front edge to match the angle of the sides. If you have difficulty getting a clean cut, use a sureform to smooth the edge.

For the top, cut a rectangle of ductboard 2¼" x 21". Bevel one of the longer edges to match angle of sides.

**13.** Glue the ductboard pieces to the plywood with DAP Foamboard and Panel Adhesive. Then seal all seams with aluminum foil duct tape.

Glue ductboard to the inside of the door and let the glue dry with the door closed. This will insure that the ductboard is properly aligned.

Also glue ductboard to the top, measuring carefully so it is properly placed 1½" in from the sides and back. Loosely screw top in place until adhesive dries.

## D. Trim

**14.** When selecting a trim, keep in mind that screen molding will give a more finished appearance, although ¾" strips of plywood can be substituted.

Cut a piece of molding to the width of the oven (24"). Using ¾" brads, tack the molding in place so that it will be flush with the bottom of the oven.

Cut two pieces of molding to 21⅛". Measure ¾" up each side from the bottom molding. With the brads, tack the side moldings in place so that they are flush with the outside of the oven.

Run a bead of caulking along the outside between the screen molding and the plywood to insure a tight seal.

## E. The Glazing

**15.** The glass should be cut to 22" x 22⅞" by a glass shop unless you are an experienced glass cutter. When handling glass, wear gloves so that you don't cut your fingers on the sharp edges. Also take care that the glass isn't inadvertently chipped or broken.

Slide the glass into place; do not force. It should rest on the ledgers and be beneath the screen molding. None of the brads used to tack the molding into place should interfere with fitting the glass. If they do, remove and reset them.

Remove the glass.

## F. Painting

**16.** Paint the inside and outside of the oven with flat black spray paint. Use the pressure can for convenience, and be sure the paint you use is non-toxic. Let dry for 24 hours.

## G. Assembling the Window

**17.** Clean the glass with water. Then slide into place between the ledgers and molding. Loosely screw top to sides.

Set the oven outdoors with the window focused towards the bright sun. Because of the heat, the black interior paint may give off fumes for awhile; these will be deposited as a film on the inside of the glass. Periodically wipe off film. (It may be easier to remove the top, then the glass, for cleaning.) Once the glass remains clear, continue window assembly.

Before window is finally installed, run a thin bead of caulking behind the bottom strip of screen molding. Then slide the glass into place between the ledgers and side molding. The glass should seat in the caulking to form an airtight seal.

**18.** Glue and screw the top to the plywood sides and back.

**19.** Caulk the sides of glass, as well as the joint between the top and the glass. Or use a duct tape seal which is more easily removed.

## H. Reflectors

**20.** There are reflectors on all four sides of the oven to further raise oven temperatures. They can be inexpensively made of cardboard and aluminum foil.

For the frame, cut two pieces of plywood ¾" x 25½", and two pieces ¾" x 22⅝". Drill and screw (one screw per corner) the pieces of the frame together with ¾" wood or drywall screws.

---

Ideally, a solar device should be adjusted frequently so that direct rays from the sun are always perpendicular to the glazing; with the solar oven, this isn't as critical. Since the oven is designed to hold in heat, the food continues to cook even when the oven isn't directly aligned.

To reduce the number of adjustments, position the oven in the morning for optimum sunlight at 11 a.m. to noon. During this period, the heat of the sun is most intense, so it is important that the sun's rays hit the oven directly. Some early morning sunlight will still reach the oven, even though the oven is pointed ahead of the sun. Align the oven again with the sun between 1 and 2 p.m.

The oven can be used in winter, especially on clear days, although it will need to be rotated as well as tilted because of the change in the sun's position. To tilt the oven for winter, tip it slightly backwards and hold this position by sliding two wedges under the front. You will have to compensate for this by also tilting the food, which should be as level as possible.

Until you get a feeling for average oven temperatures, leave a thermometer inside the oven; temperatures on a clear, sunny day can range from 250 to 400 degrees F.

Remember vaporizing water consumes heat. Heat is also lost by convection through utensils and oven walls. Use wooden utensils and insulated cookers.

We recommend that you use an oven rack or false bottom of metal to prevent the insulation from collapsing under the weight of the food.

The frame will rest between the bottom screen molding and the side moldings; the top rail of the frame will rest on top of the side moldings; the side rails will run along the plywood sides of the oven. If you intend to paint the frame, do so now.

**21.** Cut the reflector wings from cardboard to the dimensions shown. Cut out all four wings. To add further rigidity and to prevent warping, use a double thickness of cardboard. Cut to the same sizes, minus the tabs.

Glue the double thicknesses of cardboard together with Elmer's white glue, rubber cement, or contact cement.

Cut strips of heavy duty, double strength aluminum foil to cover each wing. They will be trimmed to size later.

Apply glue to the cardboard surfaces. Spread carefully to insure that the glue is thinly and evenly applied.

**22.** Use a piece of Scotch tape to attach foil to dowel, then roll foil tightly around tube or dowel. Be sure that when foil is unrolled, the shiny side will be up.

Unroll foil slowly from tube onto glued surface of cardboard. Be sure the foil lies flat; bubbles will distort the reflection. If more than one strip is necessary, leave a 2" overlap. Cover the entire cardboard reflector, excluding the tab.

After the foil has been applied, check for bubbles. These can be eliminated by pricking them with a pin or by making a small slit in them with a razor. Then flatten them with your palm or with a clean cloth.

## I. Attaching the Reflectors

**23.** Trim the foil with a sharp knife, razor or scissors. To prevent the

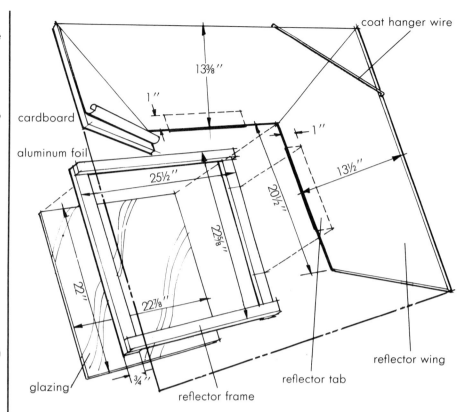

cardboard from curling, place the reflectors under a pile of books or lumber and cement blocks to weight down the wings until the glue dries. Once the glue has dried, the reflectors can be attached to the frame.

Bend the tabs for the top and bottom wings. Center the tab on the face of the bottom (and top) rails of the frame. Staple tabs to the frame using ¾" staples.

**24.** You will need supports for the corners. Use four pieces of wire 10" long. Coat hanger wire is convenient and readily available. At either end, bend the last 2" of wire 90 degrees with pliers.

**25.** Slide the frame around the oven window. The side rails should be flexible enough so that with a screwdriver (if necessary) they can be bent far enough away from the plywood sides of the oven so that you can slip the tabs of the side wings between the plywood and the frame. There will be a reflector on either side.

**26.** To secure the corners, gently push one end of the wire into the corrugations of the cardboard near the corner of one reflector. The other end should reach across the diagonal to a second reflector to hold the proper angle, and slide in between corrugations.

Do the same on all corners. The reflectors should be at an angle of 120 degrees from the oven window.

To double-check that the reflectors are functional, adjust the wings while watching the reflection inside the box on the dull black insulation. When they are focusing light on the window, insert corner pins. (This should create angles of 120 degrees.)

### Other design possibilities:

**Oven Box Construction.** Cardboard is light, cheap, and easily replaced; it may be used for the oven box, but unfortunately it is also flimsy and may not hold the weight of the glazing material. Masonite is more durable. Aluminum and 28-gauge sheet metal are other possible materials, although they demand skill in cutting and bending.

The dimensions of solar ovens may be adjusted to utilize discarded windows, especially old cellar windows. The glazing may need recaulking and the frames a new coat of paint.

**Window.** To further increase oven temperatures and the oven's ability to hold heat, a second layer of glazing may be added. This layer may be two sheets of glass with a dead air space between, or an inner layer of polyethylene, Teflon, or Tedlar.

**Insulation.** You may want to build a removable insulating cover to place over the window whenever the sun is no longer adding heat to the oven. Even throwing a blanket over the glazing will help minimize heat losses, especially from high temperature cooking. A cover also will aid in keeping the glass dust-free.

**Reflectors.** Corrugated cardboard to which aluminum foil has been glued is the cheapest solution, but it is difficult to get the foil absolutely flat. Other possibilities include polished sheet aluminum (which is lighter in weight), pieces of light-gauge sheet metal riveted together and hinged to the oven box, or almost anything as long as it will remain flat and is shiny and smooth. Half-inch Thermax (urethane foam backed on both sides with aluminum foil) may be used; it is expensive.

Far superior to aluminum foil is aluminized Mylar. It is more durable and much more reflective. It should be applied to the cardboard wings with a solution of epoxy-resin. Mix equal portions of hardener, resin, and 80 to 95 percent alcohol together. Then apply a thin smooth film to the cardboard. Roll Mylar onto the wings following the instructions for aluminum foil.